BLACK & BLUE SARI

The cost of leaving a toxic relationship and how
the transition can prosper you and others.

D0976416

Reprint - First Edition Feb 2012.

Copyright© 2009 by Kamal Dhillon

Printed in Canada
First published as a Lotus Speaking & Writing paperback 2009

Library of Canadian Cataloguing in Publication Data
Kamal Dhillon, 1961-
1. Biography & Autobiography

ISBN 978-0-9813869-0-4

Lotus Speaking & Writing
Surrey, BC

1 2 3 4 5 6 7 8 9 10

BLACK & BLUE SARI

The cost of leaving a toxic relationship and how the transition can prosper you and others.

DISCLAIMER

Names, places and dates have been changed
to protect the innocent.

DEDICATION

To my four beautiful children and my grandchildren whom
I love deeply...Thank you for all your support, patience
and understanding. Most of all thank you for walking this hard
and difficult journey with me. You are the real heroes of this book.

And to the countless men and women who have been touched
by domestic violence. For those who have lost loved ones
through this kind of tragedy, I dedicate this book in honour
of all the sisters that have had their lives cut short.
May you find some comfort in reading this book.

ACKNOWLEDGMENTS

I am so grateful to...

God Almighty for the strength that he has given me. If it weren't for my Lord and Saviour, I wouldn't be here today. He has truly turned my life around from Ashes to Beauty. Thank you, Lord, for using me to be a small vessel in your kingdom.

To my precious and incredible children. You were the reason I chose to live and not give up. Every morning and every night, after seeing your faces, I knew I had to fight to live just for you. You showed me how to be a teenager again and to see and laugh and cry. You have made it possible for me to write and help countless numbers of people through my speaking. May you all live a life full of purpose. You are the true heroes. Not to forget my best friend, Prince, my dog who has always sat beside me day and night while I worked on this book.

Dr. Barry Buzza, thank you for believing in my story and encouraging me to keep writing. Thank you for your prayers and always being available to me.

Dr. Jay Martens, thank you for adding your special touch to this book. You have an amazing gift Jay. I will always treasure our friendship. Bless you.

Jennifer Roberts, thank you for your time which you spent on the cover and the layout. I will never forget your kindness and your dedication to this project. Many thanks to you, Jenn.

Tina Goetz, I thank you from the bottom of my heart for all your hard work and the long hours you devoted to this book.

Acknowledgments

To my dear friends Darlene Davenport, Judy Lynch, Aaron Rogers and Rose for reading this manuscript over and over. You never said no to me. Your support and directions have made a big difference. Thank you.

To my dear friends that have stood beside me and never gave up on me despite my whining. I am so blessed to have the best friends in the whole world. Thank you Cheryl, Daphne, Idellete McVicker, Maralee Dawn, Madhvi Rogers and Caroline and Peter Reimer. You never let me give up on my dream even when I was ready to call it quits. You all stood with me. Thank you all for your contributions towards this book.

ENDORSEMENTS

Black & Blue Sari written by Kamal is both a quick and intense read. This is a riveting autobiography of a young Indian girl, traditionally raised in India, married at age 19 in Canada who faced years of severe and sadistic abuse. This abuse which occurred in Canada and in India repeatedly was at the hands of her husband. The abuse included beatings, being tied up for long periods of time, doused in kerosene (and given matches), being hanged, sexual assaults and even being placed in shark-infested waters. Except for one suicide attempt when she gave up hope temporarily, the author wanted to live. The reasons that helped to keep the author alive was first her fantasy of what could be, then her extended family, then her precious children and when the sadistic abuse was most severe, fantasy once again became her coping skill. Her last chance was to leave the husband's family home in India, but without her children. In despair she began to cry at the airport when a female stranger showed kindness and shared the Gospel of Jesus Christ with her. Her personal relationship with Jesus began a challenging journey of getting her children back, while still experiencing the stalking and harassment of her husband. The final chapters reveal how forgiveness freed her from the past despair and fear and how God was the one to get revenge or to provide justice for her. This true story is a testament of a young girl's desire to survive and to not let an abusive husband and his family destroy her. The book is an encouragement for those in the terrible grip of abuse to not give up and to get help. May it also be an inspiration for each of us to not ignore the evil of abuse; we may be the one person that God wants to work through to help free another person from such a terrible bondage.

Review/Endorsement by GEORGE F. RHOADES, JR., PH.D., *Clinical Psychologist; Director of ALERT, GAiN-Canada; Director of Trauma Training, ALERT, GAiN Canada; Trauma Psychology Executive Council (Division 56) and International Society for the Study of Trauma and Dissociation Executive Board.*

* * *

Bloodshed. Confinement. Forcible submission. Torture. Rape. Am I referring to the atrocities that occur at a medieval prison? A WWII concentration camp? Is the victim a helpless prisoner of war? In some ways, yes. However, this conflict did not take place in the jungles of Vietnam or the bloodstained beaches of Normandy. No... in the case of Kamal Dhillon, the enemy was lying in bed beside her and the battlefield was her home.

As a medical doctor I have witnessed tragedy and I have seen my share of pain. In each case I strive to intervene for good, to promote healing. Sometimes my efforts do help, sometimes my efforts fail to bring about the desired change, and many times I need to call for help. In almost every case though, I find a way to start the process of healing regardless of how remote the possibility of recovery is. This is why Kamal's story has absolutely crushed me... To hear her story is to define afresh the word despair. I found myself pondering how to help such a woman as Kamal... but no matter how hard I try, I cannot find a place to even begin. In her shoes I am as helpless as she. With only one possibility of escape, only one way to heal the bruises of the black and blue sari.

J. D. MARTENS MD

* * *

This book is for YOU, and for each one who wants to "help/love their neighbour". With drama and intimacy Kamal will take you on an extraordinary personal journey, as you walk with her you may see your sister, mother, friend or perhaps... a mirror of your own life! Kamal will lead you to discover truth that releases courage and strength to proactively embrace freedom in your life. The great freedom of choice that can take you to a safe place ...and Kamal will show you how. I love this book, because the message is relevant and must be trumpeted by courageous men and women.

REV MARALEE DAWN *(producer and TV host Passionate Women)*

Black & Blue Sari is a compelling story of one woman's courageous journey to freedom. Abuse and violence are met with wisdom, miracles and faith on every page. This is a story of LIGHT in darkness and HOPE in despair and will encourage women everywhere.

GWEN MCVICKER, *Linwood House Ministries*

* * *

"Blindfolded through an arranged marriage with a wealthy handsome husband, Kamal Dhillon's white wedding dress was soon splattered by an unending storm of blood and pain. Will fear keep her in the dark corner of her cold prison? Kamal's riveting life story of abuse, betrayal, and her struggle for survival, will captivate your mind and draw you to the light."

Friends and Mentors,PETER REIMER B.SC, B.ED, PGD *(High School Teacher/Firefighter)*. CAROLINE REIMER B.ED., BA *(High School Teacher)*

FORWARD

I've always loved Cinderella-type, happy-ever-after dramas. Whether I'm reading a Walt Disney story with big, colourful pictures beside my grandchildren, or watching a "Sleepless in Seattle" or "Slum-dog Millionaire" movie on the silver screen, I get thrill-chills up my spine when the girl gets the guy, or when the poor boy finds the well-deserved pot of gold under the rainbow's end.

But better than any of the fantasy novels I've read or seen could ever be, is when the story is actually true. A biography of an unknown teen from a far-away country taking home the gold in the Olympics; a gifted single mom from the other side of the tracks winning "America's Got Talent" or a skinny black kid who grew up in Indonesia becoming President of the United States. Those are the stories I love most of all.

And that's why Kamal Dhillon's, "Black & Blue Sari" has become my new favourite. I've known Kamal for about twenty years. She first appeared in our church as a somewhat introverted, obviously distressed and economically deprived young, single mother of four. At that time in the late 80's, she was in great need, but never asked for anything. I saw in her, despite what I knew of her story, an inner serenity and strength that I deeply admired. When she and her children had to move to another part of town to find affordable housing, I was sad to see them go. Even though I prayed for blessing on Kamal's life, I never imagined how the next few years would unfold for her.

Over the last months, as Kamal and I have become reacquainted, I have looked at and listened to her with awe and enthusiasm, as well as admiration. When I first read the manuscript of "Black & Blue Sari", I could not put it down. Her story of the abuse she endured shocked me; but at the same time, she helped me understand what an abused woman feels and why they often stay in the hostile environment.

As I came to her concluding chapter and read of Kamal's forgiveness of her husband and her wellness of soul, I marvelled at her character, courage and God's grace in her life.

Kamal's truly a Princess now. Although her body bears the scars of abuse, she is whole in her soul.

You will be gripped by this true story; you will grow in strength as you come to know Kamal, and you will want to pass "Black & Blue Sari" on to as many friends as you can.

Thank you Kamal, for your bravery, humility and grace. May you wear your crown with joy as you continue to teach, encourage and inspire thousands of women and men with this story.

DR. BARRY BUZZA, *President, Foursquare Gospel Church of Canada; Pastor, Northside Church; Author, Life Journey, Life Purpose, Secret of Happiness and Good Mourning.*

REFLECTIONS OF A FRIEND

Usually authors ask other famous writers to write a piece for their book. I am neither famous nor a writer. I am simply a sister in the Lord who has been blessed to call Kamal a friend. I first met Kamal when she was the guest speaker at our monthly fellowship group, a small intimate gathering of friends who pray and seek God together. As she shared portions of her story, I kept asking myself how it was possible for someone to forgive and be healed from that level of continual abuse. How does one become "normal" after being treated like that? I had come through a dysfunctional marriage with some emotional abuse. I struggled with issues of self-esteem, co-dependency, and healing in my ability to relate to God as my husband. I walked the hard path towards forgiveness. I knew that the resentment, anger and sense of injustice could rear its ugly head again and again at the slightest provocation - the playback of a distant memory, a psychological button pushed, a hurtful remark - could all shatter the forgiveness I had worked so hard to extend. Then I would go back to God in obedience and ask for His strength to again pardon my offender. But what I had endured paled in comparison to Kamal's experience. How does one come out the other side of such a nightmare?

On our own we cannot. What is impossible with man is possible with God. Kamal's life has shown me that the power of God's love to heal is greater than the destructive power of abuse, manipulation and control. The power of the risen Christ, whose final cry on the cross was a plea for forgiveness for his torturers, is sufficient to deliver us from our natural desire for revenge and the unrelenting hold of unforgiveness. I still see Kamal endure ongoing physical pain from her reconstructed jaw, a result of it having been broken numerous times. Yet I see a spirit set free by choosing to respond according to God's principles time and time again.

Through the testimony of Kamal's life, we see the divine paradox of suffering; its bittersweet nature. Although the pain may seem more than we can bear at times, yet as in childbirth, the fruit of its labour is blessed in the new life it brings forth.

Some may find parts of this book difficult to read. If you cannot finish it all, I ask that you make sure to read the final two chapters, for it is in their message that the purpose of this book and redemption of her story is revealed.

When put in book form, we get to see the end of this story of abuse. For some you are still caught in the middle of your story; you despair that there is no final chapter. May Kamal's life bring you hope. Kamal contributed to her ending the relationship by stepping out in courage, but she was not alone. Just remember that you also need not go it alone. The same One who took Kamal by the hand will also be there to guide you.

This is a rags to riches story. It helps us believe that there still are happy endings.

JUDY LYNCH, *Friend*

CONTENTS

CONTENTS

CONTENTS

PREFACE

The woman sat trembling at the foot of her master. He despised her and tried to control every aspect of her life. She had inadvertently displeased him again, although she could never have anticipated beforehand what small violation would set him off. Grabbing the gallon container of kerosene, her tormentor stood menacingly over her. She knew what was coming by the icy look in his eyes.

She glanced at the sharp utility knife on the table behind the kerosene, her mind grasping for a possible way out. She quickly discarded the option of using the knife to protect herself, knowing that he would overpower her as he had done so many times before.

She knelt before him with clasped hands, as if praying to some deity, but found no mercy there. Her weak begging landed on deaf ears. The sight of the blood coming from her cut mouth and her pleading cries seemed only to fuel the man's anger and heighten his sense of power over her.

He cunningly had her in a defenseless position, bowed in the corner of the kitchen. He slowly began to tip the container, watching with satisfaction as the caustic liquid soaked his victim. He took his time, savouring every moment of her indignity. After all the kerosene had been emptied over her drenched form, he shook the container for emphasis to make sure nothing was wasted.

She pictured scenes from an Indian movie where a young bride had been burned. The horror of ending her life through such a painful death engulfed her and made her weak with fear.

Her mind raced to thoughts of her four children, feigning sleep only a few feet away in the same room. Who would look after them if she was gone? Would they be left to the mercy of this monster?

His tobacco stained fingers fanned the matches before her face, taunting her, daring her to light them. The stench in the room was overpowering. The woman gagged as the volatile fumes of the kerosene swirled around her. The man was breathing fumes of his own frustration, as he grabbed her by the hair, lifted her off the ground and flung her into the shower. He muttered something about how filthy she was, about how much she stunk. Then he left the woman, her skin burning, not from kerosene or even the allergic rash that was spreading over her body... Her skin was burning from shame.

That man was my husband. The woman was me.

INTRODUCTION

I woke early this morning with a violent headache. I considered cancelling this morning's scheduled talk at the breakfast meeting. Even though I have spoken many times in this condition on the same topic, the emotional and physical stress never seemed to lessen.

I received an email from the organizer of this meeting informing me that there would be approximately one hundred and eighty women in attendance. They were looking forward to hearing this amazing survival story. I agreed to speak and suggested there be several boxes of tissues on hand. Even men had been so touched by my story that they too had shed tears in my previous talks.

As I walked towards the stage, I felt myself tensing up. The host introduced me, "Kamal is a survivor, an inspiration for many and an amazing woman".

As I gathered my composure, I asked: "What is the most difficult thing you have done or have been asked to do?" I heard the audience muttering various comical responses, such as 'getting married,' or 'living with my mother-in-law,' or 'sleeping next to a husband who snores all night.' I interrupted, "The most difficult thing for me to do was to forgive".

I continued, "Like any other young girl, I too had a dream—not an unrealistic dream, but a simple dream. Through the years, with every tear I shed, my dreams washed away. And through all of those years, I never imagined I would be standing here, sharing my story of survival with strangers. One of the hardest things that I have ever done, or been asked to do, is to share the humiliation of those years with others. But here I am, doing it.

"The dreams of my childhood are gone, but I have a new one. My dream is to share my story with as many people as I can, in order to help anyone who is as lost, alone and hopeless as I was. My dream is to help put an end to abuse, in all of its forms. My dream is to inform people about the truth; to be a living example of not only surviving abuse, but thriving, growing and becoming a new person."

"During those years, the only question on my mind was, 'what's next? What new way would he come up with to torture me?' In those days the only question on my mind was—'will I always be black and blue on the inside as I once was on the outside?'"

CHAPTER ONE

Mischievous Years

I was the seventh of nine children from a traditional, hardworking upper middle-class family in India.

My dad met my mom when she was a young girl growing up in a carpenter's house and they were soon married. Though he was a Sikh and mom was Hindu, no one objected to them getting married because mom was well respected in the community. We were altogether nine siblings, four brothers and five sisters. Ravi and Kuldip, the oldest were sent to Universities in another part of the country to further their studies. Later they went on to be high school teachers. The third, my sister Nina, married a businessman while the fourth child, Bobby decided that school wasn't for him and chose to be a farmer. He secretly smoked and drank beer in the sugar cane fields with his buddies. Then Harp the brother after him came to Vancouver to further his studies in accounting. After him was my sister, Sukhi who spoke little, she was the envy of many girls simply because of her light complexion. And then I came, followed by my younger brother Ronny and the youngest sister Billie. Needless to say, mom and dad were very busy parents.

All nine of their children attended a private school because our parents wanted us to have a good education. In my child-like mind, I thought that the nuns were also nurses as they dressed the same as the nurses at the local hospitals, which were also referred to as "sisters." Almost every year I had to go to the local health centre or the hospital and get poked by these "sisters," so I wasn't too fond of seeing them at school.

I was a mischievous child and in my first year in Class One at St Mary's School, my 6-year-old curiosity over the nuns was growing daily. The nuns seemed mysterious and I wondered what was under their veils. I asked my older brother one evening. He told me they were bald and had to cover their heads. I knew that I had to see this for myself to believe it. I was forced to go to school with ponytails and blue ribbons, sitting on the floor every morning while mom sat on the chair, combing my hair with her black, fine-tooth comb. She wasn't always patient with the three girls who remained at home, especially after rising up before dawn and cooking breakfast and lunch for over ten people. My two older sisters were happily married and their ponytail days were over. I couldn't believe that some women didn't have to go through the torture of doing their hair, so one day, when Sister Patricia passed by my desk at school, I quickly got up and flipped her veil. Seeing her hair, I yelled to the class that she wasn't bald! As my punishment, I had to sit next to her facing the class for the rest of the day.

That wasn't my only encounter with Sister Patricia. I enjoyed chewing gum—that big pink bubblegum—and one day, Sister Patricia noticed me chewing, which was forbidden in the classrooms. She pointed straight at me, with a stern look on her face, and said, "Kamal, come to the front of the room and throw the gum into the rubbish bin." As I made my way to the front, she was heading to the back of the class, so I purposely missed the bin and placed the gum on the teacher's chair instead. As punishment this time, I was sent to spend the afternoon sitting in the hot sun to do my work, all by myself, facing the classroom.

My mischievous attitude eventually stopped in school but

continued at home. I was brazen and often said whatever came to mind, always asking many questions - though only a few were ever answered. I was unstoppable, even though my parents were very strict—especially with us five girls. In my culture, most parents were strict with their daughters, because, if we acquired a 'bad name,' they would consequently be unable to get us married. We lived in a small and humble farmhouse that my dad had built with both my grandfathers. Because there was no running water available at that time, they had to dig a well. My older brothers had a habit of scaring me and would tell me stories of how someone had fallen into the well and drowned. One day, I determined that I would see for myself how deep the well was and whether there was a dead person down there. I gathered some big rocks and started throwing them in, one by one. I was staring deep down into the well and all I saw was darkness down there. Suddenly, I felt someone pulling my hair and turned to see my mom standing behind me, her hand raised, ready to slap me. Mom was a little bit chubby, so I was able to out run her to escape any punishment.

Eventually we outgrew our farmhouse and our parents decided we would have to move. We were the only ones in our community to have a brand new car, and the road wasn't designed for cars – only for tractors, horses and cows. So we moved to a newer and much bigger two level house on a busier street, which had a grocery store downstairs .The house had nine bedrooms and was well designed but I didn't really like it. I missed the familiarity of our farmhouse and the few friends I had made in our old neighbourhood. This new house was in a crowded area. Every time a vehicle drove by, dust flew all over the place. There was no privacy in this home. Strangers on the bus could see us no matter which part of the house we were in. This also meant we were always under the microscope of my oldest brother, Ravi's, watchful eyes. The Indian family is usually patriarchal. The eldest male is considered the head of the family. The sons continue to remain at home while the daughters were married and sent away.

Because our yard was big enough, mom planted lots of vegetables and had chickens and a few milking cows, so we always ate fresh food. One interesting fact about Mom was that she had four kitchens. She always wanted her kitchen to be kept clean, so when one would get too disorganized, she would just add another kitchen. I guess she stopped adding more when she realized people were laughing at her. There wasn't much land left to build on either.

Bobby, who became a farmer, was arranged to be married and the wedding was coming up. He got married within the month in a *Sikh gurdwara*, (temple), instead of the girl's house. Some families would choose to have the wedding at the *gurdwara* because their properties weren't big enough to accommodate the hundreds of people who were invited. My brother's wife, *Bhabiji*, as we called her respectfully was a nice daughter-in-law who helped mom with all the chores.

My job was to feed the chickens every morning and every evening. Before feeding them, I would throw stones toward them, hoping to see if I could fool them, but those chickens were so smart, somehow they always knew it wasn't food. Our live-in maid, Saroj, always came to their rescue and gave them real food. With all their clucking and cooing, there were many times when I thought those chickens were talking about me as I passed by. I knew they didn't like me very much.

I graduated from St Mary's primary school to start high school in January 1975. Compared to St. Mary's, this school was extremely large. There were probably four times more students attending, from many different public schools. Most of the students were from an Indian background and as a general rule we were not allowed to be too friendly with the opposite sex. We could only talk to them in class during our projects. Ravi my older brother happened to be my science teacher. He was a very strict teacher. In the first year of high school, my class was right next to his science room and every time he passed by, he would give me this look as if he had caught me doing something I shouldn't have. He talked more with his mean-looking eyes than with words; one look from him would give me shivers. I always felt that he was spying on me, even though I had grown up and had stopped being mischievous and was a good student. I guess he felt the need to watch over me and took his role as the eldest seriously, ensuring that the family name was well-protected. He was not a tall or well-built man but, because he had the title of "head of the science department," he had authority in and out of school. He hardly smiled and always had a stern look on his face. During the car ride to and from school, I was made to sit next to him in the front seat, because the seat behind was usually full. I made sure not to make eye contact, in case he remembered something that I had done earlier. I was embarrassed to sit near him, knowing that a lot of students feared him and most didn't really like him.

But Ravi wasn't as bad as the principal—who was a cruel man. Compared to him, my brother was a charm. The principal was nicknamed "Hitler" by some of the male students and he didn't disappoint them – he mercilessly lived up to his name. Everyone knew that he was always looking for trouble so that he could exercise his powers. We were careful to stay out of his way. Almost every morning, he would ask for the attendance sheet and check for absentees. One time, I remember walking past the principal's office and seeing terrified students standing there. I felt relieved that I wasn't one of them. But one day, my name was called out to go to the principal's office because I had missed school. I had been home sick and Mom felt that I should stay at home that day. This unfortunate day many of us were standing in his office, some girls and some boys. We all stood in a line waiting for our turn in front of the tyrant. From my classmates, I had heard that he would make the students either bend over or stick their hands out to be whipped with his thick belts. At that time, the law did not protect the students, so he was free to discipline them in whatever manner he chose. We stood waiting nervously; the school secretary called out the name of each student before he or she had to go into the principal's office, where the principal stood waiting. From outside, I could hear noises of beatings. I was so terrified of having to go into that office that my knees started shaking violently and I wanted to run off and call my brother to defend me.

When the first student came out he was crying; his face was red and he showed the red welts on his legs as he walked out. The principal had the look of death on his face – a ruthless snarl. As he waited for his next victim, he would keep folding the belt in his hand, testing its strength. I wondered if his belts ever broke and if he kept spare ones in his office.

I quickly walked over to the secretary and asked why the students were being beaten and he replied that the principal believed that these students were skipping school and hanging out in the town. I told him that I had been sick and at home with my parents, and that Ravi and my parents were my witnesses.

* * *

Was this how responsible educators disciplined the students? A school is supposed to be a place where informed professionals teach and model good standards; and not setting the stage for serious emotional and behavioural problems in later years. Was corporal punishment the only way to combat this problem?

In the principal's mind, the answer to that was yes; hitting was the only way to instill fear in the students so they would be compliant and obedient. Would this brutal punishment or so-called discipline not actually create violent adults? It teaches children to bully when angry. Many of these students were not only being beaten at the schools but the punishment was continued at home.

* * *

Finally, my turn came and I began to shake, holding on to the doorknob and knowing that the door was the entrance to a secret world that I didn't want to enter – a world of cruelty and beatings.

When I walked into the torture chamber, I quickly introduced myself to the principal saying "Sir I am Kamal, Ravi's sister, the head of the science department". With my head bowed down slightly I continued: "I was home sick". I kept my hands in my dress pocket, trying very hard not to show him how sweaty and shaky I was. He showed no emotions and just stared at me. Although I was afraid of being beaten up by his thick black leather belt, I summoned the courage to suggest that he had no right to beat me because my brother knew my every move. Thankfully, he grabbed the slip from the secretary, signed it, and motioned for me to go back to class. As I walked back, I promised myself to never miss another class, so that I would never have to face this cruel man again.

I felt very sorry for the other students who were beaten so badly and wondered if their parents knew how the principal beat them, or if perhaps their parents were as mean as this man. I suddenly realized how much power this man had over everyone, as he was not only the principal, but he also owned the school. Sometimes he even made students scrub down the hallways and walls of the school and his house that was adjacent to the school. Some students had to mow the lawn. Many students wanted to sneak away, but they knew the consequences all too well. He felt that he not only owned the school but the students as well. I could not wait to finish that school, but I still had a few years to go. I just couldn't imagine having to be there that long.

Then one day I got my lucky break. My brother Harp, who had been living in Canada, decided to sponsor us to immigrate there. My family and I began planning and preparing for our medical exams to immigrate. It was a very exciting time for us.

CHAPTER TWO

A New Country

My older sister, Sukhi, whom I depended on and loved dearly, was older than me by three years. Once she completed high school, she got married to a man from Vancouver, Canada. He was a nice man and our families were close to each other. They had a beautiful wedding in our home. Our home had a big yard and so a tent was pitched in our back yard to celebrate a traditional Punjabi wedding. Lots of people attended. Even passers-by stopped to see the celebration.

I was very happy for my sister, yet sad, because according to custom, the bride leaves her parents' house and goes to live with the husband's family. My sister was my roommate and the one who was in charge of keeping the top floor of our house clean. I wasn't ready to take her place and felt the responsibility was overwhelming. I also knew she would be leaving for Canada in a few days and it would be very different without her. She was a quiet person who laughed silently at anything. She was very well liked because she never complained and did whatever was asked of her whereas I would protest. Mom and Dad were extremely proud of her personality. Because of her light complexion and light brown eyes, I decided to call her the "white one." She was about 5'2", not very tall, slightly bigger than me. I was medium complexion and a whole inch taller than her, skinny with dark black shoulder length hair. I envied this older sister. There were many times I tried to imitate her so that others would feel the same way about me.

When the day came to see her and her new husband off at the airport – a week after her wedding – her eyes were filled with tears as were mine. Everyone was crying. My aunts were consoling my mother, who was losing her favourite daughter—the apple of her eye. I remember her having to spend more time with her in-laws than with us, but every opportunity I got, I ran over to her with tears rolling down my cheeks and hugging her. I kept reminding her to phone us and send us pictures and she nodded while wiping her tears away.

I cried for hours after the plane took off and went to school the next day with swollen eyes. When anyone asked about my sister, tears would well up. I couldn't wait to go home that day, but dreaded it also, knowing that everything would be different without her. I wished I had been nicer to her. My mind was crowded with thoughts of Sukhi throughout that day.

* * *

My older brother Ravi had a fascination with planes. He knew when a jumbo jet would be landing and would take us and park his car close to the airport for the best view. I once told my parents that I would become a flight attendant so I could see the world and be all the other girls' envy. Everything about those hostesses fascinated me. They were so well-groomed and beautiful too. They traveled the world for free and stayed in hotels. They always smiled at everyone even after a long flight. Their life was just so perfect and I wanted to have what they had and be just like them.

Little did I know that my flight of fancy would be a start to my tribulations?

* * *

As the climate in India can get very hot in the summer months, we mostly stayed indoors to keep cool. We were lucky because our home had a nice breezeway, but I did enjoy the rainy months when it was cooler. I would sit by the window and watch the heavy rains, the lightning and the fierce winds. Mom would make 'chai'—spiced tea with lots of milk—and prepare some fresh salty snacks to go with it.

I was glad we were never forced to go outside and gather firewood or even cook under a shed like most other families did in our neighbourhood. Even though I loved the rain, I would not step in the mud because it was just too filthy. I was also very scared of frogs—they were little dark animals that were always jumping and looking for food. When it started to rain I would hear them croaking and start jumping as if they wanted to come inside the house; I would quickly jump onto the safety of my bed. The other creature I ran from was the gecko. These little reptiles always seemed to be fighting with each other on the ceilings and sometimes they would fall to the ground. I remember that one time, a gecko fell on my head and I screamed for a very long time. I had to have a long shower, hoping to wash away anything that may have been left behind. If I spotted a lizard in any room I was in, I would either leave or get inside the mosquito net.

Mom and Dad had furnished the upstairs and downstairs of our house very nicely. Our upstairs balcony was built all around the house with a metal railing. The main living room had vinyl couches, a wall unit with a stereo and some black and white family pictures. The windows had white lace curtains. The dining set was hand made by my maternal grandfather with large wooden chairs. All nine bedrooms had at least two single beds or a double bed depending on the size of the room. The two toilets and showers were separated from each other. This was a wise idea, considering the number of us living in that house.

***

In the fall of 1977, three months after my sister left for Canada, at the age of sixteen, along with my parents and my younger brother and sister, we immigrated to Vancouver. This was my first experience on a much bigger plane. I closely watched the cabin crew pass by with beverages and a happy expression on their faces. I told one of our attendants that I was going to become a hostess just like her one day. She smiled and said that she missed her husband and children whenever she was on a long flight. I quickly suggested that I would bring my husband on my flights and enjoy visiting as many countries as possible. She gently touched my shoulder and wished me success.

The airport in Vancouver was huge, compared to the airport we had departed from. Even the plane we traveled on was so much larger than any I had travelled on before—there were at least 8 flight attendants. My younger siblings and I made a game of putting the window shutter up and down until we got the look from mom. It was exciting, even though we had left two married brothers and two married sisters behind. It was very sad to leave them and we cried a lot.

When we arrived in Vancouver it was the beginning of the fall season. It was very cold for us and I was sure that we were in the middle of winter because it was foggy and raining most of the time. We chose to live in Richmond where my parents and my older brother bought a house. I was overwhelmed by different things that seemed so strange to me. There were so many cars on the roads and even young sixteen year olds were allowed to drive. This really impressed me. Everyone spoke (or tried to speak) in English to each other. Most of our neighbours chose to keep to themselves, unlike back home where they would come over uninvited and make themselves comfortable. Mom would have to make them tea and offer lunch. Here even the mailman didn't have to knock – he just shoved the mail in through the slot in the door.

A week later, we started school and I was already feeling very homesick. We would wake up when it was still dark and come home in the dark. The students weren't friendly and I just didn't seem to fit in. My clothes were different, my accent was different and everything about me was different. Students were allowed to wear their own clothes; girls wore makeup and had funny hairdos. There was a smell of perfume and cigarettes inside the school. The office had fresh coffee brewing all day and the students ate in their classrooms and drank pop during class. I felt that there was no discipline in the Canadian schools; it was a total culture shock for me. The school had these red lockers that I wasn't used to and I had no idea how to use the combination locks. When the students began laughing at my struggle, I stopped using my locker and carried my bag around – trying to spare me any further embarrassments. I began to hate school, but I somehow made it through and even made a few friends. Students and most teachers called me "Camel" others called me Carmel and finally, after correcting them many times, I responded to anything that sounded close enough. I was trying very hard to be like those cool students, some of whom even drove at my age. Seeing the way that the schools were run here, I would often wonder how my brother would react to seeing the students so free. They said whatever came to their mind and called teachers by their names instead of "sir or madam."

We walked to school every day. The mornings were very cold and foggy, especially where we lived in Richmond, the city across the river from Vancouver. Even at eight o'clock in the morning it was dark, but the afternoons weren't so bad. Once at home, my job was to help my mom with the dinner and to take care of my little niece, whose mother worked an evening shift. I didn't watch much TV because we only had one and, most of the time, the men—my dad and my two brothers— were watching their programs. Mom joined them for the six o'clock news everyday even though she didn't understand much English.

During this time, I began hearing compliments from families that I had grown up and was looking quite mature. They had observed that I was very helpful at home, doing my share with the housework, which is very important when you get married. It's sort of criteria for marriage—that you must know how to cook and clean. Mom and dad were always talking about marriage, saying that, until their daughters were married, they carried a heavy burden. I think I felt that I must have been a burden to them. They kept an eye out for any good family that may be interested in me. In their old fashioned thinking, they found no good reason for a daughter to remain single after high school. Some families did send their daughters to college or university, but my older sister had only gone to another state in India to earn a University degree because she had a slight disability. Mom and dad felt that in order for her not to be a burden to anyone she should be well educated in order to get married into a good family. And eventually she did—she married a highly educated man who didn't mind her slight limp.

By the time I was in my late teens, while still in high school, a few marriage proposals had come in. I was pretty relieved that my parents had somewhat good taste in men. One young man that I had seen was dressed quite nicely except his pants were two inches above his ankles. I thought he was getting ready for the floods. I was eighteen and really didn't want to get married, but in our culture it was very common for girls to be married at eighteen and even younger. I was afraid that if I said no there would be consequences. None of my sisters ever rebelled or disagreed with my parents' decisions, so I didn't really know how they would react if we did rebel. I didn't want to find out, because I had heard of other parents disowning their daughters for life and even killing them in some circumstances. If they believed that their daughter might have a boyfriend, they imagined that they were probably involved sexually; this would bring a lot of disgrace to the family. I feared the unknown of disobeying my parents, so like a good girl; I went ahead with their expectations.

* * *

Almost all Indian children were raised with the expectation that their parents would arrange their marriage. This holy matrimony is deemed essential for virtually everyone in the Indian community.

Some parents begin marriage arrangement on the birth of a child but most wait until later. It is seen as a mandatory social and religious calling towards maintaining family and community bonds.

Finding a perfect partner for one's child can be a very challenging chore. Many families use their social network to come across the potential mate. Often times the parents and other family members decide on behalf of the couple. Sometimes photographs are exchanged and the boy's family narrows down to a selected few. The bride-givers are considered inferior to the bride-takers.

If there is resistance from a son or daughter, enormous pressure is put upon them to submit to the parents' wishes. Sometimes the families use emotional blackmail, other times threats or violence. The last thing a family needs is for their child to bring 'shame' and 'dishonour' to their name. It would be a disgrace to the family if their daughters were not married. The pressures imposed on young women are even greater. I was one of those daughters. Their well-being and blessedness would depend on how the in-laws, especially the mother-in-law, treat her daughter-in-law.

For me life turned out to be so different then what I had visualized. I had always dreamed of a happy life with my husband. What did I do so wrong to deserve this? Should I just accept my parent's decision as defeat and learn to live with it? Am I supposed to live everyday superficially when people around are full of hatred and animosity? I now live amidst lies and hate.

* * *

CHAPTER THREE

An Intriguing Visit

I was out of high school when serious marriage proposals started coming in for me. I knew my parents had been spreading the word that I was now eighteen and they would welcome meeting good marriage prospects. My two older sisters had been married shortly after high school, so I knew it would be my turn soon.

I had started working at McDonald's at the beginning of the summer break to earn some extra money for makeup, shoes and all the other things teenagers want. I had never taken public transportation, but now I had to because I didn't have a driver's license and there was no one to drive me around. To get to work, I needed to change buses three times, although, some days I got lucky and someone would offer me a ride. Needless to say, I became acquainted with the bus route to Vancouver.

On the way to work, I would fantasize about what my ideal husband would be like: I dreamed of a humble man who would treat me like a queen. We would be best friends and we would work together and complement each other and I'd feel accepted and worthy. He would have a nice car, a beautiful home, money and of course, good looks. I wondered what kind of career I would have. I knew one thing for sure; I didn't want to make a career in a fast-food restaurant. My dream had been to become either a flight attendant or a registered nurse, but I didn't do well in science so I wasn't admitted to nursing school. And a career in waitressing on the plane – that dream died as quickly as it was conceived. I had applied for nursing and wrote the test. I was disappointed in myself and realised that I shouldn't have rushed into writing the test without being fully prepared. Despite this, I was hopeful that someday my dreams would come to pass.

In the meantime, I faithfully fulfilled my duties at McDonald's, serving customer after customer with a smile and a pleasant manner. Every day for lunch, I would have a Filet-O-Fish, a small order of fries, a small Sprite and an apple pie. The apple pie was the best part. This lunch special lasted a few months and surprisingly, I did not gain any weight, but stayed at about a hundred pounds.

My weight was something that vexed me. Every morning, my Dad would peel almonds, grind them and add butter and give me a heaping tablespoon of this mixture, perhaps hoping that it would help me to gain weight. I tried to eat lots of food, but nothing helped and everyone in my family made fun of me. They cautioned me not to go out when it was windy, saying that I would be blown away, considering I was such a lightweight. They would go even further and say that if they sneezed hard enough, I might fall over. They had nicknames for me such as, "Dried Mango Pickle," "Stick" and most often, "Agent" since I was usually the first of my family to get any sickness. I hated these nicknames and made my feelings known by ignoring them whenever they called me by one of these names. To get even, I found names for each of them and this seemed to work because they didn't like the names I called them. Slowly I won the right to be called by my real name.

Life at home in Richmond was much the same as in India, except for the weather. My parent's attitudes didn't change with the country. Their customs, strict up-bringing and traditional values still continued. Our two-story home was very close to the railway tracks, so at least once a day we had a mini earthquake.

I lived with my mom, my dad, two brothers, a sister-in-law and my younger sister. We were expected to show respect towards our older siblings by calling them either 'Veerji' for brother or 'bhenji' for sister. Even for guests or visitors, calling them by their names was very disrespectful. Every older person had a title, whether they deserved it or not. Our oldest brother was a teacher – so out of respect everyone started calling him Masterji, including us. I was always called by my name by my younger siblings. There were strict protocols, but I was used to it and never went anywhere socially. Whether it was to the mall, grocery shopping or to family gatherings, we all went together.

Mom and Dad continued their passion for gardening in Richmond and planted garlic and other vegetables during the fall. Mom learned to freeze cilantro for the winter and also kept chili peppers, tomatoes, green beans and garlic in freezer bags. She was very proud of her accomplishments. One thing I missed in Vancouver was her amazing mango pickles. India had either hot or mild weather all year round, so everything that Mom needed was in our backyard—including the mango trees. The mangos in Vancouver were brought in from Mexico and by the time Mom got her hands on them they were getting ripe. Not good for pickling. Since we couldn't get the right kind of mangos in Vancouver, she tried making apple pickles instead, but they didn't taste half as good. There were many different foods in Vancouver that I did love though, such as the pastries. I've always had a sweet tooth.

During Christmas time, while I was still employed at McDonald's, my parents told me that we would be having visitors. This wasn't unusual; we had visitors come over often, so I really didn't see any need for Mom to tell me that. I sensed that maybe there was more to these visitors – why else would she mention it? Then she told us to tidy up the house and reminded me of some unusual rules. I was told to make tea for our guests and bring it out with an assortment of snacks. I asked who was coming over, since I wasn't very fond of entertaining and pretending to enjoy conversation. Mom didn't always answer my questions completely, often just giving a yes or no response. Whenever we had company, it was made clear that leaving the room was rude. Even if we were bored, we still had to sit there out of respect. I was careful not to say much in case it offended someone, but it was hard to always bite my tongue. My younger sister, Billie, also knew my weakness so we began to use certain code words and hand gestures to talk and make fun of people. She was the youngest and she could get away with a lot of mischief. I was always reminded that I should be the responsible one of the three, so most of the time I got in trouble because I was in the wrong place at the wrong time. Mom and Dad weren't the kind of parents that would ask details from us. It was always easier to blame the oldest; so many times I got caught while my younger siblings laughed as I was yelled at. Billie took advantage of the situation. I began to get good at making fun of people without being caught by my elders.

Around three o'clock in the afternoon, the doorbell rang and Dad hurried to answer the door in his neatly pressed shirt and pants. I sneaked a peek from the balcony and saw unfamiliar faces; however, I recognized the man who walked in last—I had seen him before. The visitors made their way upstairs to the living room.

Mom quickly came into the kitchen and told me to make some tea and put out the best china. I poked my mom and, in a low voice, asked her who these people were. She told me the older man was Tarlochan Nayyar "He is a big businessman," Mom explained. He was a tall skinny man who had made a fortune in textile and metal industry.

Still not very interested, I wondered how long they planned to stay. Mom went back and forth between talking with the guests in the living room and checking on me in the kitchen. Everything had to be just perfect.

Then came that big moment, "Take the tray full of loaded tea cups to the living room without spilling it," she told me.

I shook my head and tried to look busy, hoping she would carry the tray herself. My *bhabiji*, Mona came in to help and I handed her the tray and took the snacks, just to be safe. I followed her into the living room and said, "*Satshriakal*," which means "Hello" in Punjabi, and greeted each visitor with my hands held together as if I were praying. With a quick smile I slightly bowed my head, to show respect.

I briefly sat down on the floor, since there was no room on the couches and all six dining room chairs were also occupied. The men sat on one side of the living room and the women on the other side with the children, which is customary in our culture.

The conversation was boring, so I excused myself, pretending I had to use the bathroom. Instead, I headed to the kitchen to wash dishes. A few minutes later, the women entered the kitchen with the empty teacups. The guests were in search for a nice girl who would become their daughter-in-law. The women would glance at me every so often, dropping hints. "Was that the reason they came with the man that we were familiar with? I wondered if he was the middleman." Now it began to make some sense. That's why mom was acting so anxious, but wouldn't tell me anything. I couldn't figure my parents out. They knew that this family was coming over to see me and possibly talk about marriage but they did not want me to know. I continued to look busy and avoided making eye contact with the guests. Our small kitchen suddenly felt much smaller and cramped. I was feeling very anxious with all the attention.

The older woman, Tarlochan's wife, Padma was a petite woman covered with expensive jewelery. Padma focused her eyes on me before heading to the kitchen table. She spoke softly and occasionally glanced in my direction. I knew they were talking about me. I turned to the other group of women and listened in on their conversation: they were talking about their small children and work—nothing exciting—and I would occasionally nod and smile.

The men in the front room were very loud, obviously having more fun than me. My brother was the bartender because, in our culture, it is the obligation of the girl's family to see to it that the other family is always taken care of. My family waited on them with big smiles and hands joined together—as if worshiping them—and only ate when the other family had finished eating and drinking. It almost seemed to be a servant/master relationship, as if my family were trying to make themselves lower than these visitors. Some of the men from my family, who would ordinarily never pick up after themselves, were now doing so and, for me, it was quite funny to see. But at the same time it made me mad to see how much the girl's family was expected to do for the guy's family. What made them feel so much higher than us? I watched an Indian movie once and never forgot the comment that was made by a guest at a wedding. Someone asked this particular guest who was from the girl's side and who was from the guy's side and, smiling at the question, the guest responded, "the men that you see with joined hands and their heads bowed and agreeing to every demand is the girl's side." How true that statement was and still is.

Then the announcement was made by someone that they should be leaving soon. "Wow, what a relief". I had been waiting for this moment a long time.

Gathering at the bottom of the stairway for goodbyes, Tarlochan extended an invitation to my family to a dinner party at a relative's house the following weekend. He assured my Dad that his son would be there as well. There seemed to be some special significance to this and I had begun to suspect that, although they were interested in me, they were being careful not to commit since their son wasn't around. Just seeing their facial expressions gave me a hunch that I had received the first round of approval. For my part, I thought the other family looked good.

After we had said our goodbyes, we headed towards the kitchen to clean up. There was also plenty to clean up in the living room empty glasses, dirty dishes, alcohol bottles and crumpled napkins everywhere. Even the furniture had been rearranged. The women started cleaning the living room first although we were all pretty tired. All I wanted to do was shower and head straight to bed.

Mom and Dad talked about this family for a little while and I tried to listen in, hoping to hear something about me. "Did the other family say anything nice about me, were they interested in me, or had they just come to visit?" My parents often didn't include us in their conversations, so we had to either sneak in on them and listen, or have one of the siblings sit with them while they talked. Even if something concerned us, we would be the last ones to find out; it seemed they were oblivious to our feelings and I'm not sure if that was a cultural thing. Our parents simply made all the decisions: what we had to wear, what we should become and whom we were to marry. As children, we did everything to please our parents.

Exhausted, we all went to bed after cleaning up and I slept like a baby. Even though I shared a double bed with my youngest sister, that night I didn't even notice that she was beside me. I woke up feeling good, and hoped that somehow I would get my mom to let me in on their conversation.

The next morning, mom and I made breakfast together—cheese omelettes, which were the family favourite, and some tea and toast. Punjabi teas are quite a speciality. The tea bag is boiled for a long time in water and then heavy milk is added with lots of sugar, *Elaichi* (cardamom), *Saunf/Sanchal* (Fennel seed) and *Lavang* (Cloves). Either you liked this tea or you didn't and I always felt that if it was cooked a little bit longer it could be some kind of a soup. Mom would always spread lots of butter on the toast for my dad because he loved it. Dad added butter to everything - to his *dhal* (lentil soup), *roti* (bread), almonds and even some kinds of curry. I had heard that people from India were known to love butter and my father lived up to this. For the rest of us, there was some butter on the toast and lots of strawberry jam. We all ate quietly and I sensed that this breakfast was rather odd. We usually talked a lot, about the weather, gardening, family stuff or housework. I wondered the impact these visitors had on our family because we seemed to be somewhat cold towards each other. I could tell that my parents knew much more than they were saying, but they didn't want to share anything. Maybe because we were all there, my parents couldn't talk about grown-up things in front of us children.

The silence was finally broken when my dad asked what time the dinner was. My mom replied that it was around seven p.m. I started eating slowly, so I wouldn't have to get up right away and miss out on the conversation, which had started heating up. My parents and my brother and his wife all joined in the conversation. My brother, his wife and their daughter, along with my parents, my younger brother and sister and I lived on the top floor of our home. Everyone was asking questions, talking over each other and answering each other; it was getting exciting. Then someone asked my dad about the son in question and Dad said that they were looking for a wife for him. Dad went on to say that the son was ready to get married now and would be in town soon. Apparently, he was a smart man who had a university education.

I knew they had visited our house for a reason. Although our families weren't close, they knew my parents from back home and so they also knew there was a girl here; I guess my parents had told them I wasn't spoken for yet.

My mother asked me to clean the kitchen, maybe because they had gotten carried away in their conversation and I had heard a little bit too much. I obeyed and started my work, all the time thinking about this marriage possibility.

My head was crowded with many thoughts. "Was I really being considered as a possible bride for this family's son? Was I ready to get married? I was only eighteen and I didn't know how to cook much. Neither was I skilled to do any real job outside of my home. I had only worked part-time at McDonald's. Did the family really like me, or were they just in a rush to get their job done as parents? What if this guy would see me and not think much of me? What if they found a better girl somewhere else for him?" There was so much to consider that I developed a headache from thinking about it.

I could hardly wait another week for the party. I was anxious about seeing this guy. Mom gave me permission to wear a sari, so I bought one with the money I had saved. It was a beautiful sky blue sari with sparkles all over. The *palla*, or wrap, is very heavily decorated, and is to be draped over the side of the shoulder. Saris are perhaps the most beautiful costumes for Indian women, and while they are traditional, they are definitely flattering and bring out a woman's grace, elegance and glamour.

My older sisters taught me how to put my sari on and every day I would practice a few times, trying to master wearing it. A sari can be from 5.5 - 9 meters, plus a half meter for the blouse. Walking in it was the hardest, trying to manage the pleats and the long hand piece, all the while wearing high-heeled shoes.

Then finally the day came. It was cold and dreary. I regretted that I could not fashionably wear socks or a heavy sweater with my sari. I knew it would be warm inside the house with so many people, so I would just have to make sure I found a comfortable place to sit down.

I was apprehensive about meeting the other women at the party. From previous social functions, I knew that these women liked to dress in expensive clothes and were very conscious of social status. I was unsure what kind of welcome I would receive. Chances were they knew the family had already paid us a visit for their son. They had not seen me in a sari before and I knew it would somewhat confirm to them that I wanted to be presentable to this man. Older women like it when young women dress traditionally because it shows that they have good values instilled in them.

I was also nervous because I knew how much these women loved to talk about others. They were very good at giving each other meaningful looks. Gossip seemed to be their number one preoccupation. I imagined them calling each other the very next day, talking about everyone's hair and their outfits. I didn't want to be close friends with these women because they seemed catty. I had seen people confront each other, and there were a few occasions when things had become very violent. I remember a time when one of the women in that family began spreading gossip about another woman. It didn't take long before the victim found out about the false rumours that were going around like wild fire. So, she decided to confront the perpetrator that same evening with her husband and another adult male. After loud confrontations, came a pushing and shoving match. While the men were busy damaging the property, the women shouted and swore at each other. It was a scene that alarmed some of the neighbours and the police had to break up the fight. That too became gossip that was spread throughout the community that very night. They were always confronting each other on different issues. I had always been afraid to talk about people behind their backs because I wasn't big or tough enough to scare people and I had never been able to defend myself.

Finally, we all got ready and the whole family herded outside to the car. There were seven adults and a toddler and all of us had to fit into one car. We had been on small trips many times before, and we knew how to fit ourselves into a cramped car. This time I may have complained a little because I was sure someone would step on my sari. There was no way I could go back into the house and fix it.

I was polite and let the back seat passengers in first, but then there was hardly any room for me. Half of my body was on the seat and the other half pressed against the door. During the ten-minute drive, all I hoped for was that my sari would still be intact when we got there. I didn't want to be laughed at or talked about.

Finally we arrived. My brother, who was driving, couldn't find anywhere to park and while he was generally a nice man (and somewhat of a comedian), on this evening he lacked patience. So, we all got out of the car quietly and left him to find a parking spot on the street.

Once we had made our way inside, my family and I greeted everyone and found some room in the corner. The house had been decorated with balloons and crepe paper. There were children everywhere running, crying, playing and teasing—and I hoped it wouldn't be a long night. Tarlochan and his family arrived soon after us and were given a warm welcome. The daughters were dressed in elegant saris and expensive jewellery. They were quite a stunning family. They had it all, the looks and the wealth.

The host (the same man who had brought the two families together) was a very loud man, admonishing everyone to be on their best behaviour. There were alcoholic and non-alcoholic beverages available and, to my shock, I saw some of the women pass by the pop and reach for a beer or even a rum and coke. I began to wonder about these women. When I was growing up, women were not allowed to smoke or drink. Did these women smoke as well? I guessed their husbands were allowing them to drink, but what if they got drunk and made fools of themselves? Even as these questions were running through my mind, my thoughts were interrupted by urgent shouts.

My heart started pounding. This was the moment that I was secretly waiting for - to finally see him. "What if he turned out to be not so attractive and my parents still decided to pursue this potential marriage? What if he already found himself a girl since he had been living on his own for a long time?" I was anxious to get a good look at him.

It was then that I saw the bachelor. He was a very handsome man indeed. He was well dressed and tall, with a light complexion and an attractive body. Every so often I would look at him, only to find he was looking at me. I would quickly look away, hoping no one had seen him looking at me or me at him. Did he know anything about me? I guessed that he must have searched the crowd of about fifty and figured that I was the only one of the right age group there. Besides he must have gotten some hints from his mom and sisters of what I looked like.

He appeared very different from what I had imagined him to be as I secretly spied on him. I caught him looking at other women in the room. As the evening went on, I noticed that he would make a point of making eye contact with most of the people. There was nothing different about the smile and the look I received, but I felt good about it anyways, knowing that he was acknowledging me as well. Maybe he was just playing it safe so no one would talk about his flirting behaviour. He must be used to the family gossips. But I did feel somewhat insecure when the other women were getting the attention from him. Some of these women smiled back and others just stared back. I guessed he was trying to show that he was a friendly guy and I began to notice even more little things about him. He was neatly shaved and polite, and his full head of hair was hand-somely combed. I tried hard to find something wrong with him, but he seemed like the perfect man. I even saw him with his hands joined together while greeting the elders, one of whom happened to be my dad. At one point he even offered his seat to an older man. He was soft-spoken and kind to everyone and I had to give myself a bit of a shake when I realized how intently I was observing him.

I slowly looked away while trying to fix my sari, hoping that no one had seen me checking this guy out. My eyes first landed on my mom. Oh yes, she was giving me a look that said: "I caught you." Were there others in the room that had noticed it too? I thought it best to keep my eyes off this man, if I could help it. But how could I? This was the first man I had ever met with the potential of becoming engaged to, whom I also considered very handsome. He seemed to have it all—a good family, money and good looks. He presented him-self very well and made a good impression on me, and the other women as well.

I caught him looking at me a few more times and thought, "This must be good." I was sure his family must have told him about me. Then I realized I was blushing and sweating and I began to wonder if I had put on my deodorant! I couldn't excuse myself to go to the bathroom and hope that someone had left a deodorant there. After being paranoid for some time, I decided to slide behind my sister and quickly checked if there was any sweaty smell. I was fine. It must have just been nervousness. All the symptoms I had heard a girl supposedly experiences when she meets a boy—the sweaty palms and anxiety—were all happening to me.

Some families expect their daughters to be dressed in traditional *Salwar-kameez* that covers the body well and also has a *dupatta* that is used to cover their head, which is a sign of respect. We were expected to live under the rule of our parents and be respectful to all men. The parents did not want their daughters to be seen with any man other than their father or brothers. There had been times when people had ruined marriages by telling the groom's family that the girl was "not of good character." Even after the daughters were married, they always had to be sure to protect their parents' reputation because it was important to look good in the community; otherwise, if they had any other daughters, they might not be able to find a good husband for them.

The young man seemed to be having fun with all the other men. They were being served drinks and appetizers by the host family. Every so often, some of the men, including this fellow, would go outside. It didn't take me long to figure out why they were leaving. Some of them, including this handsome guy, were smoking and I finally figured out what the smell was that lingered for such a long time after they came in.

No one in my family was allowed to smoke because my dad was very strict about both drinking and smoking. Although one of my brothers, who didn't enjoy school, started smoking in his early teens, he did his best not to smoke in front of dad. I wasn't sure whether he was afraid of dad or just being respectful. I remember dad always complained about my brother's smoking and drinking habits to my mom.

As soon as the introductions were over the men moved to one side and the women made their way towards the kitchen and dining room. Dinner was being served. We all found somewhere to sit and eat. Kids were spilling soft drinks everywhere because they were tired. I was too. The place was becoming noisier and noisier, and I couldn't wait to get back home.

Finally, Tarlochan gently got up and announced that they were leaving. Everyone got up as a sign of respect to say goodbye. Men were shaking hands with each other for a long time and women gave casual hugs and waved their goodbyes. I thought, "Finally, we can go home too." My parents and my older brother didn't like to party late and we were not allowed to dance, so I knew we'd be leaving soon.

We said our goodbyes and gave formal hugs as we made our way to the back door. It was very cold outside, but I didn't mind one bit. I was just relieved to be out of there. I couldn't wait to get out of my sari and into my comfortable, warm pyjamas.

Again we crowded into my brother's car. I wasn't complaining anymore because I had much more important things on my mind. Actually, no one was talking much. The others were all tired and probably wanted to change and go to bed as much as I did. I couldn't shake off the feeling that I actually liked the young man. But did he feel the same way about me?

Before long, we were home. I was the first to run upstairs and change and my sister followed right behind me as if she wanted to say something. She was all smiles and in a bit of a teasing mood. I ignored her until we went into our bedroom.

My youngest sister Billie and I shared a room. One day, while casually talking to her about the engagement party, I must have mentioned that the older brother wasn't bad looking. My sister was fifteen at the time, and she behaved like any fifteen-year-old would. She began asking questions: "Do you like him? Was he looking at you? Were you looking at him?"

I ignored most of her questions because I had never been in love or even looked at a man from that perspective. Growing up, we had regarded all older men as uncles and all younger men as brothers. I didn't know how to behave. "What did the older brother think about me?" I knew he had been looking at me that night—I had caught him many times. So many thoughts about my crush were overwhelming me. To me, love was new and exciting.

My sister, Billie, couldn't contain her excitement either and told Mom. My parents had a meeting between themselves and I tried to hide behind the door, in hopes of hearing what they were saying, but I was caught and sent back to my room.

After a few phone calls back and forth, Mom announced that Tarlochan and his family were coming over later in the afternoon for tea and, once again, she quickly went over some of the house rules. In considerable anxiety, I wondered if this meeting was to talk about marriage for their son. I was nervous to the point of feeling sick and was sweating profusely; my hands and feet were shaking. I figured that by the time they arrived, I would probably be ready to collapse. I began to regret telling my younger sister my thoughts concerning this man—it was happening so quickly that I hadn't had a chance to think. I wished my parents consulted me and had a family meeting. It was all happening too fast. The thought of being nice and always smiling at the young man's family wasn't really appealing and I wondered how long they would stay. "Were we going to prepare dinner for them? Would the women make their way to the kitchen again to stare at me?"

Knowing that there was really no way for me to escape this visit, I started to think positively. Surely, this influential and wealthy family would treat me very nicely. After all, they were respected people. They treated their employees very well and support a number of charities. They were looking for a good family and my dad was a reputable man as well. Furthermore, I was of the right age and lived under my family's protective eyes. This pleased them.

I could feel butterflies in my stomach and a smile crept over my face. The marriage proposal and planning was exciting and nerve-wracking as well. I made sure that I looked my best. Who knows, they could be my future in-laws. I had to make a lasting impression on them.

It was a very cold December day, but I felt sweat all over my body. My parents cleaned the house very quickly and mom changed into a better outfit, and told us to do the same. I wasn't sure what to wear. Should I put on something traditional or stick to winter clothes? I chose winter as a more practical choice.

Then the doorbell rang. I didn't know whether to hide in my bedroom or run to the bathroom. I kept thinking, "What have I gotten myself into? Why did I ever tell my sister about my secret crush on this man? Are they going to accept me as their daughter-in-law? Will I be able to fit into their lifestyle?"

My sisters and I had been very sheltered. I definitely wasn't ready to leave my family behind either. I had only been away from home to visit my older sister for a week or two, but to be gone forever was a terrifying thought.

The visitors all made their way upstairs to the living room. There were a couple of children and about six adults. My parents had gone out of their way to be gracious. My parents are generally nice people, but to be that nice! It was obvious that they were acting like the girl's parents in a possible marriage negotiation and they considered themselves a little lower than the guy's family. Mom was busy making tea, putting snacks on plates, and setting out napkins and getting juice and cookies for the children. I was so nervous. How I wished this afternoon would be over soon and that the family would give us their verdict and leave. The pressure was intense. I was forgetting the rules of how to sit, where to sit and how long to sit for. Do I look at people or look to the floor? I knew I couldn't ask questions. I occasionally nodded at the women and smiled. What if I had to burp or had hiccups, how do I hide that without having anyone notice? I knew that I was under a microscope.

Mom made me help her take the tea to the living room and I don't think that those cups had ever rattled that much. I was sure there wouldn't be any tea left in the cups by the time I reached the living room. Once there, I had to greet every person in the room, but I avoided eye contact with the bachelor and quickly found a spot in a corner, closest to the bathroom and the kitchen. Every so often, I would glance over to the person who was talking and wondering when these people would leave. Though the gathering was about me and would determine my future, nobody really cared to involve me in the conversations. My mind went back to the times when my sisters were involved in such marriage talks and realised that they must have gone through the same emotions as me. Mom was known for being a matchmaker in India. I had seen many families enter into a marriage covenant in our own living room.

The visitors told stories of their businesses, the many trips they took around the world and the number of people who worked for them. Earlier impressions I had had of their wealth were now confirmed. Padma was tiny compared to her husband. When he spoke, everyone listened and no matter what he said, they all agreed with him—I guess out of respect. The living room seemed like a zoo; there were voices and people everywhere. The waiting was getting harder to bear. I needed to know what their decision was so that I could change and go to bed.

Finally, Tarlochan spoke to his son quietly. It was then that I found out that he had a name. He was no longer referred to as the "son" but Raj. It was a moment where everything stopped. All eyes were on these two men including mine. We watched for any facial expressions that would indicate one way or another. What if he rejects me? What if he likes me? Moments later Tarlochan approached my dad and they spoke quietly. I knew this would be their decision-making time. They must have sensed my anxiousness. I slipped out so quickly hoping everyone was too pre-occupied to notice.

I heard voices and footsteps coming towards the kitchen. The women followed my mom into the room and they all had smiles on their faces. I didn't have to wait to hear. I knew he had agreed to marry me. I wasn't sure whether I should cry or be proud of being married into a very wealthy family. I guess I felt a bit of both. Our parents had found our soul mates and they would look no further. They had found our match and the search officially ended. They assured my parents that they had nothing to worry about. With their thriving businesses, Raj and I would be traveling back and forth to India often. I knew that the rich people in India had modern homes, cars and servants.

I knew I would be treated like a princess by this family. Besides, Raj was a very handsome man.

The men made arrangements for an engagement party, while the women went along with their plans. There was no communication between my future husband and me. The only time we made eye-contact was when his family was heading out. He looked up briefly at me and then walked down the stairs. I sat stiffly, not making any eye contact with anyone, which was very common behaviour for East Indian girls. If a girl was perceived as being too forward, she was considered to be a loose woman. A respectable girl speaks only when spoken too and is soft spoken. They are to keep the family honour and not bring any shame to the family.

Mom told me the engagement party was planned for the following Saturday at our house. That meant we needed to get the invitations out and start to shop for clothes and gold. Mom knew what she and my dad had to give the groom as a token of welcoming him into our family, a gold bracelet. The groom's family would give me a sari and an engagement ring. Mom and I had a very busy week buying clothes, gold and cleaning the house.

Everything was being set for the engagement party, phone calls were made to the guests, and the menu was prepared. Everything was ready, but I was still wondering if this was the right decision. Dad and Mom had agreed to the marriage, and I knew that I couldn't disappoint them but still, I wanted to tell them that I wasn't ready for marriage. I was only eighteen and had hopes of having a career. I thought about our childhood, and how strict my parents had been from an early age. My sisters and I had never been allowed to have boyfriends or to even talk to a male friend. I remember once talking to a classmate one hot afternoon while waiting for Ravi. From the moment I saw my brother's face, I knew I had done something forbidden. During the car ride home, his eyes did most of the talking and when we got out of the car, he told my parents what I had done. I got a spanking for that. My brother assumed the role of protector when he returned from University majoring in science. I didn't have fond thoughts of him and was glad that he remained in another part of India, only visiting us every six months. He had a lot of privileges – not only was he the first-born but he was a *munda* (a boy). He had a good position as the head of the science department at our high school and he was greatly respected in the community. He seemed to be very nice to others, but I always found him to be quite mean to me. Despite his attitude towards me, there was also a soft side to him. Whenever I got sick, which was often, he would take me to the doctor, hospital or to a healer.

Since my brother was perfect in my parent's eyes, he was allowed to discipline us in whatever manner he chose. Sometimes he would punish my older sister and me with a slap or take away our privileges; this would be the occasional movie or a trip. He would watch everything we did and his looks were enough to send chills down our spine. We were brought up with the saying that "children should be seen and not heard," but it applied mostly to us girls.

Fearing that I might bring shame to my family, I kept silent about my feelings towards the engagement. For days after the marriage agreement, I cried in the shower and cried myself to sleep, so no one would know. I hardly ate. I was emotionally drained. There were a range of mixed emotions from fear to excitement.

Finally, the dreaded day came. I was ready, dressed in the sari I had bought from working part-time at McDonald's. Our invited guests had arrived and took their seats on one side of the room mostly on the floor. The other side was reserved for the groom's side. They had nice dining chairs and a coffee table close to them. Some of my cousins assumed the role of waiter or waitress. Everything was going smoothly until the door bell rang. Panic arose. Billie ran into my room to tell me that they had arrived. When they walked in, all my immediate family rushed downstairs to greet them. They were given VIP treatment again. Raj's sisters came in my room and handed me the sari and blouse they had bought for me. It was customary for the groom's family to buy a traditional outfit for the new bride. I had to put it on. My parents escorted me to the living room beside the waiting groom. I walked nervously to the empty chair. I was sure I would trip on someone and become a laughingstock. It was no different than taking a trip down the aisle.

As soon as I sat down hoping to catch my breath, he wasted no time to put the ring on my finger. That made some of the guests laugh. My sister-in-law brought two red handkerchiefs and placed them over both of our laps, so our guests would bless us with gifts. Our parents were the first to walk over and bless us with money. Both sides were very generous with their giving. I was impressed. After the money was placed on our laps, the guests would gently touch our heads. My sister-in-law knelt beside me and folded the money neatly and secured it in the same handkerchief and his sister did the same for him.

I got my mom's attention and asked her if I could go back to the kitchen. She quickly walked over to me and whispered the unimaginable. I had to touch Raj's parent's feet as a sign of respect and subservience. It was important as they were superior in age and position. I felt like shouting at my mom for this unexpected gesture. I had never been asked to touch anyone's feet before.

***

In traditional Indian culture people are required to touch the feet of an elder or a spiritual leader. There may be various reasons for doing such an act: when someone goes away or arrives from a journey, and on religious or joyous occasions. In return the elders touch the person's head for a prosperous future called '*the aashirvad*' (blessings). It is also a way of humbly acknowledging the greatness of this new family.

Imagine being thrown into a situation completely unannounced to you. No one has prepared you before. You are to get up and walk over to your in-laws and prostrate before them. You've never rehearsed this before and are not sure how long to stay in that position. Should you also kiss their feet while you're at it? Caught off guard, I struggled with feelings of resentment, uncertainty and self-consciousness. Was there another way of expressing my respect for them? What if one starts to resent this meaningless tradition? How about a simple hug?

***

Tears welled and humiliated I proceeded to bend to touch their feet one at time. They gently touched my head and congratulated me. The living room was filled with spectators. I felt like I was of a lower caste as I bowed down to them.

Satisfied with my customary obligation, my mom gave me the okay to leave. I quickly made my way to the bathroom and stared at myself in the mirror and wondered where things had gone wrong. This man, who had just put a ring on my finger, had not smiled or greeted me. He hadn't made any effort to make eye contact with me. Part of me wanted to head back to the living room, return the ring and apologize to my parents and the guests.

But I reasoned with myself that he must be nervous and shy and that he would open up soon. After all, there were lots of people there that he didn't know. He wouldn't have agreed to marry me if he didn't like me. I told myself that it should get better soon.

As I headed for the kitchen, my sister suggested that he and I could spend some time together to get to know each other a little. He followed me into a bedroom. He sat quietly on the bed and stared at my face. Neither of us said anything to each other. To break the si-lence, I managed to smile. He smiled back but with a confused look. I regretted being there with him and felt guilty that he had left his company only to find out that I had nothing to say. When I suggested that he could return to the living room, he asked why I had called him there and what it was that I had wanted to talk to him about. What I wanted was for him to tell me that I looked good tonight and that he was very happy with his decision. I just wanted to hear something —anything. I felt so awkward. I just wanted to tell him that the wedding was off and that he was the most obnoxious man I had ever met. Instead, I got up and walked out, and he followed.

My new fiancé returned to drinking and having a good time with the other men, while my brothers and dad served them, making sure they had plenty to drink and eat. I remembered how my parents had always been critical of drinking. I was so displeased at how my family had lowered their standards in front of this family.

I spent the remainder of the evening either in the kitchen or in my bedroom with my cousins. I could have jumped so high when I was told that they were leaving. I came out of my room to say my good-byes. Raj actually waved to me. I also gave a quick wave back. Both our parents made arrangements to meet at the *gurdwara*, the next day to set a date for the wedding.

After everyone had finished eating and most of the alcohol was gone, everyone left and we were left with the task of cleaning the house.

The bride adorned herself with her jewels. Her beautiful unveiled face shimmered in the moonlight as it mixed with the light filtering from the hallway. As she slowly paced her steps trying to curb her excitement and nervousness, she approached the lowly lit bedroom. Her shyness had prevented her from undressing in front of her husband, so in the privacy of the bathroom she had carefully slipped into the blue satin nightgown bought especially for the occasion. She lowered herself beside him onto the bed, and he pulled her closer. She was elated to finally feel his arms around her. The moment that she had waited for all her young life had finally arrived; the wedding festivities were over; her romantic dreams of being lovingly and tenderly caressed and loved were about to become a reality. She had imaged that her lover would move his hands into her hair, down her neck, then her back and.... tingling down her spine ...soft whispers of sweet words ... finally he was hers and she was his. She felt butterflies fluttering in her stomach.

In the young bride's excitement she had forgotten to remove the hairpins but at that moment she couldn't have been bothered to take them out. The anticipation of feeling her groom's arms embrace her for the first time made her knees weak. The only question on her mind was: "Will he find me attractive?" This innocent young woman was completely naïve about sex - she had never even been kissed by a man. The only sense of what she should expect had come from reading Harlequin novels in a faint attempt to prepare herself. Women in her family had never discussed the act of marriage with her. Sex was a culturally taboo subject.

She had imagined her suhaag raat (wedding night), after seeing many Bollywood movies, as the most memorable time of her life. The honeymoon suite would be decorated with exotic flowers, rose petals and sensual fabrics. She'd pictured a suite with strings of flowers hanging from the canopy all around the bed. Candles would be lit everywhere, soft music playing and rose petals would lead her to the bed to meet her romantic husband.

She anxiously waited for gentle words of comfort, but was rudely jerked towards him with no words of warning. Without waiting to remove her satin gown, he pulled it unceremoniously up to her chest. He climbed on top of her while pinning her shoulders to the bed. He began to force himself upon his terrified bride. She cried out in pain, and reacted by trying to move away up the bed, but was stopped by the headboard. He thrust again and again until he was satisfied. When *it was over, he turned and without another word, went to sleep. She just laid there in bewilderment, her body throbbing with pain, wondering what had taken place. This was not what she had imagined in her romantic reveries.*

The newlywed excitement had vanished. The tears rolled silently down her cheeks. The naive young woman looked at her wedding ring, and then slowly started to rotate it around her finger. Her mind was racing; still stunned ... "What had just happened?"

Was she raped on her honeymoon night by her husband?

Rather than being a mutual act of intimacy, this had been so one-sided; he ruthlessly had controlled the whole act. She felt like a used object and he had had no regard for her feelings. After a short while her husband awoke. He shook her and commanded her to get up, strip the soiled sheets from the bed, and replace it with a blanket.

While the rest of the household slept, that first morning, the confused new bride got up early. Her inner thighs felt sore and bruised; pain radiated from within and shot down her legs. It was challenging to manage and mask her pain. She took a hot shower, hoping to soothe the tenderness. Then she saw her husband grab the blood stained sheets; he proudly and casually displayed them to his mother as he passed her in the hall. His action spoke volumes as if to say, "See, here is the evidence of my manhood and my bride's purity."

She had such difficulty sitting or walking. Her husband agreed to take her to her family doctor. After examining her, the doctor informed the woman that she was ripped. In disgust, he questioned what kind of monster would do this.

She would find out the answer to that question in the upcoming years.

Would she ever be able to return to normal?

Had she done something to deserve the cruel behaviour she'd received?

Why had he treated her like that?

Was it because he hated women?

She fell to pieces after that first encounter with her husband. The inner scars from the rape remained for many years. Would she ever feel safe again? From that time, fear and terror seized every fibre of her being, whenever the memory of that fateful night was triggered by any action, event, or occasion.

What arrogance he displayed! He truly believed that he had the marital right to force himself on her. She has had to live with disturbing emotions, low self-respect, and sexual dysfunction that were rooted in the traumatic events of these early days..

She would have worn her sari for the rest of her life – if it had not been for his fierce handling of his innocent young bride.

That husband was my man. The bride was me.

CHAPTER FOUR

The Wedding

Christmas was just around the corner, but we didn't celebrate that holiday in my family. Instead, we celebrated *Diwali*, the festival of lights that happens around Halloween time; it is a celebration for the Hindus and Sikhs in honour of *Rama* and *Sita*. So, on Christmas day we didn't have a tree or any presents. It seemed like it was just another day.

A date was chosen for our civil wedding at the courthouse followed by the traditional ceremony a couple of weeks later. Mom and dad worked together as a team. The day was approaching quickly and Mom and I were going shopping almost every day.

The day of the court marriage arrived. The weather was miserable outside. The streets were slushy and slippery from the snow fall. My gracious brother suggested that he drop us right at the door of the court house to avoid falling. He knew that my high heels would land me not in front of the Justice of Peace (JP) but on my butt. My family and I packed into my brother's brand new Chrysler New Yorker. In about an hour I would be married.

Raj's family had arrived before us and were comfortably seated in the lounge. After handshakes, smiles, and complaints about the weather, we made our way to the office. I looked towards Raj and noticed that he had a smile on his face. With his flashy new suit and a fresh haircut he looked stunning. As we made our way to the front of the room to say our vows, he asked me if I was nervous. I nodded "yeah". Now I felt guilty for thinking all those bad things about him. 'He's actually a nice person,' I thought. He was joking with the Justice of the Peace and my brother. When the JP asked for the bride and groom to come forward, Raj walked side by side with me. We made sure there was no physical contact between us. The ceremony started immediately. Very shyly I repeated the marriage vows. Raj was more confident in his response. He was asked to put both rings on my finger. Then it was my turn to put the ring on his finger. We didn't kiss each other. I guess the Justice of the Peace was familiar with East Indian customs and knew not to suggest it.

Both families congratulated each other, by hugs and handshakes. I was promised a good life by my new husband's parents. I was assured that they would stand beside me along the way. They knew I was very young and that he was six years my senior and had seen the world. He had spent three years in India studying medicine and then had come to Canada and studied engineering. Though he had not completed either of his degrees, he was a very smart man.

Even though I was now officially married, I went back to my mom and dad's house. I was not allowed to live with Raj until after the traditional Punjabi wedding in the *gurdwara*. That was scheduled for a couple of weeks later. Raj and his family moved into our basement for a month, but we still didn't have any communication with each other.

***

Punjabi wedding celebrations are notoriously elaborate and can go on for about a week. My wedding was on a Friday night and there were lots of things to do to get ready. The culture of Punjab is very rich and Punjabis are generally known as large-hearted, cheerful people who live their life joyously and vigorously. Sikh marriages are a festive family event and include many rituals, such as a day of *Mehandi* (henna). Ladies *sangeet* is an evening of celebration complete with music and dance. The bridal party dances to the *jagoo* (Indian folk dance) with a decorated copper vessel on their heads with lit candles. Some of the ladies carry a long stick with bells tied to the end and they dance around with it while singing and performing *gidda* a traditional dance. The following day a paste of turmeric, milk and cream is applied to the bride by all the women in her family starting with the mom. In India and other countries, henna is arranged in intricate lacy or floral patterns on the hands or feet, which symbolizes good health, fertility, wisdom, protection and spiritual enlightenment. The deeper the color, the more fortune will come upon her. Our weddings are the big reasons families get together. Some would travel from different parts of the world to attend the wedding.

***

At last, we made it to the *gurdwara* for our wedding ceremony. It started with the Priest telling us about the obligations of married life. We were to walk in tow around the *Sri Guru*, four times at set intervals. First the priest read a *laav* (one of four prayers) from the *Guru Granth Sahib*; then the musicians began to sing the same *laav*. Then we were asked to get up and circle the *Granth Sahib* in a clockwise direction. I got up during the first call, only to find that my fiancé had fallen down. "Was he drunk?" I was shocked but I pretended that it was okay. He said in a rather loud voice that his knees had locked. I didn't acknowledge him or feel any pity for him. I was sure that people in the *gurdwara* were talking and definitely coming up with their own reasons why he fell. At this point I really didn't care. I wanted the wedding to be over.

We didn't go anywhere for our honeymoon and stayed in our

basement with his parents. Out of respect for his parents, brothers and sisters, Raj decided that I should change and go to sleep without him. He went back to the family room and I closed the door behind him and quietly went to bed. When I heard the door open, I quickly shut my eyes and pretended to be a sleep. He undressed partially and slowly went on the other side of the bed. It took a few minutes before my drunken husband passed out on our honeymoon night. I looked forward to another night—a better one than this— with only the two of us.

CHAPTER FIVE

A Rude Awakening

During the first month of our marriage, while we were living in my parents' basement, Raj kept me away from my family. They were just a few feet from me, but I didn't see them much. He would either take me out to meet his buddies, or we would go to his sister's house where the only thing everyone did was gossip. They made sure I knew that their family was very wealthy and that no daughter-in-law would be entitled to their hard-earned money. They also complained that their parents hadn't given them enough money to buy their house. Their talk would put me to sleep.

I began to take more notice of the amount of alcohol Raj was consuming. It was always hard liquor and he drank more than the others. He was a chain smoker as well. The ashtray in front of him would be overflowing with ashes and cigarette butts. The room would reek of alcohol and cigarettes.

Part of me wanted to suggest that Raj should stop drinking and smoking. I wondered how he could possibly be enjoying himself and his companions. I quickly realized that I did not like his friends. Almost every other word that came out of their mouths was a foul word and they had little respect for women. It was already clear to me that they didn't treat their wives very well. When we got together, the men would sit in the living room drinking, and the wives would sit in the kitchen. There wasn't much laughter among the women. We would make small talk and always kept an eye out in case one of our husbands was listening in. The men always ate first and the host wife made sure that the men always had beer, water and alcohol supplied to them. While drinking, they ate finger foods that always had to be warm. There were foods such as fried chicken, lamb and curry; it didn't matter as long as everything was spicy and warm. The men seemed to enjoy being waited on.

Within a few weeks, Raj and I moved into our own suite not far from my parents. He continued to drink and have a few drinking buddies join him whenever they felt the need to be together. One evening he joined a bunch of his friends for drinks at a nightclub. I didn't like the idea, so I tried to stop him. I stood in front of him with my hand blocking his path. He pushed my hand away while grinding his teeth. The other men were standing around as if they had come to watch a fighting match before heading to the club. One of them encouraged Raj to show me who the boss was. Raj thought that was a brilliant idea and turned and pointed his finger to my nose, and said, "Don't ever embarrass me in front of my friends."

These friends all had wives and children at home. I never was formally introduced to these men. All I remember about them was that they were skinny and dark. I made little eye contact – hoping that they would leave. I wanted to be rude to them so they would never return. I tried to explain to Raj that I wasn't embarrassing him; I just didn't want him to drive after drinking. His friends began calling him to the car. One of them made a comment that I wasn't worth the time and that they were getting late. "You let your so-called friends talk to you like that," I said. "They don't care what happens to you – all they care about is having a good time. When will you start spending some time with me?"

The next thing I can remember, I was on the kitchen floor, bleeding profusely from my nose. I was shaking and crying and scared. There was blood on the floor and all over my clothes. My face seared with pain with Raj's backhand strike. I had lost my balance and fell. "See what happens when you talk back to me? Just remember I am the one who pays the bills around here, not you!"

In a loud voice, he shouted at me to put my head up so it would stop bleeding. He walked to the bathroom and returned with a towel. He handed it to me, suggesting that I clean up all the mess. The mess that he started, I had to clean. I had never been hit that hard in my life and I could feel my nose swelling. Mom and dad had spanked us as kids, but I had never seen blood like this anywhere. And while I had seen women with bruises on their faces, I had never thought it would happen to me. I began to think that this man was a liar and that he shouldn't have married me if he didn't like me. After waiting around for ten or fifteen minutes, he left to meet his friends and told me, on the way out, to behave myself while he was gone.

I slowly made my way to the bathroom and stood, stunned, in front of the mirror and thought to myself that this was not what I had looked like when my parents had given me in marriage. I thought of something that my dad had said— that if a man raises his hand on a woman once, he'd do it again. I wondered if this was the start of a cycle of violence but hoped against hope that it wasn't. Crushed, I phoned my parents and told them what had happened and they promised they would come over in the morning and talk to Raj.

***

Do abusive men consider it their right to punish and control their partner's actions? Did he feel he succeeded in convincing others that his behaviour was rational and she needs to be taught? Does he believe that his special status as a man entitles him with rights and privileges to hurt her? It is important for him that she not disagree with him, especially in front of other people. No matter how badly he treats her in his mind they should not raise your voice – He only has the right to be angry. Does this sound familiar?

A young girl is forced to get married and then fall in love with a man she hardly knows. From the beginning there are signs of rejection, isolation, physical pain and control. A one-sided relationship dominated primarily by the husband. He insists on making all the decisions because they are the right decisions. He treats her as if she were his personal servant. They are careful not to show this behaviour to any one of their friends or colleagues.

The floor was usually covered with stains of violence, a place of loneliness and trembling.

The beautiful young virgin he had married just weeks ago, who proudly displayed the wedding pictures in the living room and bedroom now stood staring. The girl in that picture was dead. She had been beaten away by a ruthless man. The wise thing to do is to remain silent because to agree or disagree would also provoke. All she does is bow her head in shame. He strikes on the face as if verbal abuse wasn't enough and makes her believe that it was her fault again. The marriage is nothing more than loveless and lifeless. What had she done and could she do anything to correct her mistakes? I don't think so.

***

I got a mop and washed the floor. With every painful move, the mop got redder and redder. I felt like throwing the mop away. It was covered with innocent blood. The bathtub where I emptied the pail of water was also stained with blood. I threw away the soiled clothes. I didn't want to keep a reminder of such a painful and humiliating experience. After a long shower, I took my pillow and a blanket and lay on the couch staring outside. I had just been through a terrifying experience. The hope for a loving and peaceful relationship was shattered. I was now nursing a swollen nose and a bruised face. I was flooded with thoughts of regret and self-blame. "Why did I embarrass him in front of his friends?" I thought of the hockey players who resumed playing after the fight. The swelling or the bruising didn't bother them much. They proudly gave interviews – they were committed to their game. I too was committed to this marriage.

I wondered if Raj was enjoying himself with his friends after hitting me so hard in the face. How late would he stay out, or would he even come home? I cried myself to sleep.

Some hours later, Raj rudely awakened me. He was drunk and could hardly stand straight. The stench from the alcohol and cigarettes was overpowering. He pulled the blanket off me and demanded that I stand up immediately. Terrified, I got up quickly. He pushed me into the spare bedroom, threw me down and closed the door behind him. He told me I must never talk to him in that manner again. He said that he knew I had called my parents and that they were not allowed to come to our house.

I was shivering not from the cold, but from fear. His eyes were red and he clenched his teeth together. He was about a foot taller and weighed much more than me; there was no way I could stand up against him.

He gave a gentle push and turned away leaving me in the spare room. He slammed shut the door behind him. There was nothing in that room to keep me warm. I remembered that my pillow and blanket were in the living room. I stood against the wall for a few minutes wondering if he was psychotic or did he possess a dual personality. He enjoyed all his friends' company but not mine. I heard sounds outside my door and thought he was doing something in the hallway – But what? Curious I decided to slowly open the door. 'Was the door stuck?' I looked all around to see whether something fell and if I was blocking it. I tried to pull it harder with both hands. Nothing was working for me. I was convinced he had done something. The room had no furniture in it yet, so I yelled and begged him for a blanket, but he didn't respond. There was nothing I could do but lie down on the bare floor. The window was too small for me to crawl out. Even if I could, where would I go? The area was fairly new to me. Off and on I drifted off to sleep, but most of the time I lay awake with the question "What had I said and done that made him react so strongly."

After some time, I could hear the landlord walking upstairs. I assumed it was early morning. I started to knock on the door to get Raj's attention. I wasn't sure if he was even in the house. My body was aching and I was cold. All I wanted was a warm place to lie down.

Then I heard footsteps outside my room. It was him. He decided to open my door. He looked tired and hung over and motioned for me to come out of the spare room. Very quickly, I got up and headed towards the bathroom, but he called me back and told me to make his breakfast. I longed to take a hot shower and sleep for the rest of the day.

I thought that we would talk over breakfast. Wanting so much to hear that he felt bad for what happened and he would never do that again. As soon as I had finished making his breakfast, he went into the living room and ate it while watching TV. I tried to get his attention, but he totally ignored me. He left his dishes and told me to start cleaning the house, saying that women should get up early to cook and clean.

My parents did end up coming over that day. I invited them inside; needless to say they were shocked to see my face. My mom, in a rather loud voice, asked where Raj was. I motioned that he was in the bedroom, that he wouldn't be too happy to see them. They made their way to the living room, angry to see me so swollen and bruised like that. Mom continued to ask me questions about the incident. I didn't want to talk about it; there was so much shame and pain attached to it. I knew how difficult it was for them emotionally. I said very little. Dad asked me to call Raj. He refused to come out of the bedroom. I asked my parents to go and promised them that I would call if he hurt me again.

In our Punjabi community, people rarely talk to each other about their personal issues because of the huge concern – "what will other people think of us?"

As soon as he heard their car leave, Raj came out. One look at his face sent chills down my spine. He was very disappointed in me. Now his anger was multiplied. I stiffened. He kept coming closer to me. I kept moving backwards until he got hold of my arm. He asked with a firm voice why my parents had come when he had told me that they were not welcomed. I apologized, promising it will never happen again. He pushed me onto the couch and pointed his finger at my face. I couldn't breathe. What if he slaps my face again? He told me never to call them again. If he ever caught me talking to them, I would be very sorry. If I wanted to be happy, I would have to obey him. Fearfully, I agreed.

Then he invited me into our bedroom, and I was allowed to sleep. He held my hands and gently reminded me that I was his wife and no longer my parents' daughter. They had no more say over me. The day he had married me, they had lost all their rights over me; I was his now. I turned towards him and told him that I was in pain and that he should never hit me again. He said that he didn't like hitting and that I should not provoke him or tell him what to do. He said that he didn't like to be told what to do. I was too tired to get into a discussion and just wanted to take advantage of the opportunity to sleep.

It was a long time since he showed me some affection. I wanted him to love me so badly. I had not enjoyed our sexual intimacy at all in our few weeks of marriage, but I didn't want to give up this opportunity to be with him and to show him my love for him. And since I had no experience, I was willing to learn and enjoy our lives. Our culture strictly prohibits sexual intercourse before marriage and I had been proud to keep myself innocent for Raj. I had looked forward to enjoying the love that comes from that. But our honeymoon was in our basement next to my in-laws room. Though the whole event lasted only a short time, it left me with an intense pain and not wanting more.

This particular day however, I felt wanted, loved and desired. He was a gentleman. Within a short time, I forgot the physical and emotional pain he had inflicted on me and enjoyed being with my new husband. Now my marriage had meaning and we were united.

There were a few days of peace afterwards—he didn't drink much and I didn't say much to him either. I made sure he didn't find out when I talked to my mom on the phone. He frequently asked me if I had called my parents, and I always denied it. My parents knew not to call when he was home.

Raj often called his parents back home in India. It didn't matter to him that he was racking up the telephone bill. When they asked how I was, he told them a completely different story—that I had been very mouthy and was fighting with him. He told them that he slapped me to teach me a lesson. He continued, telling them how hard he was working outside the house and then at home he had to clean and help cook. He said that I had lacked the basic household skills. He asked why my parents had never taught me anything. I couldn't believe how much he could lie in front of me. I wondered how much he lied when I was not around. He laughed and joked with his parents, completely ignoring me. He poured himself drinks and smoked while telling them stories of things that had never happened.

Then he called me to the phone saying his mother wanted to talk to me. He whispered in my ears to be respectful to his mom. She reminded me of all the rules of marriage. Laughingly, she asked if I liked being hit. She said she knew her son loved to drink and I should keep my mouth shut in order to keep peace at home. I said alright and handed the phone back to Raj.

They continued their foolish talk for a while longer and when he had finished talking to his parents he repeated the same stories to his sisters. He also told them about my black and blue eyes very proudly. They asked what had happened. He said that I talked too much and he had to put me in my place. I walked over to the bathroom and shook my head in disbelief. He gossiped and lied. He had told me to not talk to my parents, but here he was talking to his parents, long distance, and telling them many lies. And why was he telling them all the details of our lives?

"Why had I gotten married? Maybe I should have just gone back home with my parents. Why hadn't I left the night he had hit me?" I had so many questions, but I didn't have any answers. If I left Raj, what would people say about us? Would my family be able to show their faces in our community again? Would they be respected? I had another sister who would one day get married. I didn't want to do anything to jeopardize my parents' reputation. I didn't have any way out. I felt trapped.

He totally dominated our sleeping patterns. Whenever he needed me, he would face me, other times it was his back towards me. He would mostly turn over and go to sleep. I didn't really mind since he was so abusive. I couldn't get over the incident when he had hit me out of my mind—or the lies he had told his family. I was forbidden from speaking to my parents. But he could talk to his whenever he wanted. He began to exercise his power over every aspect of my life. I felt it was better that he didn't touch me.

A few weeks after his first violent outburst, Raj told one of his closest relatives that I could babysit her young boys. He said that I was doing nothing else at home and that taking care of the children would keep me busy. He told them I had too much useless time on my hands.

I was shocked that he hadn't asked me first. He proudly told her that they could save their money. My services would be free. She was elated and couldn't wait to phone her previous babysitter and cancel her services. I slowly walked away from them, thinking, "What's next?" This man was full of surprises and I couldn't keep up with him. I wished he had talked it over with me before telling them I would babysit. I didn't mind taking care of the children, but I also wanted to go to school and have a real job—I wanted to be paid for my work, but now I knew there would be no chance of that. The relatives phoned a couple of their friends to announce the good news.

The children's mother wrote up a list of things I would be doing with her kids. The list was posted on the fridge. The little ones seemed excited to be spending time with me. The first few days, they brought snacks and a packed lunch, but after that, there were no more snacks and eventually, the lunches stopped as well. I was required to make their lunches and come up with creative snacks and one day, their mother called and asked if I would give both boys a bath and I agreed. It ended up being part of the routine and there were even days when they would stay for dinner without any invitation. I was getting very frustrated with the arrangement.

Finally, after a month or so, I voiced my concerns to Raj about the food bill and the lack of respect on their part. My complaints seemed to fall on deaf ears, until one day when the two of them had a disagreement. It became rather heated. I removed myself from the living room and went into the bedroom, where I could still hear everything. They swore at each other and accused each other of gossiping. Finally, Raj kicked them out of the house and told them that I would no longer be babysitting. He said that he had realized we had been taken advantage of.

I was so relieved to hear Raj sticking up for me. It was about time he stood up for me. I felt proud and somewhat powerful. When they left, he had told me that they were never to come back to our house.

CHAPTER SIX

Pregnancy and Policemen

Raj put on a charming face outside of the home. A sharp split from the private to a public image. Though he was enraged at home, he would be a different man outside. He laughed and helped friends and neighbours. With me he would pick on almost everything. The clothes my parents had given me looked cheap to him. He always came up with something. If it wasn't me, then it was my family. No one came close to his expectations. He always looked down on people, constantly making negative comments. I wanted to remind him of things that would open his eyes to the truth about him and his family—that they were not the perfect family that they had portrayed themselves to be. They were liars, drunkards, and very unkind people. I tried hard to be a good wife, to keep the house organized and to his standards, so I could have some peace and sanity when he came home.

With time Raj's confidence grew. His abusive behaviour was getting excessive. He began to blame me for anything that went wrong. He slapped, pulled my hair, pushed me against the walls and would verbally attack me. He also fought with the landlord. He could no longer keep his phony nice guy image.

About a year and a half later, I found out I was pregnant. I was overjoyed, but Raj didn't show any signs of happiness. He asked me how that happened. Although it was supposed to be a happy time for us, I couldn't break the silence between us. He made me work even harder at home, saying that if I kept active, my pregnancy would be a breeze. I helped him fix cars in the garage on evenings and weekends. One night, looking for a fight, he decided that he wanted something else for dinner. I told him that dinner was already cooked. I wasn't feeling well, and I needed to lie down. He pulled me up from my bed and demanded that I cook what he wanted. Trembling I headed towards the kitchen quickly. He came in the kitchen with a rage. With one hand he held my face very tightly and with the other he grabbed my hair. He told me never to talk back to him. Fearing for my baby and my life, I agreed. For every one of his violent behaviours he blamed me. My punishment for that night was to wash all the walls. It was early in the morning before I was finally allowed to go to sleep.

A few weeks before our baby's arrival, Raj appeared to be in high spirits. He was drinking and played his music rather loudly. He would come around me and start smiling as if he had a big surprise for me. I didn't bother asking what it might be. Later in the night, he asked me if I wanted to see how built he was. He punched a hole in the living room wall. Terrified, I hurried back into my bedroom. He followed me there and told me to get ready. I asked him where we were going at that time of the night, but he said it was a surprise. I was beginning to get very scared. I put on a sweater and shoes and went out with him to the car. He went around back into the house to get the German Shepherd his friend gave us a few days earlier.

I knew the streets of Richmond, where we lived very well. I realized fairly quickly he wasn't going to my parents' place. So where was he going? He stopped the car on the side of a main road and told me to stay inside the car. I knew the people whose house we had parked in front of, but I couldn't figure out why he was going there. He did not get along with them. Why had he come here then? Is this the surprise he was telling me about? Within minutes, I heard screaming and saw a lot of commotion in the house. People were yelling at him to leave. He ran back into the car and sped off. I asked what had happened, but he replied "nothing". From the opposite direction, a fleet of emergency vehicles with sirens and flashing lights sped by us. He even slowed down and moved to the side for them. I had no idea what happened in that home. I was too afraid to ask.

Then he broke the silence. "I need you to protect me." Protect him, I thought, now he's asking for my help. He must be in big trouble to come to this level.

During the short ride home my body went numb. I asked him what he had done, and he said that he'd had to straighten some things out with this family. He wouldn't say anything more. My head was spinning, and I felt ready to deliver my baby. The next words were a threat. "If you tell the police anything, I will kill your family first and then you". Did he already kill someone there? Am I next? I was so terrified. Trembling with fear, I assured him I would not say a word. He gently put his hand on mine.

He rushed me inside and shut the door. He returned a minute later. Pretending to be calm, he heated his dinner and sat watching TV. Just then we both jumped to the loud knocks on the door. Raj opened it and about ten police officers stormed inside. They immediately handcuffed him and took him outside. A few officers remained inside and asked me what had happened. I told them that he hadn't told me anything. I had no idea what had happened at that house. One officer bluntly asked where the gun was. Totally shocked at this question I told him that he didn't have a gun. But they didn't seem to believe me. There were a couple of nice police officers who told me he would most likely turn that same gun on me one day. They told me that he had threatened to kill some members of that household while flashing the gun in front of them. I knew that the police were genuinely concerned about my safety.

The police went from room to room checking everything—the drawers, cupboards, under the beds. They couldn't find the gun.

They knew Raj was drunk and they saw the hole in the wall, but neither they nor I knew much about the gun.

I knew that the police were searching the whole neighbourhood for the gun. A few hours later, they left without making an arrest. The look of victory was all over his face. He had won this battle and it gave him a big boost. This only intensified his macho behaviour. Part of me was angry that Raj hadn't been arrested. I felt even more terrified of him. He came over and thanked me for protecting him. I wasn't sure how I had protected him. For some strange reasons I thought he would now treat me better.

I had nightmares about the gun all night. The next day, he got up earlier than usual. He didn't ask me to get up and start his breakfast. He went out and was back in ten minutes. Before I could ask, he said he had gone out for a walk. I believed him.

When Raj returned to work a couple of days later, I called my parents. My mom was very angry and said she didn't want to ever see him again or have anything to do with him. She told me that he had a gun and had been threatening to hurt some people. I told my mom that I had had no idea he had a gun. I hadn't seen it. It turned out that my brother and his family had been present at that house when he had crashed their party. I was deeply ashamed and apologized to my mother and hung up.

I wondered if Raj really did have a gun and where it could be. Would he really hurt my baby and me one day? I knew that my mom was terrified of this man and I also began fearing for my family's safety. Raj seemed to have no regard for anyone. I felt responsible for his actions. Were they blaming me as well? After all, I was in the car with him. They didn't know how he was treating me.

I started thinking about my unfortunate life with this man. I had been a pretty good girl most of my life. I couldn't remember ever hurting anyone. I had made people laugh. I had sometimes disagreed with others, but I had never done anything like what Raj was doing. Was I having a bad dream or living in another reality—everything seemed surreal. I knew I was sinking deeper into a quicksand and I had no clue how to get out. I wanted so desperately for everything to get better. I had a lot to look forward to; I would have a baby soon.

Raj was a smart man. He did well in school, winning a few awards. I had seen his potential. He was very intelligent. Anything he put his mind to, he could do it. I wondered if there was something wrong with him that he had become so violent.

One afternoon, Raj told me that he was going to a football game. He had bought tickets for this game. I had gone with him a few times, but that day I wasn't feeling well. He gave me permission to spend the evening with my parents. I spent most of the evening lying on the couch, watching TV. Around 11:00 pm I drove home. Raj was back.

Halfway there, my water broke. I panicked and stalled my standard car at an intersection and a few minutes later, I got home and rushed in to tell Raj that we were going to have the baby soon. He was asleep and told me to call an ambulance and reminded me that my younger brother was on standby.

Around four a.m., I woke Raj up and he drove me to the hospital. After he checked me in he went back home to sleep. He had lots to drink at the game. I was scared and felt very alone at the hospital, but there was also an excitement in me. I would soon be a mom and things were about to change. Raj would be a daddy soon.

The child was terrified by her mother's screams for help. The sight of her father's thick belt buckle imprinted on her mom's tiny body was unbearably painful and confusing to the little child. Those awful occurrences increased in frequency and violence each time. She dreaded the next explosion and fear kept her up most nights. How could she feel safe when her father, who was supposed to be her role model, was spiralling out of control?

She could never speak in her mother's defense for fear of making things worse. She would just sit there being a sad helpless onlooker to the dreadful on-going saga.

The abuse that this six-year-old had witnessed was overwhelming. Where were all of her mom's and dad's relatives when she needed them? Why were they turning a blind eye to all that was happening? No child should have to live under these circumstances and be a continual witness to such mind-boggling abuse. She felt trapped and had no choice but to continue living with her harsh, distant, abusive father and seemingly voiceless mother. The nightmares and hallucinations plagued her nightly.

Where did all the blood on the floor come from? From her mom? Chills ran through her body as she stood paralyzed in shock, yearning to release the screams that arose within her. Her days and nights were spent crying and feeling extremely alone. Fear was her constant companion.

Did her father love her?

Had she done something to cause her dad to act like this? He seemed so hard-hearted. Maybe if she tried her best to be very, very good, he would stop.

The impact of this situation caused her to experience difficulty in expressing herself both at home and in school. She became increasingly withdrawn and began having frequent panic attacks. As a result, her grades in school were negatively affected.

Her mom was being bullied and treated like a servant. It baffled her why her mom was dealt with worse than their real servants.

At the same level, she loved her father – but resented him and felt that he didn't deserve the title of father. How did her mom do it? How did she raise her and her younger siblings under such extreme brutality?

She lived with the constant fear, "when I wake up in the morning, will my mother be alive"?

The child alienated herself from the world around her. She had thoughts of running away. She found it hard to trust others - especially grown-ups.

A sense of familial duty and obligation caused her to rally around her mother. Her dad was very unstable and unreliable. He drank and smoked all the time, totally disregarding the fact that her mom was very allergic to cigarette fumes. She wondered how many more times she would have to watch him beat her mother ruthlessly, "Please no more....!"

In between his beatings, he would tell the child that he was disciplining her mother and she was welcome to join in to hit her.

Truth or lies? She knew that they were lies, but it almost seemed like a relief to believe them because of how convincingly he said them and often the lies were being crammed into her head.

Why was he rampaging on about how her mom had wrecked his life? More lies?

She could not bear the sight of her mom being grabbed by her throat again. What would be next?

The petrified child hid in the corner of her bed and wept. She was shaking uncontrollably. The tiny space that she called her room became her shelter and her place of refuge. Her whole fragile world seemed like it had been thrashed. She often wondered when the season of mourning and anger would end.

When is it ever going to be okay?

She was the bravest survivor of all. She survived the horrific atrocities. She suffered alone; hiding her secret well and making sure others didn't learn about the abuse in her home. She feared abandonment and the repercussions. She had endured so much loss, uprooting and separation. Her home had become a battlefield. Inside there was only audible silence. There was no joy.

The outbursts from her father were frequent, unprovoked and unpredictable. There would be a litany of abuse inflicted on her mother by her father. She felt it was her job to protect her mother. She tried to take on adult responsibility but at the same time she herself was being deprived of the security and care she wanted and needed. Intimidation pervaded her daily life. She did not know a life of peace. Violence had been an integral part of her family for as long as she could remember.

She longed for a home where there would be no more shame and embarrassment. She felt like a child held hostage.

"Not a word from you, young lady. I will deal with you later, unless you want to end up in the same place as your useless mother", were the hateful words that came out of her father's mouth.

The thing about her dad was he seemed great in front of others. He made sure that her voice remained silent. She had tremendous ambivalence as to who the enemy was.

The child often stayed behind after school to help clear the desks with the teacher. Then she would walk home very slowly. Anything to be away from home: School was an escape from her domineering father. It helped her forget the most painful aspects of her life at home.

Her mom was her idol. She knew her to be a loving woman who covered her children's faults. She would take the blame herself. Whenever her dad was away, the child noticed her mother wearing make-up. "Wow mom, you look so beautiful. I want to look just like you when I grow up", she would proudly tell her.

Little did the girl know that she would be helplessly watching many more tragedies to come. Yet in the end she would burn up all her built up anger, rejection and lies with him. She would eventually find the strength to let it all pass away.

That man was my husband. The child was my daughter.

CHAPTER SEVEN

Hannah

I moved around my small room in pain, too embarrassed to cry out very loudly. Every so often, a nurse would check on me, smile and say I was doing very well. I didn't feel like I was doing well at all. Three long hours later, they wheeled me into the delivery room.

Since my doctor hadn't arrived yet, there was some panic because the nurses knew they had to take charge as the delivery was progressing rapidly. I tried to cooperate as much as I could. Finally, they said, "Well done!" and I heard a baby cry. The nurses talked softly among themselves and told me they would try to get me some sedatives. Before I passed out, I remember the nurses saying, "Congratulations! It's a beautiful baby girl."

I woke up a few hours later. I still hadn't seen my baby, so I called for a nurse. My family doctor and a nurse came to my room, but the look on their faces wasn't very comforting. I quickly sat up and asked if my baby was okay. They assured me she was doing well, but said there was a small defect. They thought it would be best to prepare me before they brought the baby in. They said the baby had a black birthmark that covered her entire arm. I asked if she could move her arm and they said she could. After answering all my questions, they told me referrals were being made to have a plastic surgeon and a team of specialists look at her arm in the next few weeks.

Then they rolled the baby's cot into my room. She was a beautiful baby girl with lots of black hair. I immediately moved the shawl to see her arm and was shocked because I had never seen anything like it before. I just stared at her arm, making her tons of promises for a brand new arm just like her other one. I was so lost in my thoughts that I forgot to feed her. My nurse came in and started to help me. They gave me a mini orientation on how to feed and change.

It was late afternoon when Raj arrived. By then the baby was back in the nursery. He said he had had a bad hangover and needed to sleep. He asked to see the baby. I told him about the arm before the nurse brought her back to me. He gave me that look of disappointment. He either stared at the floor or straight through me.

I wondered if he was excited about the baby; he hadn't brought me flowers or hugged me. He stood at the foot of my bed staring at me as if I had brought this problem on our baby. I didn't bother asking him if my parents knew. I had my precious baby – and I wanted to enjoy her. I tried my best to look somewhat happy. I didn't want the nurses or the new moms next to me to think something was wrong with us.

A nurse brought the baby over to us, all wrapped up in pink. When she opened her eyes for a second, I saw her beautiful black eyes and began to fall in love with her. I forgot for a moment about the birthmark, until Raj walked over, lightly touched her face and immediately started to remove her clothes. He was shocked to see her arm and stood there staring at it, not saying a word. There was a big empty silence in the room. The lady from the bed next to me was in the lounge with her family. I hoped she would come back to her bed to break the silence in my room. Our baby went back to sleep quickly. I leaned over and picked her up. Bringing her close to my face, I whispered that I loved her no matter what.

I heard footsteps and looked up, assuming that my neighbour had come back. Instead, there was a team of doctors, who introduced themselves as dermatologists. They were there to provide some comfort about the birthmark. The team leader assured us the birth mark wouldn't cause our daughter any harm. They would eventually remove it. They made several suggestions, although none of the procedures would be performed for a number of years. They needed a large area from which to obtain skin for a graft. They told us the baby was perfectly healthy otherwise and admired her hair, since a couple of the doctors were losing theirs. She had long fingers and the most beautiful eyes I had ever seen. I knew this girl would be very special. I held her close to my face, kissing her almost non-stop until a nurse finally interrupted. She wanted to show me how to bathe the baby. I was a new mom and didn't know how to care for a newborn. I observed her carefully. Raj passed up the invitation, saying that he'd rather not since he would probably never bathe her anyways.

That evening, my family came to visit. They were very excited. They brought flowers and cards. Mom had also brought some homemade food. Her first comments were that the baby looked very much like me. After the hugs and well wishes she asked Raj if I could spend a few days with them. Mom was well known for taking care of my sisters and spoiling them when they had had their babies. They were pampered for two weeks while mom and our housekeeper cooked, cleaned and took care of the babies. Then mom would send them back home with gifts and more nutritional food.

Raj didn't respond. Mom looked at me and we both knew he wasn't going to let me go. The rest of the family were pushing each other in order to get a closer look at the baby. There was so much excitement. It had been a while since we had a baby in our family.

I kept quiet, knowing Raj would have the final say. I also knew that once they left, he would make comments about my mom—I could see it coming. I had not mentioned anything to my family about the baby's birthmark. What would their reactions be towards my precious baby when they found out?

Then the nurses made the announcement that visiting hours

were over. I began to feel sad knowing that I would be left alone with him. What was he going to say to me? I hoped he would leave with everyone else. I wanted to sleep and enjoy my baby. Why wasn't he like the husband next to me? He was such a proud dad. He was so happy. He even asked his wife if he could spend the night there. Very lovingly, she said no and he kissed her goodbye and repeated, "I love you" a few times, both to her and their baby.

Raj sat on the chair beside the bed and stared at the floor while I tried to nurse the baby. He looked at me and asked why my mom would even think of asking that question. I shook my head. I knew he would bring up this question. I ignored him. He asked if I had told them about the birthmark. I said no. Then he told me that no one should ever know about it. I figured that was another reason he didn't want me to go to my mom's house. I nodded, knowing he had just found the perfect excuse. If not the birthmark, it would have been something else. He didn't like my family.

We brought our baby home. Raj began to hold her a bit more. A couple of hours after we got home, he called his parents and updated them on her arm. He told his parents already. What a rascal. Just two days ago he warned me not to tell anyone. Do his rules apply only to my family? I couldn't believe he had told them. Pretending to be religious, he asked his mom to pick out a name for her from the *Guru Granth Sahib*. In the Punjabi culture when a child is born the first initial is picked from the *Sikh* scriptures. The priest opens the book and picks the first initial. That is the beginning of the newborn's first name. My heart sank because I wanted to pick a name for her. They had a lengthy conversation about the birthmark. My mother-in-law suggested she would go to a witch doctor, which was very common, to find out what had happened to the baby and get a cure for her arm. They promised to call back the next day.

I began to clean the house slowly while Raj sat on the couch with the baby beside him, watching TV. He gave me a list of things he wanted for lunch and dinner. The menu was posted on the fridge.

I was tired and needed rest. I envied my sisters who had been pampered by my mom. I wished our still nameless baby would cry for milk. That would give me the much needed rest. She didn't cry much—she was a good baby.

Mom was allowed to come for short visits. She would bring warm food with her. Immediately she would attend to the baby. She would apply warm oil on the baby's head and gently massage it. Although mom was very fond of massaging the babies and was pretty good at it – Raj told her that she did not have to do all that. I knew that he did not want her to see the birthmark. My younger sister Billie helped me in the kitchen. I was very thankful to them both. But this help was very short-lived.

Raj's parents called back with a name. He was over the moon and started filling out forms with that name. I gently suggested another name, but he said he could not disappoint his parents. They had asked Raj to invite all his relatives for dinner. They hadn't spoken to each other since their fight. Raj obeyed his mother and called all of the family right away.

They all came for dinner the next day. When they found out the baby's name, one of them suggested a nickname for her. She named her Hannah and Raj agreed. I was losing control of my own child's life. It didn't matter what I thought about anything, although I did like "Hannah" better than the traditional name Harjit.

A week after Hannah was born; Raj had to have surgery on his ankle. He was hospitalized for a few days. Mom took care of Hannah when I visited him in the hospital. Mom saw the mark on Hannah's arm. I told her to keep it a secret from the rest of our family. Mom asked him if I could stay with them while he was in the hospital. He said I would be fine at home. He made frequent calls at night to check up on me. I didn't get much rest, with him calling and having to feed and change Hannah.

He came home with a cast on his ankle. One of his relatives needed him to buy some materials from the lumber store. Raj obliged.

We headed to the store after lunch. Hannah slept on my lap peacefully. As we approached a traffic light, we were hit head-on at the intersection by another vehicle and dragged a few feet into a parked vehicle. Hannah fell from my arms. At that time we did not have a car seat. She made no noise; I was in shock. All of us were taken to the hospital. The doctor assured us that the baby was fine; however, I had some injuries and needed some tests done. My face was bleeding. We were sent home with some painkillers.

The pain was unbearable. It was swollen like a balloon on one side of the face. It was difficult to take care of Hannah while doing all the housework. Raj insisted that he couldn't help because he too was healing from his ankle surgery. He would not let me rest. Instead he would tell me how much pain he was dealing with and that he needed rest. I was on the brink of a breakdown.

He showed no consideration for me. He yelled obscenities in my face, saying that I looked even uglier now. I had to stay up late waiting on him until he went to bed. Every day, it was pretty much the same routine. Raj would call from work to check up on me. I was physically and mentally exhausted. I was like his slave. The only place I could go away from him and the baby was in the bathroom. I made a point of making frequent visits to the bathroom and called it my asylum. My day included the list of chores Raj wanted me to do: wash the walls, clean the cupboards and sort out his tools; the list would go on and on. He would come home and check if the chores were completed. If not he would make me finish them after dinner. There was absolutely no way out of this. Not only was I tired, but I was also feeling extremely frustrated with him. I was beginning to despise him. There was no way I could tell him or show my emotions. It would make the situation worse. On the other hand, he freely verbalized his feelings towards me. He often made comments that he regretted marrying me. I had to change my entire lifestyle to keep peace in the home. Raj considered that it was his right to punish me because he had given me freedom to visit my parents. To irritate me further he'd ask if I had a mental problem or if I was uneducated.

Hannah had lots of doctors' and specialists' appointments in the Vancouver area. Knowing that Raj wouldn't take us, I secretly asked my sister to accompany me. I was getting used to his temper. Whenever I went out, he would time me and if I was late, I would have to prove where I had been. I never told him that I had spent a few minutes picking up my sister at my mom's house. That would give him another reason to fight. He always seemed to feel good after a one-sided fight—I guess it made him feel like a strong man.

Once Raj needed my younger brother's help, so he asked me to call him. I didn't mind at all. I was very happy to call my family in front of him. It didn't take long for my brother to come over and help. Raj suggested that we go over and visit my parents. I wondered if he was up to something. I jumped at his offer and quickly got Hannah ready before he changed his mind.

He was very nice towards my parents. They sat and chatted for a long time. He had a few drinks and enjoyed my mom's food. We left on a pleasant note. As we drove out of their driveway, he asked me if they knew about Hannah's birthmark. "Should I try and explain to this man, who had a short-term memory, that mom was babysitting Hannah when he was in the hospital. Is he that dumb that he couldn't remember? My mom and my sister had the baby for hours at a time. Wouldn't they change her diaper, give her a bath and put on fresh clothes? Did he think that her birthmark would mysteriously disappear when she was there?" Fear struck-had anyone talked about her birthmark to him? Why was he questioning me? Or was he testing me? Whatever the reason was, I knew he was looking for a reason to fight and maybe going to my parents' house had just been a set-up, giving him something to fight about.

This would be a long night. This was his way of punishing me. He saw how happy I was and he couldn't stand it. He repeatedly made negative comments about my parents. Their kindness meant nothing to this low-life. He was demanding superior privileges as a son-in-law. This man's thinking was completely distorted. Whenever he wanted, he would twist my words to suit him. That gave him a reason to fight. He felt he was entitled to call the shots anytime.

Fear was evident on my face. I placed my hands where he couldn't see them shaking. That would prove to him that I was scared of something and would suggest that I was hiding something. In his eyes, I was always guilty and he needed to discipline me.

I held the baby close to me and hid my hands under her blanket. Every so often, Raj would glance at me and give me the look of death. I had been so happy at my parents' place, feeling free, able to smile and enjoy a moment of peace. Now, it was all slipping away, I sensed a rough night ahead. Part of me hoped that my baby would be very fussy tonight, so I could attend to her instead of sitting in front of the devil and listening to all the nasty things he would have to say about me and my family.

It was usually the same things. I was getting good at knowing when he would pause, when he would reach for a drink and when he would make the same ugly face he did whenever he described someone in my family. Most of the time what he had to say was about my mom—he just hated her. My mom cared about my well-being and was concerned about me, especially with me being a new mom and the car accident. She also knew Raj was very abusive. His mission in life was to isolate me from my family, from my few friends and from the community. He was succeeding.

The short ride home was quiet. He kept giving me dirty and frightening looks. I got out of the car and gathered the baby bottle and diaper bag while he walked ahead of me. He went straight to the bathroom, which gave me a quick moment to wake Hannah up. I undressed her and tickled her so she would be fully awake. Bless her heart, she woke up.

When Raj walked into the room with his hands on his hips, he asked me again if I had told my family about Hannah's arm. I shook my head. "He is really out of his mind. Should I even bother reminding him of his hospital stay?" Part of me wanted to shout out the truth, but it would land me in hell for screaming. I started to get angry at my family, thinking that one of them accidentally brought it up with good intention. Was it my brother, my dad, my mom? Who would have done something like that; especially after had I told them not to?

Raj kept staring at me, hoping for a confession, but I kept quiet. He walked over and slapped me across my face so hard that I saw stars. Just then, the baby started crying. He grabbed me by my hair and told me to put her to sleep quickly; then he would deal with me. I quickly grabbed the baby's bottle and headed to the kitchen, with one hand on my face. It was burning with pain and anger. I began to sweat in fear. He grabbed the baby from my hand and no matter where I moved in the kitchen, he followed with Hannah in his arms. If I looked at him, he would slap me again, but these slaps weren't as hard as the one before. I guess he was holding the baby and couldn't use his full strength.

It didn't take long for the water to heat up for the baby's milk. That meant that as soon as she was fed, the saga would continue. How I wished that she wouldn't sleep, but unfortunately, she did. Raj got up and motioned for me to take her to her crib, and he followed. Once she was covered, he pushed me outside the room and shut the door behind him. This time, I didn't make it to the kitchen. He grabbed me by my hair from the back and slapped me again on the same side. I was still nursing the place where he had hit me when another blow came. Then, as punishment, he sat me down on the floor and laid out the rules again. I was never, ever to contact my family or even think of going to see them. He was going to monitor my phone calls. He said that either he or someone else would always keep an eye on our house to see who came and went.

After he was finished talking, around midnight, he told me to cook him some lamb and rice. I got up and walked towards the kitchen. I rolled my eyes and swore at him under my breath. Ever so slowly, I took the meat out and began to thaw it. Sensing my disgust he walked over to tell me to speed up. The menu became longer; now he wanted salad and tea as well. I cursed and swore at him, but thankfully, he couldn't hear it. I began cooking, the curry smell spreading all over the house. (What I didn't like about cooking Indian food was that it left a very strong smell which gets into the clothes and even makes your hair smell. Often in school the non-Indian students would ask some of us why our food smelled so bad).

That night, I was pretty sure our landlord was listening to what was going on in our suite. The sad part was that they did nothing. I knew they didn't want to get involved and I didn't blame them. No one wanted to get between a husband and wife, especially with this man involved. They knew him well from a previous encounter, when the police had come after Raj had threatened my family with a gun. I knew the landlord and the neighbours preferred to keep their distance. They probably wanted us to leave because Raj was a trouble maker and drank most of the time. There was also the constant smell of smoke around the house. The TV was on until late at night, and the landlord and his wife had young children, who went to bed early. They were very patient with us.

Raj and I stayed in that place for about eight months, until he got into an argument with the landlord. A few days later, he served us with an eviction notice. I wanted to leave quietly, but Raj didn't and purposely spilled ketchup in the fridge, on the stove and the carpets. We moved closer to my parents' house, but Raj's rules still applied. I did break them occasionally. I often sneakily called my parents to let them know I was okay and because I was also concerned about their well-being. I thought that, after all, Raj made numerous long distance calls to his parents and talked for long periods, so I was entitled to talk to my family at least occasionally. Most of the time, when he talked to his family, he complained about my mom or me. They gossiped about the other siblings, and his mother complained about her daughters-in-law, who lived with them.

I learned to keep secrets from him, only sharing what was necessary. I would often agree to his demands to his face to keep some peace, but I didn't always abide to every rule he made. Sadly it had become a way of life for me. I could never hate my family, and I wasn't going to avoid them because of him. As long as he didn't find out, I was safe.

The verbal and physical abuse had become a lifestyle for me. Instead of enjoying the peaceful days, I wondered if this was the calm before the storm.

One day he decided that he would stop smoking. He kept his one and only promise and surprisingly did well. Maybe someone told him that he would die from smoking. He valued his life and decided that cigarettes weren't worth it. The downside to that was he was always hungry. I had to cook whatever he wanted, whenever he wanted. I tried to talk to him on good days and ask him to stop hitting me. He was six-foot-two, one hundred eighty pounds. I was five-three and weighing ninety eight pounds. His response was that I had to stop provoking him. He said if I did everything right, he wouldn't have any reason to get angry. He explained that he had to punish me for my own good. He would say that I was getting out of control and I needed to be saved and protected from that kind of behaviour.

Moving into an apartment was a wise choice. I knew there were many neighbours around us and they would call the police if they suspected a fight. That was comforting. Maybe this would be the turning point in our marriage; maybe now Raj would accept me. He might be a bit more sensitive towards my needs. That was very wishful thinking.

Hannah was growing into a very healthy toddler and talking more. She was drawing closer to her papa. He liked the attention he got from her. I didn't mind at all because it gave me some space to be by myself.

Soon after we moved into our apartment, I found out I was pregnant again. I had hoped the news of another baby would bring some change in Raj. I knew Hannah would like to have a little brother or sister to play with. I figured the children would keep us busy so there would be little time to fight. I just had to find the right time to tell Raj about my pregnancy.

Raj had just applied for a position with a bigger company closer to home. He was a good worker so he got the job. He made new friends at work that also enjoyed having a few drinks after work. They would meet at a local pub after work. He often came home late. Other times, he would go to a nightclub and come home early in the morning. I had planned to announce our pregnancy over dinner. That night he came home around two in the morning. I had been worried about him, thinking he'd been in a car accident. When he came home, however, I found out he had been to a nightclub. He was so drunk he couldn't walk straight. He just made it to the couch and fell asleep there. I went to bed, feeling very let down. We should have spent that evening together, sharing good news, but he chose to be with other people that night.

I had never been to a nightclub, and I had no idea what took place there. "Did Raj go with someone, or was he meeting someone there? How did he get home when he could hardly walk; did someone drop him off?" I tried to think positively, assuming that this would be an isolated incident. As I settled into bed, I hoped it would never happen again. I turned and faced the crib and fell asleep.

In the morning, I noticed him taking painkillers. He said he had a bad hangover from the night before. I asked where he had been and he gave a good story, somewhat believable. He said it was a friend's birthday and the friend had insisted he go along since he had no family here. Raj said he had felt sorry for this guy since he was new to Canada. Raj wanted to help him out and then he'd gotten carried away drinking. He said he didn't realize how drunk he was until he started driving. He acknowledged that he had made a mistake. He should not be drinking and driving.

I slowly found the strength to tell Raj I was pregnant. He stared at me and asked how it had happened again. "Maybe you had something to do with it", I wanted to say. Instead I told him that I would be looking for a doctor closer to us. The previous doctor was too far to go to. There was no excitement or discussion on this matter. He spent most of the day sleeping. Hannah and I played with Barbie dolls for a while. I told her that soon she would have a baby to play with. She was excited. I was glad that someone was.

On one weekend, he asked me to cook his favourite dish, goat curry. I was busy in the kitchen when he came out of the bedroom very well dressed. I thought he would ask me to get ready to go out and celebrate with him. Instead he reached for his keys and waved to Hannah, saying, "See you later." I followed him to the door and asked where he was going, but he just kept walking. As he closed the door, he said, "See you in an hour." I hadn't seen him dressed like that since our wedding. "Why was he in such a hurry, and where was he going?" I continued to cook, hoping he would be back soon.

Eventually, Hannah fell asleep waiting for her dad. I kept looking out the window, hoping to see his car. The entire evening passed in this fashion. Drifting in and out of sleep, I wondered why I hadn't tried to stop him from leaving. Was he avoiding me because he wasn't happy about the pregnancy? What was so wrong with me that he needed to be away so much? I began to believe the things he often said to me—that I wasn't pretty and educated enough. That he could have done so much better than me. He'd come close to my face and point out things that made me look ugly. My nose was too big, I didn't have a model-like figure, and I wore cheap clothing. Nothing was ever up to his standards.

I wanted so much to be like the other beautiful women that he admired and praised. I began to wear a little bit more make-up and dressed nicer. He hardly acknowledged my new look.

I did not have much support from my family. I didn't have any friends left. I felt lost and alone in my life. What I did know was I wasn't happy at all in this marriage. When I got married I hoped to do things with Raj that I wasn't allowed to do at home when I was single. Now I could go to a club, to the movies, friends' houses and anywhere else that he would take me.

Instead I was a lonely woman. The little self-esteem I had, quickly vanished. It seemed like my life was being sucked out of me. Day after day it got worse. I wished that I could just walk out with my daughter. Raj would easily convince my parents that this was an isolated incident and it would not happen again; that I was causing harm and embarrassment to myself and he had to use some force to save me. With his charming looks and sweet talk, he would win them over. Knowing the consequences too well, I would remain silent. That would only prove that I was guilty, and that I was not strong enough to be on my own, especially with a young daughter. I had never lived alone before and the thought terrified me, yet I felt suffocated being near him. He controlled every aspect of my life. He had begun to pluck out my own sense of beliefs and replaced it with his. I was on the verge of losing my sanity. I began to live one day at a time, beginning to believe his words that I would never make it without him—that I needed him.

I must have been feeling jealous; I didn't want another woman sharing my husband. I dreaded the thought that he would be out having a nice dinner with someone else. Even though I didn't want to be with him, I also couldn't live without him. I was stuck in this dysfunctional marriage.

It was very late at night when I heard the door opening. I quickly jumped out of bed to see if he was okay. He was drunk, but not too drunk to push me out of the way. To avoid him, I went to the bathroom. When I came out, he was sitting on the couch, waiting for me to get out of the bathroom. He called me over and pointed to his neck. My immediate thought was that he had been in a fight and someone had tried to choke him. Concerned, I turned on the light to take a closer look and saw what appeared to be a bruise. He grabbed my hand, pulled me down and told me that I was a useless wife. He said he had found someone who loved him. "Poor woman, she has no idea who she is dating", I thought. Then he began to spill out the events of the evening. He had met a young woman somewhere and they had gone for dinner. Then they went for a few drinks at his favourite nightclub. After that they had gone to her place. He kept smiling, feeling so proud of his action. He must have felt so desirable.

I went completely numb. I wondered which was worse him beating me up or him having an affair? I felt sick to my stomach. Why was he doing this to me? Did he hate me that much? He was a liar and an adulterer. Any little love that I had for him, vanished that moment. I looked at him with disgust. I spent the night on the couch at his request.

The next morning, I went through Raj's pants pockets and wallet while he slept. I couldn't find anything other than some loose change and his cigarettes. I checked for any smell or lipstick stains on his shirt, but I couldn't find anything. I felt betrayed and dirty. Now that I was pregnant again, where could I go? I didn't have any money. I didn't have any skills as I had never worked a real job. I would have to talk to my mom and get her advice. I would call on Monday after he left for work. I walked around the apartment, totally numb. I was in no mood to play with Hannah. She had no idea of the turmoil her papa was putting us through. She would jump onto the bed and try and wake him up. He slept the whole day.

It was late afternoon when he got up. The thought of having him around us made me furious. If I voiced my anger at him, he would definitely act like a mad man. Besides I didn't have any proof other than him talking in his drunken state. He had been good at twisting things around. He didn't believe that I should ask him any personal questions. He was in control of his life – not me. He was the bread winner.

How was I going to make his filthy bed? How many other women had he had affairs with? I began to despise him in my heart. He had done many other hurtful things to me, but this was the worst. After a long shower, he grabbed a beer and headed for the couch. Hannah ran after him, but he wasn't in the mood to play with her.

I was enraged with him and debated whether I should tell him how I felt. I wanted so much to leave. He had been taking advantage of me. He knew my weakness very well. I had little skills and no support. As I began to rehearse what I would say, he appeared in the kitchen and grabbed my hand and took me to the living room. He told me to sit on the floor in front of him and when I refused, he pushed me to the floor. He bent towards me—I could smell the alcohol on his breath—and he held my face so tightly I thought he would break my teeth off. Then he pushed me back.

Hannah started to cry at his violent behaviour. When he saw how scared she was, he called her closer to him. Her eyes filled with tears. He began to tell her that I was the worst mommy ever and all he was doing was disciplining me. Placing the distraught child on his lap, he began to brainwash her into believing that I was a bad mom. He began to tell her that he would give her a better mommy. One who would love both of them and they would be very happy. She nodded okay.

I sat there for a long time as he began to give out details of his affairs. He compared me with these other women. Then said I came nowhere close to them. He said I should be thankful that he allowed me to stay in his house. He talked proudly of how generous he was with me. He felt sorry for me since no one else wanted me, so he was stuck with me.

I was only allowed to get up to get him or Hannah something to eat. He assigned me a place on the floor in a corner. He related me to his old shoes. Their place was on the floor just like mine. After handing him his drinks, I would have to take my seat on the floor again. He cuddled with Hannah and told her to laugh at me because it was so funny seeing me on the floor. He told her I was being punished because I didn't know how to take care of them.

He asked her what else they could do to make me learn his rules even faster. Poor Hannah was caught in the middle. Her eyes were filled with fear and sadness. Reluctantly, she would suggest something, and he would make me do it. Once she said I had to face the wall, and he made me stand in the living room facing the wall. At first, I refused, but he quickly jumped to his feet and slapped me across my face. After seeing stars all around me, I quickly did as I was told. Then he made me turn around and asked if that had felt good. I didn't reply.

"If you had listened to me the first time and not refused, I wouldn't have had to slap you," he said. He blamed me for his violent behaviour. "I know what is best for you. If you continue to disagree with me than I will decide which path is right for you. When I am talking you need to shut up."

He fed Hannah and then ate his own meal. The whole time, I stood with my back to them. As he ate he'd ask me to turn around so I could see how much he was enjoying his food. Later in the evening, he put Hannah to bed, a role he had never taken before. Proudly he came out, expecting a medal for his achievement. Still smiling, he dangled my knee-high nylons in my face. "Was he now dressing like a woman?" I wondered in disbelief. This man was full of surprises. Just then he began to tighten the nylons on his neck as a demonstration. I began to shake, thinking that he was going to strangle me. I started to look towards the door hoping to run for my life. Should I scream at the top of my lungs or reach for a knife? Begging only heightened his excitement. It had taken two years for me to accept him as my husband. But at that moment, I began to hate his voice, his presence, his smell and everything else about him. Was it a mask he had put on that first day I had seen him? He talked more with his eyes than his rotten mouth.

As he walked closer to me, he began to stretch the nylons to see how long they could get. He had a devilish smile on his face. I began to sob and shake with fear. Was he going to strangle me? How long would it take for me to die? Should I start banging on the walls to get the attention of the neighbours? How I wished I had superwoman powers at that time. I wanted to break his hand and throw him out the window.

He took my hand gently and walked over to the couch. We both sat down. He reached for his drink and asked if I would like some. I refused. He lit a cigarette and blew the smoke into my face. When I coughed, he deliberately continued and asked me if the smoke was bothering me. It really didn't matter whether I said yes or no; he continued to do whatever he wanted to do. I noticed that he had put the nylons down on the coffee table; they were still within his reach. I kept hoping the stupid nylons would vanish mysteriously. He noticed that I was still shaking with fear. He put his arms around me and told me not to worry, but to enjoy myself. I relaxed a bit, thinking that maybe he had been joking with me all along—after all, he was showing some affection towards me. Thank God I hadn't screamed for help. That would have been so embarrassing, and he would have been very angry with me.

It was much later when he suggested that we have dinner together. I still couldn't get the nylons out of my head. Why had he brought them out of my drawer? I wasn't going to bring it up in case he forgot about it. I was clearing up the dishes when he called me into the living room. He got down, grabbed one of the nylons and pulled my feet together and started to tie it. When I began to resist, he got up, slapped me across my face and told me to shut up and cooperate. I had been such a fool to think that he had innocently brought my stockings out. He really was a cold hearted torturer.

Once the nylon was tight enough, he sat comfortably on the couch and demanded I walk around the coffee table. Feeling totally humiliated, I cried and begged him to take the nylon off. I quickly got down myself and started to untie it, but he pulled me back up to my feet. Then he reached for the other nylon and tied my hands behind my back. He asked if I liked that and, as usual, he blamed me. He was a sick monster who was motivated to torture me to satisfy his sadistic wishes. If I had obeyed the first time and done what I was told, then he wouldn't have had to punish me further, he said. I could feel my hands and feet getting colder and colder. He ordered me to walk around a few more times. I shook my head and he gave me a good push. I fell. I struggled to get up while he looked on. He was getting a kick out of it. To avoid a third nylon, which he probably would have used on my neck, I went along with what he demanded and tried to please him.

The monster then stripped my knee length nightie off and raped and sodomized me. I pleaded with him not to do such a sick thing, but my pleas fell on deaf ears. The more I pleaded, the more violent he became. When he was done, he untied the nylons. I just covered my face and cried. I hoped Hannah wouldn't come out of her room and see her mother in this condition. I knew how devastating it would be for her. She was still a little child and she didn't need to be exposed to this kind of abuse at her tender age. I made sure I wept quietly. I wished for this animal to be paralysed, so he would never do this to me again. I had never heard of these kinds of acts being done to anyone. Was this what marriage was about?

When he was finished, I slowly got up and headed for a long shower. There was nothing I could use to cleanse myself from the filth he had poured onto me. If I could have used bleach and erased my memory somehow, I would have. The remainder of the night, he made me sleep on the floor next to his bed. He pulled the dresser in front of the bedroom door so I couldn't leave. He must have known that I was thinking of running away with my daughter. I didn't care where to. I just wanted him out of our lives.

It was a very long night. Every part of my body ached. I was so relieved when Hannah finally woke up the next morning. I pushed the dresser out of the way to get to her. He woke up and watched my every movement. He came out of the bedroom and lay down on the couch and watched me even when I went to the bathroom. I wanted so badly to phone my parents and tell them that I had married a monster, but how could I tell them what he had done to me? My parents had a very good relationship with each other, and my siblings and I had never been abused. Would they even understand my pain and the kind of fear I was living with?

For the rest of the day, he watched TV and played with Hannah. Later in the evening, he came over, gave me a hug and suggested that I rest and take it easy. There was lots of leftover food from the previous night, so I didn't have to cook.

My pregnancy went okay, considering what I was going through. Raj started accompanying me to the doctor's appointments so I wouldn't say anything about his behaviour. I still had very little contact with my family. I had talked with my mom a few times, for a few seconds, while he showered. I hadn't told my parents anything about his abuse or the nature of it.

CHAPTER EIGHT

Tony

A few months before my second delivery, Raj opened a welding shop a short distance from our house. He took Hannah and me with him everywhere he went. Most of the time, we sat in the car, while he talked to people. He made sure he parked where he could see us. Some days, it would be very hot and Hannah and I would sweat from the heat. If he was in a good mood, he took us inside with him; otherwise, we had to make do with a newspaper fan.

The business officially opened a couple of months before the baby's arrival. But his business always came first. There was also a lot of work to be done before the shop opened. He quickly realized how much work was involved in running an entire business by himself. He began to teach me how to get things ready for him. I stayed with him till late into the night, working in the back. I managed the office, took care of Hannah, swept the shop and did my housework. My nose, ears, hair and clothes were covered with grit.

Around that time, we also bought our first house. It was an older home with a huge yard. I didn't like the house very much but it was his choice. He said he had big plans for that house, which was small with a large attic. I had been hoping for a newer house.

One day, while we were working at the shop, a social worker

came to talk to us about my health as a pregnant woman, as well as Hannah's health. She was concerned about the dust and the effects it would have on us. Raj got very angry and accused her of being racist. He demanded that she tell him who had reported to her that we had a child in the shop. When she refused, he looked at me suspiciously. He asked the social worker to leave and she did.

That day, we went home earlier than usual. I was happy to get out of there. After we had had our showers and finished cooking, Raj asked me to put Hannah to bed right after feeding her. He walked into the kitchen and took the belt out of his pants. One look at his face, I knew he was in a fighting mood. Immediately I felt excruciating pain in my tummy. "What now? Things had been slightly better and then this social worker appeared. His hands were probably aching to hit". If he did something to me tonight, no one would hear me. Our neighbours kept to themselves. Our properties were big and were separated by hedges. They were either busy with dinner or watching TV. He had been doing well—in the last few months there had been the occasional slap here and there, but nothing like before. He came up to my face and dug his nails into it. He said that he knew who the culprit was that had called the social worker. I pleaded with him, saying that it wasn't me, but he wouldn't listen. Then he accused my mother. He shouted that it didn't matter who called but I would be punished for it. He had to teach me a lesson. He pushed me against the wall and began to strike me with the belt wherever he could. With every strike, I screamed louder. I tried to move to avoid the beating, but he took the buckle end and whipped me several more times. I didn't realize that he had stopped because I was mentally preparing myself for more pain. Slowly, I turned around and saw him nursing his hand. I guess the belt must have left red marks on him. He threw the belt away and told me to put his dinner on the table.

How badly I wanted to poison his food! He kept reminding me how sorry I would be if I ever decided to leave. He was not going to leave a single member of my family unpunished. I was not prepared to put my family in any danger, especially from this man. They were good people and I could not let them suffer.

A few days later, I was booked into the hospital for delivery. I looked at this delivery as a mini vacation to recuperate my black and blue body. I was so excited at this news. The doctor felt I was overdue by a couple of weeks. When the nurses asked me to change into a hospital gown, I hesitated because I knew it meant they would see all the bruises on my legs. Eventually I consented but pulled my socks higher. Raj was with me the entire time making sure nothing slipped out of my mouth. I knew the nurses had seen the bruises; no one could miss the multi-coloured designs on my legs. Very little of my own skin color was showing. I was so embarrassed showing all my colors of torment to the nurses. I had expected the nurses to ask me in front of Raj what had happened to my legs. No one did.

Then just before midnight, I delivered a healthy baby boy. Raj appeared to be very happy; he now had a *munda*. In our culture having a boy is an asset and a girl is considered a burden. A family isn't complete until a boy arrives. It is almost always blamed on the woman.

He called my parents first, then his parents. He kept making calls to his numerous relatives to announce the arrival of our son. I was exhausted and dozed off; I hoped naively that things would change now and Raj would treat me like a person. He looked very happy. Our family was now complete with a girl and a boy. We had everything materially we could have wanted.

When Raj left the hospital that night, I had the best night's sleep I'd had in months. I dreamt of a fantasy world for us, a world of peace and laughter: a world where I was a princess with a loving prince. A world where fear did not exist in a home.

It's amazing how the mind will grasp onto the smallest ray of light and place so much hope in renewed dreams, despite strong evidence that such hope is unlikely to be realized.

CHAPTER NINE

Bread and Blood

For a couple of weeks, people came over to see the new baby. Most of my extended family came with gifts and food. They hadn't done this when Hannah had been born and I knew that was because this time I'd had a boy and everyone wanted to celebrate with us. Our house was livelier. Raj offered drinks to anyone that came over. It gave him a reason to keep on partying.

***

The birth of a baby girl is more muted than for a son. There is a strong cultural bias towards males. The girls have been victims of fatal neglect or even murder. Girls were cared for less than their brothers. The girls were seen as a liability. They would move away and live with her husband's relatives and with her goes the dowry. The girls have been viewed as watering a plant in someone else's home. You nurture them, spend money on their education only to be married and sent to her husband's house. So why bother.

Parents favour boys for many reasons. Sons are generally pampered and spoiled. They hardly ever have to do any chores at home. They will continue to live with their parents and take care of them in their old age. Another benefit was they enhanced the families' capability to defend themselves and their sisters. Sons also conduct funeral rites for their parents. They also add to the family wealth whereas the girls drain them through dowries. The *munda's* carried the family lineage and get their inheritance.

The boys are generally spoiled by their families.

***

I was going through the postpartum blues, feeling weak and depressed. As with Hannah, this baby was named by his *Bibi* and *Papa*, their grandparents in India. They named him Tejinder. One of his relatives was given the privilege of nicknaming our son. He came up with Tony. One big difference between Hannah and Tony was that Tony cried a lot. In many ways, I welcomed his cries because they offered me some relief from his father's abuse. Noises irritated Raj, and I was glad to have an excuse to spend more time with this baby, away from Raj.

By this time, we had hired several workers for our shop since the business was growing. The downside to this was that Raj was spending more time at home. With two little ones, it was difficult to keep the house clean and have three meals ready on time. I could never get enough sleep. The demands of being a new parent, taking care of the house and attending to Raj's needs were all very overwhelming. He assumed I had given him the power to yell obscenities at me when he wanted to. Was I just an object to serve him? Did he think that he was the king and I his grateful and adoring subject?

About three weeks after the birth, Raj suggested my parents babysit Tony so I could go back to work with him. Hannah still accompanied us to the shop. Because we had enough workers in the back, I was to take care of the office. I set up a small area for Hannah so she could play and sleep as well. She was such a good little girl. She gave me so much joy in the midst of so much turmoil. Eventually, my helpful mother kept Tony overnight, knowing we would be working late.

One evening, we went shopping at the local Safeway. Normally, Raj picked the food from the shelf. He was in charge of the groceries. I noticed that he had missed the bread section, so I decided to pick up a couple of loaves of bread. When the cashier started to punch in the groceries, Raj noticed the bread was a bit pricier than the ones he normally bought. His glare was enough for me to ask the cashier to take the bread out. He smiled and told her it was okay to leave the bread in the bag. I felt good that he hadn't made a big deal about it. Once in the car I was caught off guard when he swung his hand across my face. I screamed at him, which was something that he had forbidden me to do. I even said a swear word as a way to show him that I had had enough of his behaviour. Hannah began screaming and crying in the back seat. He looked around to see if anyone was nearby. With no one in sight he began pulling my hair and hitting my head against the window. He punched my face again and again until it bled.

Satisfied with the result, he began to leave the parking lot. What would he do when we got home? Fear gripped me. For a dime, he inflicted that much pain on me. Was there ever going to be an end to his injustice? What would he do once we were inside our home? Why wouldn't someone help me?

But today was to be different. Someone was watching over me. Help was on its way. With Hannah screaming in the back of the car and him shouting, we must have caught some people's attention. The grocery store wasn't far from the police station. I heard sirens and saw flashing lights. They blocked our car from leaving the parking lot. Then the police ran towards our car. Raj looked at me with utter shock and told me to stay in the car. Ignoring him, I got out and ran to one of the officers. They saw blood flowing from my mouth. All I remember saying to the police was, "Please save me!"

One of the constables pulled Raj out of the car and handcuffed him. I went to get Hannah out of the car who had been screaming. He denied ever hitting me and said I had a mental problems and he had just been trying to restrain me. I begged the officers not to believe him. I wasn't crazy, just terrified of him.

I thought that this might be my only opportunity and I wanted to tell all. I talked as fast as I could to tell the officers everything I had gone through with this evil man behind closed doors. He couldn't hold his anger any longer, and in our language he threatened to kill me if I had him arrested. The officers asked me what he had said, and I told them the truth. He was arrested for assault and threatening to kill me. To my relief, he went to jail. I drove home, got some clothes and called my parents to tell them what had happened.

My parents feared for their own lives, as well as ours, and they suggested that we go to a women's shelter. I did. It was hard on the children to be away from their familiar surroundings. They cried most of the night. But we were safe, and Raj wouldn't be hurting us anymore.

Early the next morning, I called mom, only to find out that my parents had received calls from Raj's parents in India. They wanted me to get him out of jail and work things out. I could tell that my parents were caught in the middle and they wanted to see us back together. My parents had no idea what I was going through. I hadn't told them everything. I wasn't sure if they would believe me.

Raj had told my parents that he felt I was losing my mind and that maybe it was due to childbirth. He always presented himself very well in front of them. He was very skilled at leaving a good and lasting impression on people. Most of the time, he was polite towards my parents and didn't talk much when we visited them, letting me do most of the talking. He had them fooled. I guess anyone looking at me could tell that I was not myself. I was losing my mind. I wasn't taking care of myself. I wasn't putting on makeup or combing my hair. I was very weak and looked physically sick. I never had an appetite due to the on-going violence and had fallen into a deep depression.

He was released on Monday morning, after spending the weekend in jail. Adherence to a restraining order and good behaviour were the conditions of his release. For a few days, he made contact with my family and me through a third party. One day I had gone to the store to get some things for the children and I noticed he had followed us there. With his head bowed and his hands joined as if he was praying, he approached me. He was very apologetic and showed some remorse for his actions. He began to make promises about going to counselling and working things out. He admitted his failures repeatedly and asked me for another chance. I told him I would think about it and left.

He followed me to my parent's house, ignoring the court order. They were willing to talk to him. He looked weak and dirty. He started his conversation by apologizing to them. This time, he blamed the police for what had happened to him. He told my parents the police were the reason I had overreacted and he forgave me for that. He said I was vulnerable and that they had wanted to arrest him because they hated him. He assured my parents that he wasn't angry with me at all and, in fact, he felt sorry for me because I was so naïve.

My parents accepted Raj's apology and asked him to stay for lunch. He tried to put on a show in front of them by being extra kind to me and telling me over and over that he wasn't angry with me at all and that I should relax. I finally told my parents that he beats me up a lot and it was getting extremely difficult for me to stay with him. No one took me as seriously as I had hoped they would. After that, I chose to remain quiet, knowing that complaining would only make me look worse in everyone's eyes.

After lunch, Raj asked my parents if he could take us home. They agreed. He told my parents it would be wise for me to go to court and withdraw the charges; otherwise, the police would make my life very difficult. My parents counselled both of us. "Be respectful of each other and do not fight" they told us. It was obvious that they were blaming me, as if I was the one completely at fault. As we walked towards the door, I saw sadness and concern in my mom's eyes. My eyes welled up. "Would my parents have sent me home if they knew the extent of my torture? It was my silence that would keep me locked in his prison. How could I tell my mom about the sexual torture? Besides, Raj was the master manipulator. He had a way with words and always presented himself as the polite one. If I wasn't ready to leave, it was wise just to keep quiet." We didn't talk much on the way home. This time I knew I had very little support from anyone. If anything were to happen I didn't think anyone would believe anything I said.

I was able to withdraw the assault charge against Raj. The other charge threatening to kill remained. He assured me his lawyer would deal with it, and I didn't have to worry about it.

Her: "Why do you keep pushing me?"

Him: "Stop being a drama queen and keep walking."

Her: "What are you doing? Let's just go home. It's getting really late and the babies need to go to bed".

She trembled with fear. She knew he was up to something. He walked around in the messy warehouse looking for something; anything that would do the job. All along he made sure he could see her.

Her: "Please, please, I'm begging. Let's go home."

He shoved her by her neck into the back wall.

Him: "This is f.....g bull..... You have ruined it all for me. You f...... crazy b.... Tell me what I should do with someone like you."

Her: "I'm sorry but I didn't ruin your life. I don't know why you keep saying that."

He slapped her across her face with such force she lost her balance.

Him: "Did you like that b.....? How about one on the other side of your f...... face?"

Her: "Please stop. This is enough. I said I was sorry."

Him: "Stop! You want me to stop? I'm just warming up. Did you come into my life to destroy everything that I worked so hard for? There's evil written all over you. How was I so dumb that I didn't see it coming? Since you made it your mission to destroy me, I will make it my mission to destroy you completely. When I first asked you to stop, you looked away. Now, baby it's my turn. The tables have turned on you now."

Her: "'Please I'm begging you to stop. I'll do anything but please no more."

Him: "Anything?" (He starts to laugh)

He liked the sound of her pleading. He moved closer and with a smirk grabbed her face.

Him: "Well, let's see. Since I have fallen into a depression and can't work, you will have to provide for us. I made good money – so I'll expect good money from you."

Her: "I can still work in the shop and get a part time job in the evenings, if that would make you happy."

Him: "That's not enough. With that kind of wages I'll never get anywhere. I expect more from you."

Her: "What do you mean? I'm trying to do whatever it takes so you won't beat me up anymore. Please don't hit me anymore. Again I'm pleading with you. Please let's just go home and we can talk about it there."

She knew that no one would hear her screams. There is no one there. Most working people are usually in bed at that time of the night.

Him: "No, I need a solution right now. You are not going home b....."

Her: "Can you please explain to me how I have destroyed your life? You keep telling me that repeatedly. I have no idea what I have done to you."

More slaps and punches landed on her face. By then blood was dripping from her cut lip. She heard one of their babies cry.

Her: "That's f...... enough now."

Him: "What did you say? Did you just swear at me? How dare you raise your f...... mouth to me? You f...... B.... you asked for this. I will smash your ugly face beyond recognition."

He continued to throw more punches and kicked her in the stomach. She fell to the floor, breathing in all the dust. He kicked her a few more times.

Her: "Please, please." Faintly she begs with her hand rising up as if to surrender.

Him: "Get up you f..... piece of s..... I'll show you another way to beg."

Her: "No please don't. Think of the children, please."

Him: "Don't tell me to f...... think of the children. Did you? They will be better off without you useless thing in their lives. Do us a huge favour. Get out of our lives permanently you f......b....."

She noticed he was heading towards the machinery. He rolled the arc welder towards her.

Her: "Oh my God. Why are you doing this? Please stop."

Him: "Why? Don't you wanna die? Do us a favour. Just behave and it will be quick".

He plugged it in and demonstrated the strength of the arc welder on a piece of metal.

Him: "See how quick it fixes things up. It will fix you up that quick."

Her: "Why the hell are you doing this to me? Please, please I'm begging you. Please, don't do this to me. Whatever I've done, I'm really sorry. Please give me another chance."

While she begged for her dear life, he smiled and flashed the tip of the welder in front of her horrified face. With tears rolling down, and her hands joined as if he were her God, he still did not relent.

Him: "Alright you b.... get ready and say your good-byes real quick. I don't have a lot of time. You have wasted enough of it already. With you gone, we can easily use the insurance money. Even your parents didn't want you. So they dumped you on my shoulders. I don't have any need for you anymore. You are just a useless b.... It will be a good riddance."

Her: "Please, stop."

Him: "Ready, here it comes. You will now feel that pain that I went through for two days."

Her: "F... you Aahhhhhh."

She fell to the ground. Even though he just brought it very close to her skin, it was enough. She had just been electrocuted.

That torturer was my husband. The victim was me.

CHAPTER TEN

Mental Problems

We had a few good days, during which we would visit my parents often. Raj would help out with the kids. I was glad he had spent a few nights in jail. It had made some difference. It seemed like he was a changed man. I wondered why I hadn't had the courage to charge him before with all the awful things that he had done to me. He even helped with the cooking and cleaning. Was I dreaming, or was it real? This looked very much like the man I had married. I liked the attention I got from him. This time, I was convinced that he was genuinely trying to be nice. He was making an effort to better himself.

It felt like heaven on earth. We went out often. At home we enjoyed each other's company. Raj would gently give me words of wisdom and teach me how to be a good wife. Most conversations started off with him saying, "You know I forgive you for putting me in jail, but I hope it will never happen again." He suggested that I see a doctor for my mental problems. At first, I thought he was joking. I began to laugh at his suggestion. Then he started saying things about me I had never heard from him or anyone else before. He said I was forgetting to feed the children and I slept through the night while they cried. He even said I rambled on and on in my sleep without any reason. I was very angry at his allegations and denied having any problems. He came over, sat next to me and assured me there was help and I didn't need to be embarrassed. He continued comforting me, assuring me that with medical help I would be normal again.

The old fear started coming back. What was he up to? He must be planning something else now that I had had him arrested. He would never forget that part of his life. He would make sure I paid for it. I knew that now there was no one I could turn to. How could I have been so foolish as to believe him when he said he forgave me and there was no reason to be afraid of him? Even my parents had fallen for his lies. What a manipulator he was! He was such a smooth talker on the outside but a snake on the inside. I was so confused about where my life was heading.

Until I was married, I had never left my parents' house to live somewhere else; I had lived such a sheltered and restricted life. I had never been allowed to go anywhere on my own, nor even have friends over at our house. There had always been a family member with my sisters and me whenever we went anywhere. All my life, I had shared a room with my sister. My oldest brother had been so strict with us girls, we used to joke that if he knew what we were thinking about, he would have wanted to control that too. When I was a young girl, my sister and I had laughed at almost everything. When my parents or my older brother heard us laughing loudly, one of them would come over and give us a look. We had become well-acquainted with "the look," and there was never a second look. As a child, I was so used to having someone around that I would ask my younger sister to stand outside the bathroom door at night. My brothers had a bad habit of turning off our lights at night. I was so scared that the lizards or the frogs might come out in the dark that I would scream. My brothers would laugh or they would start talking about a dead person outside the bathroom door and get a kick out of me begging for mercy.

As a married woman in Canada in the early 1980's, I was even more isolated. I didn't drive much and I wasn't familiar with our streets. I didn't have any friends and my family was caught in the middle of our drama. I wasn't sure if there was any other help for my children and me. Maybe I could talk to this doctor he was talking about and tell him the truth. I knew I wasn't losing my mind; I was just simply terrified of this man. I was living in constant fear of him. I was afraid that if I turned my back, he would quickly do something and blame it on me.

The next day he suggested that we take the children to the doctor's office for a quick check-up. There were a few people sitting and reading magazines. Raj kept whispering to me to be honest with myself. He wanted me to tell the doctor about the voices I was hearing. Totally shocked and furious, I turned to him and, rather loudly, I asked, "What voices... and are we here for me?" He smiled at the other people and apologized for my behaviour. He whispered in my ears again and said that he was referring to the voices that told me to do stupid things. By now, I was getting angry and frightened about what else he might have told the doctor. I began to pick up my children from the toy area to leave. The deceiver alerted the receptionist, and she ran to get the doctor. Raj quickly took Tony out of my hands and pulled Hannah closer to him. I asked him why he was doing this to us. I added that there was no reason for us to be here. Very politely he apologized to the people there and said I would be fine.

Then the doctor came and asked me to go inside with him. Raj and the children followed. He was the first one to speak. He began telling the doctor that I screamed at the children and would forget to feed them. Totally shocked at his allegations, I got up. When I started to interrupt and defend myself, the doctor stopped me. He gently asked me to sit down and he would give me a chance to speak. He said that he wanted to hear my side of the story. Trying to be respectful, I listened patiently, at times shaking my head at his lies. I knew it was revenge time for him.

When I just couldn't hold back anymore, I abruptly stopped both of them and said that he was telling a bunch of lies and that nothing he said should be trusted. With anger rising up in me, not only was I turning red, but I was shaking as well. All of this was working in Raj's favour. I realized the doctor didn't believe my story because he kept saying there was help for me. I knew I had to get out of there. Trying to grab my children from Raj was impossible, since the doctor stood between Raj and me. He tried talking to me gently, assuring me that I had done the right thing in coming to his office.

As my temper rose, so did his conviction that I needed professional help. He asked Raj if he should call the ambulance and have me delivered to Riverview, the psychiatric hospital in the Greater Vancouver area. I knew that once they took me there, this evil man would make sure I stayed locked up for a long time. I knew of a woman who had been in that hospital and when she was discharged she looked worse than before. I began to plead with both of them. I insisted I would take any medication and agree to see a psychiatrist instead of going there. Finally, Raj gave in and told the doctor that he would keep a close eye on me, especially that night, and if things changed, he would call the ambulance himself. As we proceeded to leave the office, I realized that there was no one there who would help me. The office was emptied except for the receptionist. "Was I such a threat to them that they had sent the other patients home? Did I look insane? I knew that I had done nothing to show them that I had a mental disability. Was there something that I was doing that wasn't normal?"

I couldn't figure out what had just happened. Why had he created such a drama in the doctor's office? Did he lie that the appointment was for the children? He was a con man. He must have been planning to do something to me. Is he leaving behind a trail of evidence to support him? Whatever it was, I knew I was trapped.

We had been married for about four miserable years. Any opportunity he got Raj would bring up his arrest again. He asked if that had been my mother's idea to make his life miserable. No matter what I said, he punched. I decided to stop answering him. Although he kept repeating the same things over and over, I kept quiet and my silence bothered him. Regardless of whether I said anything or not, he would still hit me. This time the beating was so bad. It was non-stop, kicking, pinching and pulling my hair. All I could do was to curse him under my breath. I wished all kinds of evil upon him; that he would be paralysed in the arms and legs and never hit me again. Such wishful thinking, but it never happened. Instead, I ended up with a broken nose, bleeding lips and bruises. Most of my injuries were on the upper part of my body.

A few days later, after he had been drinking for a while, he decided he was going to try something new. He went into our bedroom first and I heard drawers open and shut then he proceeded to the bathroom while glancing over towards me with an evil smile. I knew it was going to be another torturous night. He gently placed the razor blade on the glass coffee table and knelt in front of me as if to propose to me. He pulled my legs towards him and tied them with my nylons he pulled from my drawer. Then, still having that smile of death on his face, he got up, grabbed me by my hair and shaved off my hair with the razor blade around my forehead. I fought back. He threw a few hard punches and I gave in. I wished he had shaved my entire head. I could at least wear a scarf or hat and pretend that I lost my hair during chemotherapy. The more I cried and begged him to stop, the more of a monster he became. He said it would teach me a lesson for the future. I never knew what lesson he was trying to teach me.

Then he demanded that I get up, still with my legs tied together, and clean up the mess. There was hair all around the coffee table. I felt like stabbing him not to kill him, but to hurt him badly enough that he would never do this to me again. Instead, I meekly complied with his orders.

The shaved hair grew back very slowly. Until it did, I tried to cover that area with a hair band.

From here on, this evil man stopped apologizing for his behaviour. His excuse was that if I had not put him in jail, none of this would be happening to me. It was always my fault, and I deserved to be punished.

I wasn't allowed to call my parents anymore. I called them behind his back. There was no way that he would take that away from me. He continued to call his parents regularly and gossiped. I told my parents very little. I didn't want them to worry about me.

Raj had purchased life insurance for both of us. One day he suggested that he needed money for something. He asked if there was some way I could make him rich fast. I said "no". He sat down and began to suggest that I do him and the children a favour by committing suicide. This went on for a number of days. Almost every day, he would come up with a new recipe for a painless death. That was the only way he would get the money quickly. This would be my way of paying back for the misery I caused him.

One day, I grew tired of hearing it and obliged to do it. I had felt worthless; I was living a nightmare that was never ending. There was no peace anywhere, except in the bathroom for a short minute here and there. When he held that bottle of disinfectant in front of me, I grabbed it from his hand, hoping it would scare him more than me. He just stood there waiting for me to drink it. He helped unscrew the bottle and gently moved it closer to my mouth. As I began to take it in my mouth, he held my head and pushed the bottle inside my mouth. I gagged from the horrible taste and tried unsuccessfully to push the bottle away. But he kept pushing it back into my mouth until I fell. I vaguely remember him calling the ambulance and telling them that I was just attempting suicide and he was very scared for me and the children. I was then taken to the emergency where Raj showed so much concern about my mental state. He held onto the children, telling the hospital staff that the children were very afraid and asked if they could help me. I was in the hospital for a few days. Other than the times Raj showed up, those were very good and peaceful days. On the second day in the hospital, I was served with papers from the Supreme Court. Raj had gained temporary custody of the children. He had told the court that I was suicidal and would hurt the children and that he feared for their safety. He would now share custody of the children with his oldest sister, several hundred miles away. My children were sent away to live with her and her husband. She was also a victim of spousal abuse—I guess Raj had forgotten to tell the courts that important detail. The fact that the children had seen her only a few times in their lives didn't matter to them.

I called my parents and told them about the court order, that Raj had been granted interim custody of Hannah and Tony. There was a restraining order in effect for me. I was not to contact him or the children and not to be seen around the house as well. They took me home, and my dad found a lawyer for me. I also got to see a psychiatrist at the hospital; he assured me that there was nothing wrong with me mentally, but that I was living in fear and was overwhelmed with stress.

My lawyer went to court and proved to the judge that everything Raj had said had been lies in order to get the children away from me. My lawyer also asked that Raj pay child support to me. The court ordered the children be returned to me immediately. This time, Raj received a "no contact" order from the judge. This order requires the offender to refrain from making direct or indirect contact with the victim. It prohibits them from going anywhere near them or to certain places, such as work, school or the same neighbourhood. Despite this "no contact" order, I didn't feel safe. It was only a piece of paper.

I had been living with my parents for about a month when Raj sent members of his family over to talk to us. There was a lot of going back and forth with messages and apologies from his side. Somehow he convinced all of us that he had changed. He joined his hands together as a sign of respect, begging for forgiveness. He looked remorseful and had lost some weight. My parents felt that he was telling the truth. I felt sorry for him too. I wanted and hoped I could salvage the wreck that our lives had become. After seeing him in that state, I didn't want to stay angry with him. I decided to go back to him with the children. I was going to do everything that I could to build our marriage again.

The children had missed their dad, and they ran into his arms and sat on his lap. He kept pointing out that, for the children's sake, we should go for counselling and do whatever it would take to be a happy family.

For some days we were doing well. I still had some fear in me, but had hoped that it was just temporary. I still couldn't shake off the fear that Raj would do the same things to me again. I wished that he wouldn't. We talked about the things he had done to hurt me and he said he didn't remember much. He said he felt as if something had been making him do those things to me. That he had never intentionally meant to hurt the children or me, but he hadn't been able to stop himself. "I wanted to propose that he seek some mental help. I would gladly take him to a doctor that was familiar with us." Very cautiously, he would suggest that I shouldn't provoke him. If I did everything right, there would be no reason for him to get angry. Soon his attitude started to change towards me. He did not talk to me much. His excuse was that he had a lot on his mind.

The business had started to decline. He took me to work in the evenings to help him clean the shop. The children either played or slept while I worked in the back. I hated this work. It was very dusty and my hands were dry and often bled from the work. If I complained about the hard work, Raj simply ignored me. He always made sure that he had the car keys and my purse locked in the filing cabinet.

One particular day he and a few of his friends started drinking in the back part of the shop. The children were tired, and I wanted to take them home to give them a bath and feed them. A couple of times, I went and asked if we could go home and he said we would in a little while. It was late when his friends finally left. The children had fallen asleep in their dirty clothes. I had hoped to go home early that day. Instead of getting ready to go, Raj poured one more drink for himself. Before leaving the shop, he turned off the front lights first. I thought this was odd but figured he had probably just had a bit too much to drink. So I went and turned the lights back on and then started to gather up my things. He called me into the back, to come and check something. When I got there, he was holding the plug for the arc welder. I asked him if he was going to work on something. He plugged the arc welder in and started to show me how it burned through metal.

Suddenly, he grabbed me by my hair and threw me against the side wall. My head banged very forcefully against the wall, and I fell to the floor. He picked me up and threw me down again a few times. I remember inhaling the dust and trying to cough, while choking at the same time. When I got up, he began to kick me all over my body. I pleaded with him to stop. He said that I had asked for it—how dare I talk to him like that in front of his friends? I couldn't recall saying anything other than that the kids were tired and we wanted to go home. Between the beatings, I tried to apologize and asked for an explanation why he was beating me as if I were a punching bag. I had no more strength in me to get up. I just laid on the floor hoping an angel would come to my rescue. My face was bleeding and my head was pounding. I tried to feel other parts of my body to see if it was bleeding. Just then he walked over and slapped me across my face.

By then, the anger I held inside me welled up. I swore at him as loudly as I could. Every swear word he had used on me, I started to shout those foul words at him. He pulled me closer to the arc welder and turned it on and threatened to burn me with it. He did a test touch on my arm and I quickly pulled my hand away. Knowing that there was no way out, I begged for him to stop. He handed me the phone and suggested that I call the same cops who had come to my rescue before. He insisted that I call. He wanted to make a fool of me so they wouldn't believe a word I said anymore. In fact, he said the police were considering charging me for lying to them about the assault. Because I had withdrawn the charges, he said I would never be taken seriously again. He added that the doctors had written proof that I was losing my mind. The more I apologized the harder he laughed at me. He said that he was one step ahead of me.

There seemed to be nothing that I could do without him finding out. He went through my purse, closets and pockets trying to see if he could find anything to punish me with.

I was living one day at a time. Spending time with my children and giving them my love. They deserved so much more than the abuse that they were exposed to on a daily basis. They were so scared of Raj. Whenever he said something, they obeyed out of fear.

One evening, the police showed up at our door and handed me a subpoena. It was for the threatening-to-kill charge. My stomach started to turn. I knew Raj had just been given another reason to beat me up that night. He didn't say anything throughout the day. In the evening he told me that he had to go look at a car and asked me to come along for the ride. He insisted that I go with him. I figured I had no choice but to go.

On the drive back he started to slap me across the face. I covered my face to avoid more slaps. When we stopped at a red light, he grabbed my hair and began to bang my head against my window. He said he had a thick belt waiting for me at home. He drove as fast as he could while holding my hand tightly. As soon as we got home he pushed the couch in front of the door and closed all the curtains. He grabbed the children from my hands and took them straight to bed. He came out with his thick leather belt and started to beat me. I had endured this kind of beatings before from him. I also remembered the pain of that belt from the students in my high school. Those young men came out of the Principal's office sobbing. I ran towards the phone on the kitchen wall. He beat me to it and pulled the wire out and broke the phone. While swinging the belt against every part of my body, he talked about the charges and his time in custody. And how much that weekend in the jail hurt him. He stopped when he became tired and his hand started hurting.

I could not move; I just lay there on the floor and wondered if there was any help for me. "Was I really mentally insane? Who would believe my story if I told them? They would most likely refer me to the police, and now even they wouldn't take me seriously. I knew that my parents couldn't help. After giving us some space they would send me back to him. This was a slow and agonizing death. I had married the devil and there was no way out. He would keep me locked in his prison forever. Only death would free me from him. Was there any hope for me? Could I ever escape from his bondage?"

I somehow survived that night and the following nights. Every part of my small body ached. With every painful move, I called upon him swear words and curses. I began to feel sick every day. I realized I was pregnant again. It must have been from the repeated episodes of rape. How could I bring another innocent child into this family? Hannah and Tony were so traumatized by Raj. No child should be exposed to such brutality. How could I expose a third child to this kind of life? I felt confused, scared and helpless. Raj accompanied me to the doctor to make sure nothing slipped out of my mouth. It was confirmed that I was pregnant.

One evening on our way home he reminded me that the case against him was coming up soon. He said he had talked with his lawyer and they were working on reversing the charges so I could be found guilty of lying to the police. He said when he had spoken in *Hindi*; the police had not been able to understand him. I could have lied to them that he was threatening me. That didn't surprise me. He always found a way of twisting my words around. He had told his lawyer that he had been trying to calm me down but when I had seen the police, I had overreacted. I feared that he would succeed in having charges laid against me.

While he was still driving, he couldn't control his rage and threatened to shoot me in the head. That would be the end of the story. He said he would do it in such a way that it would look like a suicide. Since I had already attempted suicide, no one would blame him. Everyone, including the hospitals already knew I had a problem.

Fearing for my life, I opened the door and ran out as soon as he stopped at a red light. He quickly parked the car on the side of the street and chased me. He pulled me back by my shirt and tried to throw me back into the car. I managed to escape and ran to a nearby house, crying and begging for help. The terrified owner called the police at my request and let me come inside. He kept pounding on the stranger's door to let him in. The poor man turned off all the lights and hid me in the living room.

The police arrived after a short while. One officer talked to him outside the house, while another came in to speak to me. I told them everything he had said to me, including the possibility that he had a gun and would use it that night. The officers talked with each other and then came to chat with me. They said they would take me home and we could talk there. Helpless, I went home with the police. They gave me the phone number of a women's shelter. They had talked with Raj and he was very concerned about my physical and mental health. They wished me the best and left me with my tormentor. He was so right; there was no help for me. No one believed me anymore. My life was at his mercy now.

When the police refused to take an active role in helping me, I knew I was alone. No one, not even me, had any faith left. Raj must have told the police that I had a mental problem, detailing my past history, and they had believed him. I wished I had died when I had attempted suicide. Raj told me that my parents had given up on me and so had the justice system. I believed him. What had happened to my life? Why is he making me and others think that I have a mental problem? This had gone too far. It was as if he had hit the jackpot.

Approximately four years into our marriage Raj suggested that we go to the Bahamas for a vacation. He must have been in a good mood. Since we had not had any vacations it would be good for us, he said. He knew all the stress that both of us had been under and he felt that we needed to get away from our families. He blamed my family, the police and other people in general for our marital problems. Getting away from everyone would help us reconcile and restore our marriage. It had been four and a half years since we were married. He said that he knew how tired I was and that being pregnant didn't help. We would enjoy ourselves in the Bahamas and when we returned, we would start fresh and stay away from people who were a bad influence in our lives. I knew he was talking about my family. By that point, I was so desperate that I would do anything that could help me to love him and enable us to have a loving family. There was so much violence in our home and the children were growing up in so much fear.

Raj spent lots of time on the phone. I wasn't sure whom he was talking to, but to keep the peace, I didn't ask. He wrote the date of our departure down on the calendar. We were leaving in a few days, so I began to pack our bags. I noticed that he was packing bigger items and putting them away in the attic. I thought he was just trying to keep them safe, in case the house got broken into while we were gone.

The night before we were to leave, Raj said he had to go to somewhere. He got the kids ready and told me to hurry. I quickly got ready and followed him. He kept driving around in a deserted place. Finally he found a spot under a bridge and parked the car. He turned around and, without saying anything, began to punch me in the same way that he had beaten me before. My hair was everywhere—in my face, in my mouth, in his hand.

He stopped briefly, after the children started screaming. I began yelling and hitting him back. I was fuming with anger. I shouted at him, asking why he was doing this to me and the children. He repeated his sad story: I had ruined his life by calling the police and having him arrested. He said he couldn't put up with my actions and my insanity anymore. In his distorted mind he believed that he once had pride and dignity. But I had taken all that away from him. He said that people looked up to him. All he had now was shame and all because of me. One fist landed on my face, then another. He pulled my hair so hard that I felt the blood rushing to my head. Satisfied with his achievements, he drove home. It seemed forever before we left that scary place and headed home. On the way, he drove with one hand on the wheel, and with his other hand he held onto my seatbelt buckle, so I couldn't run away.

The drive home was filled with anger and helplessness. "If I leave, he will never give up the children. What if he threatens to harm them?" I was in a place where I could no longer recognize my own needs. All he did was blame me and isolate me from the outside world. He had been very successful in disguising himself. I was left with discredit and disbelief. Every battering incident had diminished any value that I had.

He continued to have paranoid ideas about me. He was always suspicious and looking for something, anything that could become an excuse for a fight. I tried to block him out and think of other things.

Although part of me wanted to run away, I knew there was no place left for me to run to. I was confused and began to hate myself for what I had become, a laughingstock to everyone who knew me. I longed to be back in my father's house. Even if my parents had nothing to offer me, I would still be happy there. I wondered what they were doing at this time of the night. Did they have any idea what was happening to their daughter? Would they even care now that Raj had told them I was insane and was doing stupid things to destroy our family?

Once we were home, the prince of darkness told me to put the children to bed and finish packing. We were to leave early the next morning. How could I go to the Bahamas and try to restore our marriage when it was all based on control? I felt that my role in the marriage was to be his slave. He did whatever he pleased, whenever he pleased. I had no choice.

Once the children were in bed, Raj came into the room with a rope in his hand and asked if I was done packing. When I said no, he said that we should go to the attic first. I thought maybe he was going to tie up some boxes he had taken up there earlier. I followed him. He began to tie the rope to a compressor he had bought earlier for the shop. I still couldn't figure out what he was doing. Suddenly he came over and squeezed my face with both of his hands. After a struggle, I was able to push away his hands. I was already beaten severely on my face. He gave me no time to ask why he was doing this again. Was everything he had done earlier under the bridge not enough? He grabbed me by my hair and threw me from one side of the room to the other. He would pick me up like a doll and throw me again. I landed either on my head or on my back. Blood was everywhere and every inch of my body was in deep agony. He threw me on the floor and choked me until I couldn't breathe anymore. My clothes were ripped, blood and sweat were smeared everywhere. I couldn't stand up anymore. I felt dizzy. At one point, he hurt himself when he threw me into the attic window. I guess he must have cut himself while trying to pick me up. He left me on the floor gasping for breath. Finally, he stopped. I heard him go downstairs and into the bathroom.

He returned within a few minutes nursing his hands. He said that he and the children were leaving tomorrow. While he was talking, he came over and ripped the remaining clothes off my body. He dragged me to the end of the room and began to tie me to the compressor with the other end of the rope. I was thrown face down. I landed on the compressor. Then he sodomized me, all the while telling me what a low life human being I was. He took away my right to exist, my right to speak and breathe. I had become a prisoner inside my own body. I had been so severely hurt and bruised. If I had any strength left in me, I had intentions of hurting him that night.

As he left to go to bed, he paused and gave me his plan for the next morning. He said he was going to turn the gas on in the basement. Then he would turn the gas stove on. It would eventually set the house on fire, with me still tied up in it. By then they would be on their way to wherever he was taking them. I began to cry and asked if I could please see my children. He laughed at me and left. I had no strength in me to turn around or get even somewhat comfortable. I just lay there, drifting in and out of consciousness. I wished someone would torture him the same way he was torturing me. I wanted him either bedridden for life or dead. I hated this man so much. Why couldn't he have a massive heart attack or a stroke with no one there to help him?

It was early in the morning when I heard his footsteps. I knew the torturer was up and my time on earth was coming to a brutal end. I would soon burn to death. He came up and asked me if I was comfortable there and I didn't answer him. He said I had brought him to this place where he had had to teach me a lesson not to mess with him. The only thing I asked him was to see my children. He said 'no'. Covering his face he said that I looked horrible and smelled bad. He came over, untied me, pushed me to the floor from the compressor and pointed to the bathroom.

I couldn't get up and wished I could have died that night. The pain was unbearable. I had to crawl to the stairs and it took a very long time for me to make it down those few steps to the bathroom.

I could neither cry nor look at myself. My face looked like a basketball, with cuts and bruises and dried blood everywhere. It hurt so much to touch but I knew I had to clean it. With tears of pain running down my cheeks, I stood in the shower sobbing uncontrollably. As soon as I got out of the shower, I began to throw up blood. Disgusted with the sight of vomit, he threw a towel at me. I had to use my foot to clean the mess because I could not bend over. I had just been subjected to severe corporal punishment.

He decided to phone the airline and cancel the flight for that day. He did that only to save himself being questioned at the airport. There could also be a good chance that I would start speaking against him. I slowly made my way to the kitchen. To my shock he told me to go and lie down; he would take care of the children. I went to sleep throbbing with pain only getting out of bed to wash the bathroom. He began to take care of me. He would make tea and bring some painkillers with it. He made lots of peanut butter and jelly sandwiches for us. He made sure that the children were quiet when I rested. Even though he didn't verbalize that he was sorry – he showed it in his deeds.

A few days later, we left for the airport. On the way there, Raj warned me to be careful of what I tell the agents at the airport. I was not to reveal anything about my injuries to anyone. Then the threat followed. He would cancel the flight and wipe out my family, then me. I could not bear the thought of him harming my family. I could take the pain but I would not allow my family to suffer any harm, especially at the hands of this man. At the airport, I said what I had been told to say—that I had been in a car accident. I was wheeled onto the plane for our trip to the Bahamas. As the plane took off, I thought to myself that at least for the next few hours he wouldn't be able to beat me up.

CHAPTER ELEVEN

Deception in a Foreign Land

In the Bahamas, we spent most of the time inside our hotel room. I was still in a lot of pain. There were so many bruises on my face that surely would have had people talking. The room was boring and we didn't talk much to each other. Whenever Raj asked me a question, I just gave him brief answers. "Yes" and "No" were pretty much the extent of my communication. I hated being with him in the same room and couldn't figure out why I was still with him. He was a dictator and a traitor.

I knew if I left him, my parents would be the targets of much gossip. Our culture still didn't take spousal abuse seriously. I couldn't put my parents through any more misery. How I wished it was all a bad nightmare that I could wake up from and that everything would be fine. I still hadn't seen a doctor since finding out I was pregnant, but I could feel the baby kicking and doing the same things the other two babies had been doing. There was some comfort in knowing the baby was probably okay.

Once I started feeling and looking better, we spent a couple of days touring the place. Then, one day, Raj gently suggested that we go visit his family in India. I thought about it and decided it was a good idea. I saw this as an opportunity to speak to his parents. I knew they were very influential and respected in their community. If I told them in person what he had done to me, they would be compassionate. They were mature in their thinking and I knew once they saw my scars and bruising they would feel bad. I had faith in them. I agreed, and we made plans to spend about two weeks with them.

On the plane, Raj handed me the tickets to put away in my purse. I wondered how he had changed the tickets so quickly, so I decided to take a peek. I was furious to discover that the tickets had originally been purchased to take us to India, with only a stopover in the Bahamas. He had fooled me again. How stupid could I have been to believe him once again? My eyes filled with tears and anger built up inside of me. I wanted to stand up and let everyone in the plane know what he had done to me and to the children. I wanted to embarrass him.

I turned to him and very rudely asked, "Why did you lie to me and trick me into thinking that this was our much needed vacation? That it would help us clear up things and get closer to each other?" Shaking my head in disbelief, I kept asking myself over and over why I had continued to believe him. He had said we were going on a holiday in the Bahamas, but the tickets were for India all along. He remained quiet while I cried and demanded answers. I didn't care if people were giving me dirty looks or even if they were being nosy. I wanted to vent. I wanted people, and especially him, to know that I had had enough of his lies and abuse. I was tired of his behaviour. I was sick and burned out from the torture and the lies he told people about me. I just couldn't stand him anymore. I wanted someone to beat him up in the plane. Teach him the lesson of his life. He would never lift a finger on me again for as long as he lived.

Although I felt safe in the plane I wasn't sure what lay ahead of me. Raj tried very hard to be patient with me. He wanted to give the same impression to the passengers as he had done to others. He had to show that I was the 'crazy one'. He was a good husband and a father. Unable to hold his peace for much longer, he started to mumble something with his teeth clenched together. I knew from his facial expressions and body language that he was ready to strangle me. In those days, passengers could smoke in the smoking section of the plane. He lit one cigarette after another and drank as if each one was his last drink. He leaned over and said that once we landed and were home, he would deal with me. I knew he would. By now, he was an expert at "dealing with me."

I started getting homesick. I cried in the plane. I missed my family, and the thought of losing them felt unbearable. Maybe his mom would sympathize with me. She was his mother and knew of her son's anger. Maybe she knew that he was a wife beater. I was beginning to have some hope in my in-laws.

I thought about India and remembered it as a hot and sticky place where people were laid back unlike Vancouver, where life was fast-paced and people didn't have much time for visits and family time. In India everyone was somehow related but it had been a number of years since I had left. I was certain things would have changed. I had two brothers and two sisters living there at that time, so I felt somewhat comforted knowing they were there.

I did not talk to Raj for the remainder of the trip. I made small talk with my children and made sure they were okay. Though they knew I was angry, they tried to laugh and play with their toys. My heart was breaking for them. Would they enjoy their time there? I was also concerned about the change in weather—the last thing I wanted was for them to get sick. I wasn't sure how hurt they were emotionally, and to get physically sick on top of that would be very difficult for them.

I worried about their welfare, as any mom does. To add to that was a foreboding uncertainty about the future; how their lives were being affected by the ongoing fear to which they were constantly exposed.

On the day we arrived in India, we changed planes and flew to where Raj's family lived and conducted most of their business. I had an opportunity to meet most of his family and their employees upon my arrival. They knew we were coming and were looking forward to our visit. They all seemed nice and everyone welcomed me. It was very hot. The smell of the car fumes, cow dung, and fish sold by roadside vendors was overpowering.

Raj's family lived on a huge farm. Their furniture seemed outdated and the place needed a good wash and a fresh coat of paint. The beds were different from the box springs and mattresses we had at home—they were made of rope, and some had foam mattresses. There was no bathtub in the bathroom.

I couldn't stop thinking about the beggars just outside their gates. The security guards were on hand to chase them away. The mosquitoes were everywhere. I saw a mouse running under the bed. I jumped on the bed and screamed. I scared not only my children but everyone else in the house.

The children were looking around and checking everything out. Hannah said the bed was hard and there were no carpets. I knew she wasn't going to enjoy her stay here. I comforted myself with the fact that in two weeks we would be back home and things would be normal again—except for the beatings.

Around five o'clock all the servants left for the day. The place looked deserted. I was getting homesick and cried in the bathroom, wondering if my family knew where I was. I wanted to talk to them so badly. I had a sister who didn't live far from my in-laws. The families had been rivals for a very long time.

Raj's parents had gone to the office. When the servants were gone his parents made their way upstairs. His father had a chronic cough and no one could miss him coming up. His mom kindly suggested that I take care of the kids while she cooked. Tony was fussy; he was looking for his crib and his toys. I spent most of the time in my room, away from the main house. I didn't mind because I could cry and talk to the children about anything, even if they didn't understand much. Later that evening, Raj's parents sat down with their drinks and called me over. They gave me a nice old wooden chair to sit on beside his father.

They began by telling me about themselves, how well-known, rich and well-respected they were. As the dad talked, his voice grew louder and louder. I wanted to interrupt to let him know there was nothing wrong with my hearing. Then he began to point at me: "What you did to my son is not acceptable". I began to shiver with fear. What were they going to do to me now? Was this all pre-planned? There was no one left in the house as a witness; everyone had all gone home. My father-in-law said that no one in his family had ever been sent to jail. He demanded to know how I dared to put his son in jail. I tried to interrupt and give my side of the story, but I was quickly shut down. I couldn't say anything. I cried, but even that wasn't allowed. They were not interested with my reasoning except for the well-being of their spoiled son.

Raj brought my purse, took out my wallet and gave it to his mom. She threw it into the wood-burning stove. He forgot that our pass-ports were in another bag. I hoped he wouldn't find them. Standing to his feet, his father said in his loud voice that now it was my turn to serve jail time. My life in that house would be like that of a maid. Not as a wife or a daughter-in-law. He would allow me to live in their house with the children, but they wouldn't consider me part of their family. I would be treated no differently than their hired workers. This was incredibly humiliating, considering the horrible abuse I'd already suffered. They did not give me a chance to talk and tell them the truth. They only wanted to hear their son's side of the story. Their poor son, he spent two nights in jail. Don't they want to admit that their beloved is a psychopath? Also that he was the most selfish and obnoxious individual I had ever met. Were they in denial?

I knew my time here would be torturous. I asked Raj when we would be returning to Vancouver. He replied that we weren't going back. I couldn't breathe. I was devastated. I hated this place and everything about them. They were not the same people they had portrayed themselves to be when we had first met them. Every word out of their mouths was now unkind. They made it very clear that I was never to meet or talk to my sister or any of my family. I realized that I was a virtual prisoner here.

One evening, a few days after our arrival, I was in the car with my younger sister-in-law and saw my sister. I got so excited to see my sister after a few years. I yelled at the driver to stop the car. I begged my sister-in-law and the driver not to ever mention this meeting to anyone. There would be harsh consequences if my in-laws found out. I was forbidden from talking to my sister. Since no one was around I stopped to talk to her. We shed tears and hugs and kisses and for a moment I felt that I was in my mother's arms with nothing to worry about. Everyone with her was excited until I announced that I had to leave. Then there were more tears as we parted.

Little did I know that Raj's elder brother was spying on me. This same brother kept a wife and four children, along with a mistress and the two children they'd had together. Yet Raj bragged about how respectable his family was. When I arrived home, Raj and his parents confronted me. I knew I had been busted. I couldn't even come up with an excuse. His mother kept saying that Raj should get rid of me. I was a disgrace to their family. They criticized and insulted me for a long time.

Raj grabbed me by my hair and pushed me into the wall. He slapped my face over and over again until his father finally told him to stop. He hoped I had learned my lesson. That night, Raj took me for a long ride out of town. It was very dark, and there was no one around. He pulled onto the side of the road and I noticed that we were close to the ocean. He got out and came around to my side of the car. He said that it was a beautiful night and I should come out and hear the waves. I hesitated because the children were sleeping in the back seat. He opened the door and gently pulled me out. We walked around for a few minutes; he started complaining about my visit with my sister. "Does he ever give up? Is he still not satisfied beating me up in front of his parents to impress them?" I told him that I had already promised them it wouldn't happen again and there was no reason to bring it up again. He slapped me again and started to push me towards the ocean. He knew I couldn't swim. I was shaking so badly with fear that I couldn't walk anymore. I begged him for forgiveness and said I would never do anything to make him angry again.

He finally brought me back to the car and said that he did love me. He asked if I loved him, and I lied, saying that I did. Fortunately, he couldn't read my mind. I hated everything about him. I hated him and I hated his family.

When we got back to his parents' home, Raj asked me again if I loved him. Again I lied. He wanted me to prove it. I wasn't ready for any more of his surprises. I tried to look busy, changing the children's clothes and warming their bottles, while he sat and waited.

That night, he treated me worse than he had ever treated me sexually. He assaulted me and asked me to perform the vilest acts for him. I was sick to my stomach with the complete violation of my dignity. When I began to throw up I was slapped even more. Raj concluded that I must have been having an affair with another man. That was why I couldn't stand to be with him. I actually wished it were true.

Something new came up every day. One night, supposedly someone told his parents that I had spread rumours that my mother-in-law was having an affair. Immediately, Raj came and woke me up. They confronted me. I remembered once Raj saying something, but other than that I had had no idea that she was having affairs. I tried to defend myself, but all I kept hearing was that I was a bitch. If they had their way, they would shove chilies down my throat. I was disgusted by the language they were using. Finally, my father-in-law told me to go to sleep.

I often wondered about my father-in-law. He seemed like a nice man. Did he know of his son's behaviour? Was he treating me bad just too keep his wife happy? We were given a suite behind their house. It was a small, self-contained unit with a couple of green tables and a sink. There were lots of windows but most of the levers were missing and the screen was ripped. You had to push the door hard in order to close it. It had two double beds and a crib and there were no mosquito nets and only one light in the middle of the ceiling. It was just enough for me to see if there were any bugs or frogs in the room. It also had a thick metal rod from one end of the room to the other. I did not know what use this pole had in that room. The main house was well lit. My in-laws had lots of rooms that were empty. Right next to their main suite was an older green 3-bedroom house. It was usually dark and gloomy. It was used as storage for their textiles. There was another suite around the corner. It belonged to the oldest brother. He lived there half time with his wife and four children. There was also a huge balcony that was only used for hanging clothes. I had hoped to use that area for barbequing someday.

That night there was no time to sleep. Raj took over the job his parents had begun and continued to torment me. He asked me how I had hoped to die. He said he was open to my suggestions. He also began to verbalize his fantasies about what he would do with the other women he was about to bring home. He asked me if I would still be available if they couldn't make it some nights. Then he dug his nails so hard into my cheeks leaving marks. He said that I had no one to blame except myself. This kind of talk seemed to go on forever.

The next day, after a completely sleepless night, he told me to sort out the potatoes the servant had brought over. I was expected to take the rotten ones and cook them for the chickens. I refused. I said I was tired. He looked at me and said he would deal with me when he got back from the office.

In a panic, I quickly picked up my children and my purse and snuck out of the house. I passed the security and ran to a store. A woman agreed to let me use the phone. I called my sister and told her I was coming over. I needed to hide from Raj and his family. The sweet woman asked her daughter to drive us to a nearby location.

My sister and her family were expecting us. They quickly got us upstairs and hid us in their house. My sister and I cried for a long time. Then she phoned my brother in another state and told him about me. One of my sister's security officers called my sister to let us know that Raj was outside demanding that I return. They feared for their lives as well as ours. He finally left. He told the officer that I had a mental problem and needed to take my medication, which was with him.

My family decided to have me flown back to Vancouver. The children and I left secretly the next day. I did not care to get anything else. All I needed was our passports. A few days later we were on our way to Vancouver. Everything felt so strange. I didn't know what to expect, but I knew Raj's family had ways to track me down.

That journey back was filled with fear and confusion. I had a pounding headache. I had so many regrets. How had I ended up in this horrible life? Why had I married him? I felt sorry for myself, for the children and for my family. A part of me knew I would be found, but I just hoped it wouldn't be soon.

For this tired young mother, it would have been a welcomed time away from the craziness that surrounded her. This would mark a turning point in her life, a disaster she could not see. She was a warm and soft-spoken, yet a timid woman. She had been through hell. She remained so unattached to the world outside.

Nothing about her life was kept confidential by her partner or his family. She was looked upon as a failure, and even a risk. Despite her partner's on-going bursts of rage and his mania for control, she tried her best to be a good wife. She never dared to question his authority.

She was required to confess all her secrets to the appointed doctor. They would use this to blackmail her. His family and the doctor preyed upon her vulnerability.

She was diagnosed with nothing at the time. Her case had moved from the privacy of a family home into a public arena. Initially she was afforded special attention and plenty of acknowledgment. She was promised lots of care and relaxation in the best facility.

Yet little did she know that this trip to the best medical facility would lead to a confinement. She would be put in an institution without any prior warning. The following day, she walked from one prison to another. It would become one of the most embarrassing and humiliating experiences of her life.

Accompanied by a young handsome doctor, she boarded a private plane all alone and wondered why her family hadn't arrived to bid her good-bye. She was given the window seat. Throughout her flight, she stared into space. Then she was quickly transported to a lock-up. She had no idea what had just taken place.

Terrified with the way the attendants treated her and strapped her onto the ambulance stretcher-bed she began to suspect something was different now. She became increasingly suspicious and frightened at their behaviour towards her. What was her offence? The sense of anger and fear rose within her. She detested being there. She was obviously distressed about her confinement. She tried to explain to the men sitting beside her and to the doctor who had flown over with her.

Horrified and shaken by the reality that she was sent by her own family to be punished – she began to act aggressively. Even if she revealed her true pain, it would still lead her back to the sanatorium. Even though she had never had any mental or emotional disorders, she would still languish in this asylum. Everyone who spoke with her knew she was a perfectly sane individual.

The first night of sedation was in fact the best night she'd had for a very long time. As she looked out of her tiny coop, she witnessed firsthand how people around her had completely lost their minds. They were so badly damaged in this nuthouse. Some were blind, others were crippled. Some of them just screamed, while pulling out their hair. The belief among the workers was that their illness was evil and the inflicted were possessed by evil spirits.

It was into a world such as this one, that she came. A world that was so foreign to her. She stood out. Her only illness was "Fear". She was gentle with the staff yet repulsed by the patients. After all, she was at the mercy of her new surroundings.

She had become accustomed to having 'masters' in her life: someone telling her when to sit, when to eat, when to talk, and so on had become a way of life for her.

How was it possible that a woman like her, with no signs of any dysfunction, had been sent to a place like this? Was it possible that someone like his family, with that much wealth and power, was deliberately covering up something?

How could the continued injustice to a healthy and loving young mother be justified or explained? She was locked inside a prison of her fear. Someone who was supposed to love her most insisted that she be locked up and remain under psychiatric care.

The place was formidable. But there was a fairy-tale type of ending to her plight. She met a kind and compassionate young nurse. He too wanted a way out of there. He led her to the path of escape, with a promise that she would show him a path of exit soon.

That manic was my husband. The patient was me.

CHAPTER TWELVE

Unhappy Return

Almost as soon as we got home, Raj phoned my parents. He threatened them that he had informed the authorities that I had kidnapped the children. He said he had documents to prove he had custody of my children. He said that I was suicidal and would harm the children. Knowing Raj, he was capable of anything. "Did he draw up phony papers saying that he had custody? Or was he using the same documents that once gave him custody for two weeks?" Somehow his stories were believable. He was a good schemer. Other family members also began harassing my parents. They would say that it would be in my best interest to return the children to Raj. They also suggested that when I gave birth to the third child, that baby be given to him also. They would prove that I had previous suicidal thoughts and was an unfit mother.

My parents were so lost. I knew that they wanted to believe me. They also knew that they couldn't fight with this family. My dad tried to reason with my father-in-law but that too failed. They claimed that their son was the victim and I was tarnishing the family name.

I could not stand to see the sad look on my parent's faces and I couldn't think straight anymore. What had I done to them? Were they blaming me as well? Did they believe everything my in-laws told them? I knew that I had to leave, but where would I go?

I was terrified of losing my children. After a couple of weeks at my parents' home, I decided to return; because there was no way I was going to give my children to him. The calls never stopped. During the night my mom would unplug the phone lines. We all had been living a nightmare since my return. A few times we received threatening calls. That's when I decided to return.

I left my grieving parents' home to return to the dungeon I had escaped from. I knew my parents were not happy with my decision. I also knew they had no idea what I was going through. My children were the only reason I had for living. Those poor kids had witnessed so much abuse and even though they were terrified of their father, they still needed him.

***

At this point you would be wondering why in the world I would return to hell. This is one of the most common questions one would ask. From an outsider's point of view, it is nearly impossible to fathom why I would return to the abuser. One of the many reasons was that he had threatened on many occasions that he would kill my mom and dad and my younger brother and sister who were living at home. Then he would kill me. The other reason was fear. Fear of what would he do next? I did not enjoy being beaten and I feared that my husband would retaliate even more violently against any attempt to leave him. Studies have shown that one of the most dangerous things a woman can do is to leave an abusive husband. I also felt that the abuse was somehow related to my behaviour and that I provoked his violence. I certainly did not enjoy getting beaten up but hoped that it would not happen again. I wanted to end the violence – not my marriage. I had developed some skills of survival through all of this.

***

The trip back to his family was filled with so much pain and sadness. Although I had left because of the abuse, fear was one of the primary reasons I had returned. I feared there would be more severe abuse if I refused to return to him. Part of me knew that he was playing on my love for my children, convincing me that I could not support them alone. He continued to remind me of the children's need for a father. I guess I also returned to my abusive relationship because part of me felt sorry for him. He was able to convince me that he still loved me and that things would be different from then on. Believing him and hoping for real change, I chose to return. The emotions had somewhat subsided. The guilt and shame had taken over. I hoped for better things and convinced myself that he would change. Why else would he spend thousands of dollars getting us back?

It was also very hard for me to imagine being independent. I had no idea how to take care of the everyday affairs. Also, the shame for my family would be hard to bear.

I was given a nice welcome. Everyone including the servants had missed us. His parents said that they forgave me and hoped everything would be fine.

I tried hard to think positively. I would find ways to please them. The first thing I did was to ask them to forgive me. To have some support from the elders, I would have to learn to live with their conditions, hoping someday they would accept me as their own. Raj was his mother's favourite child. This family was big on gossip and backstabbing. They talked about everyone, including their own children. There were thirteen children. Not all of them got along with each other. They were always suspicious of one another.

Part of the problem was that every member of the family wanted control of the family businesses. There were constant fights over it. One of the brothers was the sneaky one. He often held wild parties with his friends at his parents' expense. They couldn't say anything to him. He was a violent man. His parents believed anything he said about me or anyone else. I knew I had to avoid him in order to live somewhat peacefully there.

Every time Raj looked at me, I could feel chills go up my spine. What was he planning now? He had had about two weeks to come up with new ways to torture me. Why was I trapped in this relationship? I decided I would ask him to sit down and give me a rundown of what he would like in his marriage, so we all could be happy. I just couldn't take any more beatings. I thought that if he showed some respect towards me, his brother wouldn't be able to influence matters as much. I wanted Raj to trust me. I had done nothing to jeopardize our marriage. He was the only man I ever had a relationship with. I didn't spend much money, since he controlled all of it. I was a good wife and a good mother.

From the moment we arrived at the house, my mother-in-law began commenting on the birthmark on Hannah's arm. She would call her the evil one. One time she said that if Hannah were her child, she would have gotten rid of her. She told me that the reason we were having so many problems was because of the mark on her arm. I had such an urge to slap her across her face. How dare they call my child evil? They should look at themselves first. Look at the son they bore? He made other evil people look good.

Tony, in his own little ways, would try to defend me. Once he decided to throw his milk bottle at Raj hoping he would stop hitting me. Poor Tony got slapped on the bum for doing that. From that, I learned that the abuse would eventually reach the children. They would be in the same hell I was in. I needed to protect my precious children from him.

Raj and his mother laid a set of rules for me. I tried very hard to abide by them. I was to wear saris all the time, something I had to get used to. Whenever his father came anywhere close to me, I had to cover my head as a sign of respect. I had to help the maids with all their work. I had to work at this job while taking care of Hannah and Tony and also being pregnant.

I also had a very difficult time using the open fire to cook. Many times I either burnt myself or the food. Mostly, my food tasted Cajun style - another reason for Raj to hit me.

Things had been quiet for some time. Was this the calm before the storm? Then it happened. Nothing could remain peaceful in this house for long. I sensed that something was brewing.

I was told that I was no longer allowed to go to my in-laws' side of the house. I had to put a small kerosene stove in my unit. The green table was used as a counter for my kitchen. Raj's mother gave me some old pots and pans. Whatever they gave me was what I had to cook. I missed my parents and my own home. I often talked to the children about the country we had left. Sometimes I wondered if Raj and his family had tricked me in saying they had custody papers for my children. Were they just showing me how powerful they were in order to get me to fear them? They had instilled so much fear in me. I was afraid every time I came into contact with them.

For a while, I had the privilege of having my laundry washed by the family's maid and then they told me to start doing it myself. I had never washed clothes by hand, especially for four people. I saw the maid sitting on the concrete floor doing their laundry. I couldn't sit on the floor for more than a few minutes. So I decided to stand and use the washtub. My father-in-law saw this and decided it was a bit too convenient for me. I was told never to do my laundry there. He said the tub was only for dishes. The old man lied to me. All he was doing was making my life as difficult as possible.

I asked the maid if she could do some of my laundry. The maids felt sorry for me but they had to listen to their boss. They feared for their jobs. We would talk when no one was around. All the employees were overworked and underpaid, but they had nowhere else to go.

CHAPTER THIRTEEN

Manpreet

By the time I was seven months pregnant, life was getting very diffi-cult in my in-laws' house. I had stopped wearing saris and begun wearing dresses and pants. I told Raj I would start wearing my sari again after the baby was born. People gossiped about my clothes and disobedience. I didn't care anymore. I heard his mother telling the female workers that I was being disrespectful to her and her family. Every time I passed her kitchen she would always slam the door.

I started to have an allergic reaction to the kerosene stove. The fumes made my nose bleed. I asked my mother-in-law if I could use her kitchen because she had a gas stove. She replied that they were all scared of me. They had heard I wanted to poison them. That was news to me. I laughed it off, thinking she was joking. She started to give the names of employees who had given this information to her. I didn't know any of them.

The poison news spread like wildfire in the community. After the employees had gone home, the family called me and confronted me. I began to call these meetings "trials in the judge's chambers." My in-laws asked if I wanted to poison them. I said "no". I told them I had no idea who would have told them that. They asked if I would put my hand on the *Guru Granth Sahib* and swear on my kids' lives. I refused, not because I was guilty but because I didn't want anything to happen to my children. To them it was all a game, but to me it was about my children's lives and their future. Then they told Raj to discipline me in such a manner that I would never be able to talk about them again.

They demanded that I get out of their presence before they lost their tempers. I quickly got the kids and left, crying. I felt so angry, especially with myself. Why had I come back to this place? Jail would have been better; anything would have been better than living with these people.

Raj followed me back into my little dungeon and demanded an explanation. I pleaded with him, saying that I had never said anything like that and asked for names. This was another lie. They did whatever they wanted to wreck my life. He just stared at me. Finally he said he would believe others before he believed me. I shook my head and began to walk away when I felt a painful kick in my back. I turned around and screamed at him to stop. I told him how much I hated being there and being with all of them. I demanded that he send me back home.

One after another, I received blows to my body. I fell to the ground, and he kicked me a few more times in my back. I was convinced I would lose the baby. Hannah and Tony were so terrified; they tried to cover their heads with a blanket and wept. Then I heard his mother telling him to stop. She began to joke with him, saying that maybe I had brought some poison with me from my parents' house when I had come back. She said she was pretty sure my mom wanted them all dead so I would inherit their businesses. I couldn't believe the stories they would come up with—it was all completely insane and too much for me to handle.

For a few days, I was in a great deal of pain and experiencing early labour. I had started bleeding, but no one cared. Finally, I sent a word through one of the maids, asking my in-laws to call an ambulance for me. I did not have access to their rotary dial phone; it had a padlock on it. The in-laws sent word back that I should wait. That evening, I asked them again to call an ambulance for me. This time, they did. I was taken to the hospital and delivered a baby girl. She was two months early, weighing just a few pounds. She was immediately put into an incubator. I hoped that nothing would happen to her. Even though she was born due to the beatings, the blame would be on me. I couldn't win. Regardless of her size, she was the cutest baby in the hospital.

The next morning, Raj and his mother came to visit. Somehow they missed my room and headed for the nursery. I went over to talk to them about the baby, but they began to threaten me. They said if anything happened to the baby, I would be held responsible for it. Of course they blamed me for the early birth. When I found my mother-in-law alone, I asked her how it was my fault. Her son had kicked and punched me and sent me into premature labor. Why was it that everything was my fault?

She said that I was a curse to the family and that she would adopt this baby. I wouldn't have anything to do with her. Then they went close to my baby and began to check her to see if there was anything wrong with her.

I went back into my room and cried. The other moms in my room tried to comfort me. They opened their hearts to me and their kindness brought a smile to my face. These poor women didn't have much, but they had big hearts. Some of them told me stories about my in-laws; others just kept quiet. My in-laws were very well known because of their businesses. Some people respected them and others didn't care much for them. Many felt intimidated by them. These women shared their meals with me. They knew I didn't like the hospital food and no one had brought me anything. I missed my family so much. I wished somehow I could phone them and tell them about the baby.

After a couple of days, I was discharged from the hospital. My nameless baby had to stay in the incubator for much longer. She was in a critical condition. I was asked to come in at least twice a day to feed her. I would take the two children and make daily trips there. The baby was so tiny compared to Hannah and Tony. Both of them weighed over seven pounds when they were born. As soon as I was done feeding, the baby was taken back to the incubator. I usually stayed longer, just to avoid going home and facing Raj's family.

One evening, Raj brought his mother to the hospital to see the baby when she was about ten days old. His mother noticed that the baby was changing color and informed one of the nurses. When the doctors checked on her, they told us she had pneumonia. They started her on medication, and we were not allowed to touch her until she was better. My mother-in-law turned to her son and said that I had known about the baby's condition but had not informed the nurses. She began to praise herself for saving the baby's life. From that time on she began to plan my daughter's future. I had no say in anything and was told that, if she wanted to, she could take all the children from me, but she felt sorry for me. So out of the goodness of her heart, she let me stay with them.

My mother-in-law invited some people to the *gurdwara* for the following Sunday to offer prayers for our baby girl. According to their religious beliefs they would pick out a name for our baby while she was still in the hospital. Raj's parents chose a name and had it registered. They called her Manpreet and my mother-in-law truly believed this was her child. She shared with everyone how she had saved my baby's life.

CHAPTER FOURTEEN

A Horror Chamber of our Own

This house was a place of horror for me. Every day there were new surprises for me. When I was allowed to sleep, I usually awoke from nightmares. I didn't have any peace and I was afraid of the dark. Around four o'clock every afternoon, I would start getting depressed. Fear and complete isolation would grip me. I knew that soon the employees would go home and there would be no one around except for the family. We didn't have any neighbours close by, and my in-laws didn't have any visitors; hardly anyone came to their house for dinner. They lived a very secretive life. They all drank and fought before dinner and then went to sleep right afterward. Every room had locks, and my mother-in-law kept all the keys in her petticoat, hanging around her waist. I wondered if she was comfortable with all those big keys. She kept her money tied in a handkerchief inside her blouse tucked securely in her bra.

I longed for my own place in which to raise my children. A miracle happened one day. Raj, our children and I were finally allowed to move into one of the family's rentals. It was a cosy two-bedroom suite. I guess my in-laws had grown tired of having us around. They reminded me daily that I was always in their face. Some days, I would say that I too hated being there; other days, I would approach them nicely and ask for a proper suite for our family.

The new place was much nicer—I had neighbours around me and felt safe at last. There was a vegetable garden in the back and a few mango and coconut trees. I took the children out there, and we would enjoy playing and picking some vegetables.

We continued to make daily trips to the hospital. The family vehicles were no longer accessible to me. I began to rely on the Rickshaw drivers. They always showed up on time. Sometimes I preferred to walk.

After some days our food supply was dwindling. Raj's family sent word that if I wanted to eat, then I would have to work for it. They offered me a job cleaning. I thought of taking it just to feed my children, but then they decided that they didn't want me anywhere near and withdrew the offer.

I asked Raj to start working in one of his family's steel factories, but he refused. He began fighting with me again. A few days of peace were over. Now he had more to fight about than before. He used all the arguments from before how I had put him in jail and how my parents were a bad influence—but now he also used the poison story, Manpreet's premature birth, pneumonia and my wanting to let her die. Our food supply being cut off was also my fault, he said.

I was in a very difficult situation. The vegetables were gone, the cupboards were empty, and there was no milk for the children. Raj told me to go and beg on the streets. I was prepared to do it. I wanted to expose this family. I went to a corner store and begged the owner to let me have food, promising to pay him later. He agreed, and I brought home some groceries. I tried to use as little as possible so I could stretch the food over a few days.

Raj slept most of the day because he would fight with me until late into the night. The neighbours knew of his behaviour and avoided him. The women were initially nice to me, until his mother paid them a visit. Then they stopped talking to me. I hardly ever went out. There was no radio and no toys for the children. We made paper balls from old newspapers. The children would play soccer in the living room. There were only two chairs in our living room. If the children got too loud, Raj would come out and slap me for deliberately making noise so he couldn't sleep. I named him the "nighthawk". He began to look very dirty; he hardly ever shaved and his hygiene was excessively poor. He was on a mission to make my life a living hell and he was succeeding.

At last we got the news I had been waiting for. Manpreet was doing much better. She had gained some weight and after two months was out of the incubator. She was kicking and crying. I was so happy that her life had been spared as well as my own.

When my mother-in-law found out about Manpreet, she bought a crib and some clothes. The she went to the hospital to find out when she would be discharged. She and Raj agreed that Manpreet should live with her. She took my little baby to her house.

I asked my mother-in-law if I could come to her place every day and help the employees. She agreed. Her servants took care of Manpreet most of the time. She began calling Manpreet her own child, which made me very angry, but I remained quiet. After all, she was taking good care of my baby. In exchange for my work, she would give me some groceries. I would also take home any leftovers so we would have a little bit more.

Raj refused to work and kept saying sarcastically that I should ask for help from my friends meaning the police officers who had arrested him. He said we were the reason he had lost his dreams in life. I secretly wondered whether his dream in life had been to become a professional wife-beater. He would switch back and forth, depending on his mood; one time he would blame the police for ruining his life, and another time he'd blame my parents. He said the same things over and over again. He was showing all signs of insanity. Many times I thought of suggesting that he tape his words and just let the tape play. It would save him time and effort.

One evening, I was so exhausted from being pushed around, having my hair pulled and my face squeezed that I decided to fight back

verbally. I wanted very much to beat Raj with a metal rod or anything that would cause him pain. I didn't have anything like that, so
I decided to let the neighbours hear what I had to say. I was beaten
regardless of whether I spoke or remained silent. So this particular
day I decided to get beaten and not feel guilty. I told him what a
monster he was. I said he was a lowlife who had no guts to fight
with a man his own size but only with a woman half his size. He
pushed me so hard into the concrete wall. I felt dizzy for a while but
continued hitting back with my words while crying loudly. I told
him how much I regretted marrying him and told him that I knew
that he and his family had deceived me. They had portrayed themselves to everyone to be something that they were not.

While I was lying on the floor recovering from the beating, Raj began to kick me continuously. By now, Hannah and Tony had run into
the bedroom and shut the door. Those poor children did not deserve
that kind of father. I wanted to tell them to run and call the police
from the neighbour's phone. But then the police were useless. They
had done very little for me before. Once a police officer told me to behave like an Indian woman; I was no longer in Canada. Most of the top
police officers were close friends of Raj's family. They also had a close
relationship with people in high places. Some of the officers felt sorry
for me, but they couldn't do anything. They feared for their jobs.

After continuing the kicking and punching for some time, Raj did
the unimaginable—he urinated all over me. I looked up at this sick
man and asked him why he didn't just kill me. I called him as many
names as I could possibly think of. I began to curse him and said I
wished he had never been born. I received more punches and blows,
but I continued to speak my mind. He beat me until he grew tired. I
always knew when he was getting tired. He would begin to nurse his
hands. He told me to get up and clean up the mess. Then I was allowed into the bedroom for the night, but I had to sleep on the floor.

Late one October evening Raj drove the children and I back to
the ocean. He pretended he had to pick up something from one of

the factories. He drove further towards the water. When he got out of the car, I quickly locked my door and the children's doors. He had the key and would open the door. I would quickly lock it. As always he won. I gave in and he quickly pulled me out of the car. He walked me quite quickly towards the end of a jetty. "Was he going to try the same thing again, his cowardly act". This time he seemed a bit calmer than the first time he brought me here. I didn't know what to expect. As a precaution, I held onto the rails very tightly. He punched me and pulled my hair for a little bit, nothing unusual. He suggested that I do him and the children a big favour by jumping into the water so he could get the insurance money. I wanted to say the same thing to him.

Somehow—miraculously—Raj had a change of heart and took me back to the car. The children were in the back seat holding each other's hands. I just smiled at them, too scared to say anything.

The next day, I told Raj's mother secretly, what he was doing to me. She didn't waste any time telling him and he denied it, saying I was suicidal and he was saving me from jumping off the jetty. He told her that my family and I had mental problems and that I needed to be checked out.

Soon after they took me to the hospital and asked one of the doctors to treat me. I suspected that he talked about me to him. He asked me lots of questions and I answered honestly. I repeatedly told him how frightened I was of Raj. The doctor admitted me to the hospital to run some tests. He told us that there was a good hospital in another part of the country that I would benefit from. In some ways, I was happy. I would be free of Raj and would have caring people around me. I agreed. I understood this hospital to be a counselling facility. The arrangements were made to have me sent there the next day.

Other than the hospital staff, no one came to say goodbye. At the airport I asked the hospital staff where Raj and children were. I was told they would meet me at the airport. Instead, a young, good-looking doctor accompanied me. I cried all the way there. That doctor sat beside me, but we didn't talk. He suggested that I take the window seat and he would take the aisle seat. All through the flight I stared out the window. Only once the doctor asked if I wanted something to drink and I shook my head. When we arrived at the airport an ambulance was waiting. I waited to get into the taxi as it pulled up but the doctor quickly escorted me to the waiting ambulance. I was surprised to see three attendants waiting. Maybe the hospital was just being respectful towards my in-laws. Nodding politely I climbed into the ambulance and tried to talk to the attendants, but they didn't respond much. I thought that either they were shy or didn't speak much English.

One of the attendants dressed in a neatly pressed white uniform asked me to lie on the stretcher. I quickly declined saying that I would rather sit. Then the other came closer to me and firmly placed me onto the cot and began to strap me. I began to protest a little but they quickly said that it was for safety reasons. The roads were pretty bumpy and a little dangerous to drive on in certain areas. They said that that the ambulance drives fast and they did not want me to get injured. I asked if that doctor could sit with us in the back. One of them said that there was no more room in the back. Both of these aides were Indian but spoke a language I was not familiar with.

When the ambulance began to slow down, they removed my strap and I sat up quickly. The vehicle drove into a driveway through a gate in a barbed-wire fence. A security officer opened the gate and let us in. I began to question the attendants in a rather loud and authoritative voice. "Where was I? Where had they brought me? Was this a jail? Why was I here?" I ran to the doctor who had accompanied me and asked him. He said he was simply following orders. The huge gate shut behind us. I was tricked again. I began to cry and pleaded with him for answers. He said the hospital was a mental institution and I had been ordered to get treatment there. "Treatment for what? I asked." I am not psychotic, I just gave birth to my little baby girl and she needs me and my other two children need me. Please you have to believe me" I begged. He stood in front of me but made no eye contact. He motioned to the staff to give us a few minutes. Struggling for the right words, he cautiously said that we were in a mental facility. "Oh my God, this is a place for lunatics!" I shouted. "There must have been a mistake. I don't belong here. Please take me back. I would never hurt anyone. What you've done is brought me from one prison to another. I would rather go back to my former jail and be with my children." I knew that this facility was for patients suffering from very serious mental illness. I looked towards the gate and saw a sign that said Psychiatric Hospital. I told him there was nothing wrong with me; Raj was just trying to get rid of me. My eyes kept going back to the entrance trying to find a way to climb out. I was so terrified of being there and so badly wanted to hold this doctor's hands and beg for compassion.

The doctor was very sympathetic towards me and suggested I tell my whole story to the resident doctors. The impatient staff signalled to him that they had to take me in to complete the paper work. When he turned to leave I knew that I was going to be locked up for a long time. He was the only familiar face there and now I would be inside this institute with a bunch of psychopaths. In a desperate attempt to be listened too, I begged the doctor not to leave me there alone. He agreed to stay with me for a while. A couple of irritated female nurses held my hands and led me towards the door to hell. I kept looking back to see if he was still there. He kindly asked the nurses to give us a few more minutes to talk. He pulled out an old wooden chair and I sat down. I talked as fast as I could. He pulled his chair closer to me and looked into my eyes with such sadness.

He suggested that I phone my parents' and go back to them. That I deserved a better life then what I had endured. He said that I was a very pretty girl and should seriously think of leaving the country. His words were so soothing. He was kind and compassionate and wished me well. Then he left and I never saw him again.

I was grieved and scared and missed my children very much. I wondered what they were doing and if they were told where I was.

In this mad house, I had no concept of the time. I was confident that Raj's family would make up lies to draw the children towards them.

Everywhere I looked I saw these unfortunate people with serious mental problems and most of them had to be restrained. I heard the gates open for my doctor friend. I wanted to run after him so badly and ask him to take me with him, but the monster gates shut as soon as he walked out.

The first night, I was given a cozy room next to the nurses' station. They made sure the door to my room was locked from the outside. I was forced to take pills against my will but I slept like a baby. I was terrified that I would be locked in seclusion or have some other form of treatment right away. No one took a personal interest in me.

Everyone was woken up early before sunrise. My door was unlocked and I was escorted to the ladies room. They handed me a small toothbrush with a very small amount of toothpaste. There was no privacy. Perhaps it didn't matter to the psychos if anyone was watching them. But I was a sane person that cared about my surroundings. Outside a few hospital staff were hosing some of the immobile patients. They did not use soaps to bathe them. Instead they pulled their cots to a warmer side of the building so they could dry up. The smell of urine and morning breath was making me sick. Many older patients had all their teeth pulled out. The staff said that it was for safety reasons. Others were talking gibberish as I passed by them. I was careful that no one would touch or grab me. One younger woman kept hitting her head against the concrete wall as if it were a sponge. I quickly made my way back to my room. Soon it was breakfast time. The food was inedible. I passed it by and waited for someone to escort me back. Soon after my morning fast, a resident doctor came to see me. He was an older dark skinned man with hair styled with coconut gel. I poured my heart out to him. He didn't make much eye contact other than to take notes on his lap with his legs folded and reading glasses just resting at the tip of his nose. I could tell he didn't care very much, so I stopped talking. As he removed his goggles he said he knew my in-laws very well and had just spoken to Raj on the phone. Walking behind him, I asked if he believed me. He stopped for a brief second and said it was too early for him to diagnose my condition. I told him my only diagnosis was that I was a battered woman who lived in constant fear of her husband. He turned around and said he would see me again in a couple of days.

As a committed patient, I had no rights whatsoever. I was still detained though my prison had changed. I felt like I had been mentally raped. Instead of acknowledging the source of my problem and caring for me, they sent me to a nut house. Scared of my surroundings and what could happen to me with all these medications, I decided to make friends with the nurses there. One male nurse told me in confidence that the doctor was planning to do electroshock treatment on me. One of the pills that I was given was valium. Earlier in the day, while walking with a female support worker, I had heard a woman screaming. She had been strapped in for the electroshock treatment. The woman's scream was enough to give a person nightmares. I begged the worker to let me out. I also offered him a bribe. He didn't accept this, but mentioned that he was a single guy and was interested in visiting Canada some day and asked if I would show him around. I agreed.

After giving it some thought, he made me promise him that I would never mention his name. He said he would unlock my door early the next morning. He showed me the way out, but said it was through bushes and I could hurt myself. It would be quite dark that early in the morning. I said I didn't care; I was determined to flee before the day started. He was faithful to his promise and unlocked the door. I ran for my life, falling many times and hurting myself. I don't remember saying bye to him or thanking him for his deeds. I didn't stop or look back until I had reached the main road. I heard dogs barking and chasing me. I kept running. The morning dew was still on the grass and the trees. My clothes were damp and I had a few rips on my shirt and minor cuts on my hands and face. It didn't matter - I was free. I wouldn't have to face the electroshock treatment planned for me. I was proud of myself for getting away from one form of torture. I outsmarted all their so-called treatment.

I saw a taxi and flagged it down. It was going towards the town where I had grown up. The driver agreed to take me there. There were other passengers in the taxi, but I made no eye contact with them. Just in case they recognized me and reported my whereabouts to the police or my in-laws. Finally the curious driver asked why I was standing close to the psychiatric hospital that early in the morning. I wanted to play deaf, but instead I chose to give a simple answer. There had been an emergency and I needed to get there as soon as possible. I knew he didn't believe me. It was then I realized I had no money to pay the driver. "What was I going to do now? He will definitely hand me over to the police for non-payment. After all, I was a fugitive running from the mental health authorities". I got scared when he announced our fares. My destination was a few minutes away. I could run fast. Someone would have caught me. I was drawing unwanted attention on me. I waited until the other three passengers left. Then I told him that I had no money on me. But he could drive me to my brother's school and get his fare. He became nasty and started to speak profanity. He told me that he regretted picking me up and that I was probably not a good woman - one who had no character. He said that no decent women leave their homes at that time of the morning. He bluntly asked me if I was a prostitute or a runaway. I said "neither" and suggested that he drive another half mile to get the money. He agreed and took me with him to the Principal's office. The same place I had vowed never to enter again. From the parking lot, I saw my brother walking towards us. Hot tears began to roll down my cheeks when I saw the shock on my brother's face. He quickly put his arms around me and asked if I was okay. This was the same brother that I feared while growing up. He had softened so much. He even wiped my tears with his chalked hands. I looked at the driver and demanded an apology. He did apologize and my brother handed him his full fare.

Raj tracked me down. With continuous threats from him my brother took me to my aunt's house. I was safe there but I was missing my children. I could not eat or sleep. Everyone kept telling me to leave the children and start a new life. How could I do that? I could not abandon my family. They wanted me to give up the most important part of my life—my children. How could they not understand a mother's heart? They all had their children with them. To save my family further trouble and threats I went back to him. Slowly my family began to cut ties with me. They felt that I had wasted their time.

I went from the frying pan into the fire. Things began getting worse. My mother-in-law sought cures from witch doctors. She scattered ashes everywhere, saying she was getting rid of the evil. She would sprinkle some on my head and say it would bring me peace. The only peace I wanted was for them to get out of my life and my children's lives. They were the evil ones. I remember going with them to a new witch doctor one evening. I was just excited to be out of the house. This supposed healer kept staring at me and Raj. His looks were very creepy. Finally he broke his silence and asked us in a stern voice, if we were getting along with each other. Raj replied "no" - I chose to remain quiet, fearing the consequences later. Glaring at me again, this 120 pound witch doctor, wished me a good life. Then he looked at Raj and said to be careful. None of us knew what he meant and he refused to elaborate and asked that we leave. In the truck the mother and son began their own deliberation on "be careful". They both concluded that he meant that he was to be careful of me. That I could do him a lot of harm since I was the evil one. Most likely that was the reason this sorcerer wanted us out of his home.

These two took his prediction so seriously that she started to lock all her doors even in the daytime in case I tried to poison or murder them. I thought I should scare them a little, maybe leave flowers on her doorstep or sprinkle ashes. It would give me a kick to see her scared. It would give her a glimpse of what it was like living in constant fear.

I discovered I was pregnant with our fourth child. I decided I was going to take this pregnancy one day at a time. I tried to hide it for as long as I could from everyone. I stopped caring about what Raj's family, their customers, and the neighbours said about me. I only cared for my children. They were the only ones that mattered to me. That was the only way to survive in that house.

CHAPTER FIFTEEN

Prison Conditions

I had learned to numb myself to all the pain that was imposed on me. I abided by their rules. Raj's parents started calling me *paghli* (psycho). When my father-in-law wanted to be particularly nasty, he would ask if I was pregnant with my father's child. One time, I couldn't hold my tongue and replied we had had respect for each other. Our family lived respectful lives, unlike the situation in his home. He swore at me and left.

By this time Raj's family encouraged him to divorce me and get a nice wife for himself. She said the poor man had been very unhappy ever since he got married. She felt guilty for finding me as his wife. She wanted to make it up to him. So she started looking for a nice girl for him. Some girls agreed to go out with him. He would stay out late and party with these girls. A few of the parents came over to our house to find out if I was mentally disabled and if I was capable of taking care of my house. "Did they really think that he could have another wife? How desperate were these parents that they would let them live with Raj as his mistress." One older woman approached me and asked what was wrong with me. I told her the truth: that my days were numbered and that any day could be my last. Raj was trying to kill me. I warned her secretly not to let her daughter come into that house. She found out I was pregnant. The workers who sympathized with me told the visitors how I was being treated in that house.

I started to gain the female workers' trust again. A couple of them brought fresh fruit and vegetables in their bags. I would get sad at the end of the day. Eventually I poured my heart out to them and the abuse that happened after they left. My goal was to have them as witnesses if something ever happened to me. I was careful never to speak to them when others were around. I didn't want to lose my only friends. It had taken me a long time to confide in anyone. I wasn't prepared to jeopardize our friendship and their only source of income.

Raj's brothers and their wives seemed to be getting along fine, except for the oldest brother, whose wife seemed miserable all the time. Her husband had another family on the side. She had access to money and wasn't abused in anyway. She was manipulating the in-laws to get sympathy. The other daughters-in-law had their own homes and were doing very well. Their husbands were nice to them. I envied them. I only spoke to one of them. She was nice. Sometimes she stole groceries and clothes to give to me. She was aware of how the family was treating me. She had lived with my in-laws and was well acquainted with their conducts.

Any extra non-perishable food I had, I hid under the bed in the underwear boxes. I feared any day our entire ration would cease. Whenever my mother-in-law was in a good mood, I took advantage of the moment. I would kindly ask her for more food. Sometimes she treated us to meat and a can of mixed fruit.

The older daughter-in-law's children had access to the store and everything in it and they ate ice cream and candy in front of my children, but never shared with them. When my children would cry and ask them for some, they would throw it on the ground, step on it and then tell them to pick it up and eat it. They did this almost daily. It became so common that whenever I heard these children coming, I quickly gathered my children and took them inside so they wouldn't have to suffer the torment.

When Raj wanted to fight with me, he would pretend he wanted to spend the night in my suite. He would bring up the same old things and start a fight. His style was pretty repetitious. First he would demand that I sat on the floor in front of him. Then he would move closer and ask me if I was enjoying my life there. From the previous countless experiences I knew this would be another long night. I would start shaking. He would ask if I was guilty of something. Otherwise there was no need to be so frightened. Had I done something to be scared of he would ask. Regardless of my answer, he would say that I deserved this treatment. He said he had given me a good life but I had made it miserable. He said that with the help of my mother and the police, I had taken away everything he had worked so hard for. Then he would squeeze my face as hard as he could with his dirty nails. If I tried to resist, he would slap me. I would see stars. He would give me a very bereaved story about his life; the same broken record I could repeat every time he opened his filthy motor mouth. He would say that everyone was laughing at me and calling me crazy. "If they were calling me crazy, I wondered what they were calling him". Then he would hit me some more. Non-stop backhand slaps would land on my face, one after the other pausing to nurse his hand. That gave him the much-needed time to gulp down his rum and coke while giving me the look of death. Throughout all these bashings, the only thing I wished for was for him to have a near fatal illness. Luck was never on my side.

He would eat his meals with the children, while he made me watch them. Once the children went to sleep, he would pick up where he had left off. He would end the night by raping or sodomizing me. At least four times a week, I would spend the night in a corner of the room with my hands tied.

The only feeling I had towards this man was of total hatred; everything about him disgusted me. I knew he was sleeping with any woman who was willing. All I could think of was that he was bringing filth and disease near us. I would spend every waking moment thinking—what's next?

Her tormentor led her to the dark death chamber, where her execution was to take place. But what was her crime?

He forced her attention to focus on the pole at the centre of the room. It's funny that she hadn't noticed it was there before. The foreboding scent of eminent death filled this too familiar room where she was held captive. Darkness loomed in her concrete tomb.

Only a sick irrational person would premeditate such a horrible crime against a young timid woman. In fact, it was his violent actions and ignorance that accentuated his guilt. He was in a state of mind that had been driven to kill. He justified this as a worthy punishment.

She resisted taking another step. She froze. She was determined to fight even to her last breath. In a last desperate attempt, she pleaded for her life. She was once again in the clutches of the vicious cycle of abuse.

Her pleas only brought a Machiavellian smile to his lips. It was as if he had some maniacal delight in seeing her reduced to this agonizing state. Raging anger clouded his countenance; his jaws clenched and his cheeks twitched.

She cast her gaze to her innocent children sleeping around her, longing to say her farewells to these loved ones. Were they really asleep? Or would they be the ultimate silent witnesses? Would influence, prestige or money prevail over justice?

As he held her hand and jerked her towards him, she came crashing onto his chest. Her nostrils filled with the pungent odour of tobacco, mixed with sweat and alcohol. She looked up into his intensely ferocious eyes, hoping to find mercy, but instead saw only merciless rage.

One quick movement unravelled her sari around her. The psycho man slammed her against the wall in front, to keep her within his reach. He then proceeded to demonstrate the art of creating a noose from her garment: painstakingly measured every inch to ensure accuracy.

As he lowered the noose over her neck, reality crashed in and she had a flashback to her youth; A vivid memory of a lifeless body of an unknown man with a broken neck and tongue hanging to the side of the mouth.

Was this to become her fate too? Ironically her sari, the same garment that she'd worn on her wedding day, would become the instrument used in her demise.

That executioner was my husband. The prisoner was me.

CHAPTER SIXTEEN

Satveer

When I was about seven months pregnant Raj took off to another state. I felt like I had won the lottery. My one wish was that he would never return. This was my first encounter with freedom. The tiny cell now had become a home. There was a sense of life in it. We could breathe and move freely in this place. Now I could sleep on my bed whenever I wanted to.

My mother-in-law decided that I should go to the maternity clinic. One day she took me for my check up. The doctor ordered a number of tests. The results came back as anaemic. I needed to have medication given through an IV at the hospital in a couple of days. My mother-in-law sent me with one of her workers, and we spent the day at the hospital. My doctor was a very kind gentleman and very concerned about the baby and my health. There were some other women there as well. We all sat in old lazy boy style chairs. It was comfortable compared to the wobbly wooden chairs I had in my suite. I was underweight for my age. He gave me a list of things I should start eating. I was too ashamed to tell him that I had no access to any of these things and suggested that he drop the list with my mother-in-law. He must have read my history from prior visits to the hospital. He agreed. He had put a request to the kitchen staff to bring me some food. Though I generally disliked hospital food, I thoroughly enjoyed this meal. Unfortunately, the IV finished too soon and I had to leave to go back to my prison.

The children appeared happier and healthier. They made noise and played any time of the day. They hardly asked about their father. An obvious sign of how much they were affected by his behaviour. I too became a kid with them, being a referee while they played hopscotch, skipping, and singing children's songs. These events only took place when my in-laws weren't around. They didn't like loud noises when they were upstairs. I was able to rest a bit more and ate a little better, just hoping it wouldn't end. I dreaded the day he would return. I didn't know why he left or what he was doing there. He called his mother often. He never asked to speak to me. I really didn't care. I was doing fine without him.

Late December I delivered a beautiful baby boy. The only good things Raj ever gave me were my four beautiful children. After the delivery, I decided not to have any more children. I discussed with the doctors and they agreed to do a procedure on me. We all felt that it was a good decision.

My mother-in-law visited me the day after my baby was born. Afterwards, one of the employees dropped off food at the nurse's station. I had not informed or consulted them about the surgery. Somehow they had found out.

I was discharged from the hospital several days after the surgery. It was Christmas day. One of the drivers was sent to pick us up. The doctor's had given me painkillers and ordered lots of rest. The children were very excited to see the baby. They also got their mommy back home.

I was changing the baby when I saw someone walking towards me from the corner of my eye. My reaction was "oh my God, he's returned and so is my hell". I was shocked by his arrival and tried to hand him the baby, but he just looked and then asked why it had taken me so long to come back from the hospital. Why had he returned? I hated his presence so much. I nervously told him about my surgery with a brief explanation. He just stared at me. That look was all too familiar to me. He was dying to use those fists again. He left the room after giving me the cold stare.

My mother-in-law brought food for us in small containers. I was still not allowed to enter her kitchen. She feared that I could still poison their food at anytime. The atmosphere on my in-laws' side of the house sounded happy. There was loud music, a big pot of fresh goat on the stove and the men were drinking. On my side of the house there was a sense of fear and uncertainty. It did not feel like Christmas at all. Christmas in India is not widely celebrated. The markets were beautifully decorated. Some Christian churches had come to the hospital singing Christmas carols. It reminded me so much of Canada. I missed all the festivities, the lights and Turkey dinners. I longed to be with my family exchanging gifts and sitting by the fireplace.

The children and I sat around the baby glancing outside every so often. I wondered what surprise Raj would come up with tonight. "Why had he come back? Who had called him back?" It had been so peaceful without him. Now my children and I were back in the house of doom. My mother-in-law came around a couple of times to check on the baby. She would only stay for a minute. I had no visitors to share my joy with. The stores were closed and all the workers were home, enjoying Christmas with their families. All I wanted to do was cry. I thought about the other women who had shared my room at the hospital. Following tradition, their parents would come and take their daughters and newborn grandchildren to their houses. The new mothers were pampered for several weeks. Their parents would have a prayer ceremony and dedicate the babies according to their religious traditions. After that they would throw a party for the new mother. Many cultures did not allow the mom and the newborn out of the house for several weeks, fearing that an evil spirit would come near them. But there was nothing in this house for me. No form of pampering or celebrating the birth of my son. I wished my mom would send someone to stay with me for a little while. But my mom had no idea what was happening to me. I needed so much help taking care of my four little ones, cooking and cleaning not to mention dealing with the constant fear of the unknown.

Around nine o'clock, after the children had been changed into their pyjamas, Raj walked into the room, drunk and angry. With his hands on his hips, he demanded answers from me. "Who gave you permission to undergo the surgery? Did you ask me or my mother before you went ahead with the surgery? Is this your way of bringing shame to our family? Did your mother put you up to this?" By now he was inches from my face. Shaking with intense fear and with quivering lips, I tried to tell him that it was the best thing I had ever done. I did not want any more children. As the tears rolled down, I pointed to the children and asked if they had a good life living in these conditions. Then he asked whose baby it was. I just shook my head with disbelief. I told him I was not like him at all—he was the one sleeping around, not me. He slapped me across my face and asked me to leave his house with the baby immediately. I pretended I was going, so he wouldn't hit me again. The children started crying. They quickly followed me to where the baby was. He followed as well. He told me to pack all my clothes. I was only able to grab a few things before he pushed me towards the door. I quickly picked up the baby and began walking out.

I saw his mother watching from her window and called out to her. I pleaded with her to stop him. She said it was entirely my fault and she wasn't going to get involved. She refused to open the door. I realized my in-laws talked with Raj about my operation. He was trying to prove to them that he was protecting their integrity. I must be punished for my actions. We walked down the stairs and got into his truck. There was no one else on the road at that time. Tony was allowed to come with us. I was sure that Padma would take the girls and make up stories about me. She had a habit of turning the children against me.

I was certain the drunk was taking me to the ocean again. We were heading in that direction. This had become my biggest fear. Now it was the baby and I he would try to get rid of. Instead he turned towards the hospital. "Why was he going to the hospital and not to the ocean?" He parked in front of the entrance and told me to get out and I obeyed quickly, in case he changed his distorted mind. He got out and followed me inside, creating a scene in the waiting room. There were a number of people there along with the staff witnessing his foolishness. He called the doctor loudly and no one tried to stop him. The hospital staff pretended to look away. Raj demanded that the receptionist page the doctor and call him as soon as possible. I stood holding my baby, feeling totally embarrassed with his conduct.

The doctor arrived soon. Raj started demanding answers. Pointing his finger at the doctor, as if to scare him, he asked "Who gave you the right to operate on my wife without my consent?" Because of the scene he created, the hospital superintendent was also called in. They tried to calm him down, but he kept shouting. Then he proceeded to tell the doctor he could have both the baby and me! I was so ashamed to be there and to be humiliated by this evil man. I felt nauseated and wanted to run away and never face the hospital staff again. Finally, the superintendent showed Raj the door and told him to leave the baby and me there. A nurse came, took us to a room and tried to calm me down. I was shaking uncontrollably.

I apologized repeatedly to the hospital staff for Raj's actions. I had no idea he would do this to the doctor and me. The doctor said he understood what I was going through. The hospital staff told me they were aware of what Raj was doing to me and they believed me over him. People had gathered around the maternity ward from all over the hospital to watch Raj's rage. They must have heard the loud commotion and decided to get in on the action. I could hear them talking about what they had just witnessed. Some of the men, with their arms folded, suggested that they should have taught him a lesson by giving him a few slaps. I could hear them from the cracks in the door. Others blamed the family. I don't think anyone had any-thing bad to say about me – well not at least in front of me. I didn't take them seriously because I knew they were all talk and no action.

The Superintendent and a couple of nurses suggested I make contact with my family and return to them with the children. I told them Raj's family was using its power to influence people and no one was taking me seriously. I had no access to a phone or to anyone who could help me. They promised me they would look into getting social welfare involved, but I knew the welfare workers were friends of my in-laws and any request for justice would fall on deaf ears.

While we were still talking, Raj returned one more time. This time he was with the other children. He pushed open the door, threw some of my clothes at me and left. Some of the clothing landed on me and some on the floor. One of the nurses picked it up and took the baby to the nursery. I was given a muscle relaxant. I went to sleep comfortably.

In the morning the same doctor who had operated on me, came to visit. He asked if there was anyone I wanted to call. My parents had bought another house, and I didn't have their number. I couldn't remember anyone else's contact. Realizing that I was alone, I begged this doctor to help me.

The other women in my room felt sorry for the children and me. They told me stories about Raj's family. They told me that the doctor would not be able to help me, even if he wanted to. My in-laws were too influential. They bribed people in high places.

Two days later, my mother-in-law came to get me from the hos-pital. I refused to go with her, knowing that she was just trying to save face and show everyone there that she cared for me. She told the staff and the patients that I shouldn't overreact to Raj's anger. She went on to say that as Indian women, we must obey our husbands. She added that I was trying to be a Canadian in India and it couldn't work. It took her a few minutes to convince them that I should act like a traditional Indian woman, stop talking back to Raj, not act like an independent woman; but rather should have consulted Raj. She said her son is a very nice and caring man, but he was shocked and disappointed to find out that his wife brought shame on him. I turned to the women and very calmly justified that he had not been around for 2 months and we had not spoken until two days ago. That didn't go well with Padma. She quickly changed the topic while motioning to her driver to get in the truck. Like a faithful servant he quickly nodded, yes *Memshahib* and left. I knew she didn't want to be there for long, in case I began to reveal more of what was going on in this smooth talker's house. I shook my head in disbelief as to how much control this woman had over people. I left the hospital, not knowing when I would die or how I was going to die, but convinced it would be soon.

In the short ride home, I stared blankly outside wanting to exchange my life with anyone else's. I didn't want to be a part of this family anymore. I would do anything to give up my status as a daughter-in-law in this rich family for a better life in any poor family. This family was just too proud of who they were and what they had accomplished. All I wanted was some peace in my life.

It only took a day before Raj came back to my room. Within a few minutes he grabbed me by my hair and threw me to the ground. I ran towards my mother-in-law's house and demanded he stop hitting me. All I heard was foul language from him. She had promised the doctors at the hospital she would take responsibility for my safety and keep the peace. She had to live up to her words instead of shutting the door. I pushed the door and ran inside holding my tummy. All I could think of was my incision. It probably ripped. Suddenly from the back, I was kicked so hard that I fell to the ground. I couldn't breathe or move. My mother-in-law was shouting at him to stop. He continued to kick anywhere his foot landed. I heard her call her maids to summon his father upstairs. While I was still lying on the floor in pain, one half-dozen men came running to my aid. My mother-in-law was concerned and she demanded Raj be booted out of the house. I knew she was doing that for the fear of the authorities. If anything happened to me she would be held account-able. The security officer told Raj to go downstairs to cool off. They all got the same looks that I was used to. When he refused to go, his father called the police. Meanwhile they began to exchange swear words. The police suggested that Raj leave for the day. I poured my heart out to his parents, hoping they would send us back to Vancou-ver. Even though they listened, they still blamed me for Raj's actions. They said if it had not been for his arrest he would not be so bitter against me. Their advice was to do whatever he said even if he was wrong. That would keep him calm. I gave up.

He returned the next morning. His demeanour hadn't changed. I was certain the police released him without any charges or restrictions. He had spent the night at his younger brother's house. Fortunately, my incision was still intact. The kick to my back was so painful that I couldn't walk, sit or lie. Every time I moved I cursed him. I wished all kinds of evil on him. The pain was so intense that the children didn't have proper baths for a couple of days.

For this baby too, my in-laws had a small prayer ceremony in the *gurdwara* and chose a name for my youngest. They named him Satveer. I hated the name, but kept silent. Nobody cared about my feelings or about me. I couldn't stand any one of them. Everything about them displeased me. I just had to find a way to numb my feel-ings in order to survive.

CHAPTER SEVENTEEN

The Torment Continues

For the daughter-in-law of a wealthy textile and steel family, I didn't have a lot of clothes. The children wore cheap clothing bought from the local vendors. I would only be allowed out with one of Padma's trusted maids and a driver for doctor's appointments. I avoided looking in the stores. How badly I wanted to buy some new things for my children and myself, but I didn't have a penny to my name. I even thought of stealing from Raj's family to feed and clothe my children, but I was too scared of being caught. I knew I would be punished severely; I couldn't breathe in that house without someone hearing me.

I tried so hard to be quiet and calm towards Raj and his family, but they deliberately provoked me. Even then, I would walk away. The workers were told to stop talking to me. Everyone avoided me. They didn't want to get in trouble or lose their jobs. Raj's older brother continued to mock me. He was a nasty man. Any opportunity he got he would gossip about me. Once he told his parents that I had stolen the spare keys to their house. They searched my bedroom but found nothing. He insisted they keep an eye on me. They had gone through my underwear boxes as well; it was such a humiliating experience.

My groceries had been cut and I was down to the bare necessities. The children still cried for ice cream and candy but never got any. I longed to eat bread in the mornings instead of *roti* (Indian chapatti). When my in-laws decided I could have bread, it was a real treat for us. I was missing English food and longed for McDonald's and KFC.

***

Have you craved something so bad that you could taste it in your mouth? Even when you knew it was junk food? I could still smell the French fries sizzling in the oil and the patties cooking on the hot rack. My Fillet-O-Fish complete with tartar sauce and cheese was the best. Just thinking about it made my mouth water. Even better was the hash browns. I had access to bags of potatoes, many of which were rotten, but I could never make those hash browns. Who would have thought after all these years I could still hear the orders. "Can I have #2 with Coke and lots of ketchup please?" I would day dream about food and my old job to make the time pass. At that time, I couldn't wait to get home and eat my mom's roti and curry. Every summer before I got married my family would pick up a huge bucket of Kentucky fried chicken and head out for the day to the beaches. My time at the fast food restaurant was short-lived, yet it left a craving for many years to come.

***

I had no money. I was told that whatever I got was charity and I should be grateful for it. Hannah started school. She was a bright little girl. Her grandmother bought her a couple of uniforms. It was about a ten-minute walk each way. In the beginning one of the drivers dropped Hannah to school. Then she was on her own. She had many stories to share with her siblings. Soon Tony started kindergarten. He did not want to leave my presence. He cried and cried; his biggest fear was not seeing me again. I asked for permission from my in-laws to take him to school myself. A worker would come with me. We did this for a while until Tony was comfortable. It took some time before he was able to trust anyone.

Manpreet was doing very well. The doctors had given her a poor prognosis with her heart condition. She had to be monitored regularly. Satveer, on the other hand was a happy and healthy baby.

Nothing had changed in our marriage. Raj was just as lazy as the first day we landed. He would stink up my suite with his smoking and refused to use an ashtray. He was on a mission to make my life as miserable as possible. Once I heard someone call him a snake. I thought that was the best description of him I had ever heard. He was, indeed, a snake.

One day, my mother-in-law came to my suite and starting yelling profanities. I asked her why she was so rude to me. She said I had gossiped about her to her workers. I denied. She called one of the workers up to confront me. This worker said that I had told her my mother-in-law encouraged Raj to leave me and beat me up. I admitted that I had said those things. This traitor had showed concern for me so I confided about the torture I endured from this family. Part of me wanted to tell my mother-in-law about the things the worker had said about her, but I knew she'd lose her job. I apologized and turned around. My monster-in-law continued cursing. She was happy her son beat me up all the time. I told her to get out. On her way out she picked up a metal spoon and hit my head while cursing my parents. Finally, I lost my temper and pushed her out of my house. Like a little girl she ran downstairs crying hysterically and demanded that I be arrested.

The police arrived shortly after and questioned me. I told them I had pushed her in self-defense; that I was tired of being treated like a slave. The police calmed us down and left with a warning not to touch the queen mother again.

That evening there were more swearing and cursing from my

father-in-law. The loving son decided that he too would punish me. Nobody was allowed to say anything to the queen. I didn't feel too bad for my action against her. I had hoped that her cussing and swearing would stop. She had gone too far with this.

The pole in my bedroom caught Raj's attention. That night Raj found a use for it. The children's beds were underneath the pole. About two feet of space separated the beds. He walked over and checked it out and called me over. Without warning he pulled my sari off me and tied a noose around the pole. The only question in my head was, "Why? Why did I marry him? Why do I keep putting up with him? Why do I let him torture me continuously? Why can't I just leave? Why didn't I run away when I had the chance? - But where would I go and who will keep me?"

I knew he would catch me if I tried to run. I was left with only my blouse and my peticoat. He forced me closer to the pole and put the noose around my neck. I protested and begged for mercy. He walked me through the process of hanging. He would make it look like a suicide; that it was the quickest and most painless way to die. People would believe that my death was self-inflicted. Even though he would kill me, he would make it look like I had committed suicide. As he talked there was a smile all over his face. The children got up and started screaming. They were just witnessing a murder. I kept shaking my head and pleading for him to stop. I didn't know how long it would take for me to die and how the children would ever heal from seeing their mother hung and killed a few feet from them. When he began tightening the sari around my neck, I knew I had very little time. Most often he tied my hands and legs so I wouldn't move. Fortunately this time he forgot to do that. As the sari became tighter I couldn't breathe. I realized he wasn't going to let go. He was enjoying every moment of it. He ignored the screams from the children. This time he was determined to kill me because his mom had been hurt. No one cared about the bump on my head from the spoon. I quickly started to loosen the sari from my neck and screamed for help. My father in-law's room was not too far from mine and he woke up. He called out to Raj to let me go and stop his insanity; that it had gone too far. His knocks on the door fell on deaf ears. My terrified children held their blankets tight. When Raj wouldn't open the door, my father-in-law kicked it down. He was a strong man and when he turned on the lights, I was hanging from the pole. He had witnessed an attempted murder in his house. He kept yelling at Raj to get out of his house. The dad threw a towel at me to cover myself. Finally I was able to free myself from the sari.

Outside, the two men—father and son—were getting into a heated argument. I was afraid that if one of them got hurt, I would be blamed for it. I knew I would never hear the end of it. Finally, my mother-in-law intervened and got her husband back inside the house. She came out a few minutes later and asked me if I was happy starting fights. She managed to calm Raj down. She repeated the same thing she had told him many times before—not to waste his time on me because I wasn't worth it. She said he should forget about me and start a new life. She joked that someday I would end it myself. "Didn't she already attempt suicide? After all, she is a lunatic," she reminded both of us.

He felt better and went with his mama to sleep in her residence. Fear kept me up all night. He could come back any moment and strangle me. The door had been broken. I lay on my bed all night thinking of what my life had become. I stared at the metal rod wondering what its real purpose was. This evil man must have carefully planned this. He didn't have to leave the house to kill me. It could be done in my bedroom. "Where would I go and who would take us?" I had no money and no one I could trust. I started thinking of ways to keep myself alive.

Fantasizing became my means of survival. I remembered good looking men from movies I'd seen. From this day on I began a new journey. In spite of what happened around me, my thoughts were only focused on my idols. They would remember my birthday and called me by my real name. I wouldn't be referred to as a female dog!

I pictured myself eating family dinners together. My fantasy husband would help me prepare dinner and compliment me on how tasty the food was. Most impressive of all was the fact that I would be happy with my new family. I could see myself in nice clothes and makeup and imagined that we would go to movies or shopping and have special dinners together. We would even go on a vacation. As my fantasies grew, I would change from one actor to another. Then I would try desperately to remember someone else that I might have had a childish crush on. These fantasies kept me going, even in the midst of the storm that surrounded me.

During the day I felt safe but still wondered what he would do in the evening. Would it be a peaceful night or one with nasty surprises? The nighthawk didn't sleep until he did his usual ritual on me. I often wondered how he managed to come up with new ways to torture me. Did he have a reference book or was he watching horror movies during the day? Or was there a voice inside of him telling him what to do? I knew the other brothers didn't treat their wives this badly. Was there something wrong with him mentally? Why won't someone have him admitted to the same hospital I was sent to?

I wished there was a way I could get into his mind to find out what he was contemplating next. I could try to destroy all his thinking abilities. He didn't have any friends; no decent men would want anything to do with him. The only people who hung out with him were the local *gundas*. I found out the women he had affairs with were no longer interested in him either. They dumped him. So he spent most of his time at home. People in their *pind* (village) found out what he was doing to me. Rumours spread pretty fast. I was happy to hear about it. The gossips were working in my favour. Not only did he lose all the respect but I was gaining some sympathy.

One day, Raj got into an argument with a man downstairs. The man dared him to come and fight with a man for a change, instead of a woman. He asked Raj to show his mighty strength outside his home. The man spat on him and invited him to fight any time as he walked away. The moment he came upstairs he punched and kicked me without saying a word. Then he accused me of having an affair with that man. I had never seen or even heard of this man, but I was actually proud of him. Whoever he was I wanted to thank him. But what happened that night was like a story from a horror book.

The children watched their father throw me around like a toy. Unable to tolerate this behaviour any longer Tony decided it was time for him to do something. He picked up an empty milk jug and threw it at his father. It merely bounced off his back. Raj directed his anger at Tony. I quickly grabbed him and shielded him in my arms. Thankfully, Tony was spared. Raj turned to me and blamed me for filling the children's heads with lies and making them hate him. In my outrage I asked him if the children were blind and deaf. I had always tried to keep peace at home. If anyone was to be blamed, it was he—he was the one who had destroyed our lives. I had lost my mind by this point, so whatever came to me, I spoke out loud. Either way, I would be beaten up, so it might as well be worth it. "From the day I married you I have not had a peaceful moment; all you have done for me is beat and torture me in every way imaginable." He interrupted me by slapping me so hard I hit my head against the wall, taking Tony down with me as I fell. He suggested I commit suicide or he would put an end to me himself. I replied that he was the one who should commit suicide. I was now determined to live.

After that, whenever he was around, I tried hard to look busy. I ignored him. I created work for myself, so I'd be distracted from the continuous torment. He would follow me around in that small place and squeeze my face and slap me. Once I had the urge to use the small knife in my hand and threaten him. I knew it would backfire on me. He would not hesitate to use the knife on me. I didn't want to give him any ideas.

When the wife-beater felt I was ignoring him—which I was—he demanded that I sit in front of him and show him respect. I had to answer his questions and look right at him when he talked. For a low-life like him he sure demanded a lot of respect. This was a place of comfort for him. He could build up his manly skills and be proud of his achievements. Outside of the home, he was a coward. I gave the answer he wanted to hear. It would please him and spare me a black eye. I made promises I knew I couldn't keep. Why not, it spared his harsh punishment. I felt no guilt for the empty promises.

Later that night, still not satisfied with his accomplishments, he made me sit on the floor and tried to hand me the gallon container full of kerosene. I refused to take it from his hands. I knew what he was planning on doing. Was this from a movie scene? It was very common for brides to be burnt to death with kerosene here. Bride-burning incidents are sometimes disguised as accidents caused by an 'exploding stove,' and fire. It was used by men who committed this kind of crime because the abusers thought that they would not leave any evidence behind. I began to beg him not to do it and held on to his dirty, evil-smelling feet and begged for mercy. He kicked me away from him and brought up the past. "Poor thing, he was an innocent man, locked up for the weekend. What injustice to him. He was a victim to a crazy wife's cooked up story. He had spent most of his married life looking for answers and justice." I wanted to shout out those words and tell him to get over it. I wished he had never been released from that jail! He should have rot in jail. The look on his face was one of absolute determination; I knew he was not backing out of this.

This barbarian knew I wasn't going to take the gallon container, so he decided to pour the kerosene over my body himself. Scared to death, I searched for a way out. I didn't want to die this way. I yelled out that he should just shoot me in the head instead. It would be over sooner. He laughed and said that would be too easy; he wanted to make sure I felt pain. That was the reason he was torturing me, so I would remember his pain in jail. Within a few minutes, the kerosene began to irritate my skin, and I developed a rash. The smell of kerosene was so strong I began to feel sick. How was I going to get out of this one? If I burned, the children would also burn, unless he took them out of the room which would be impossible since I was closest to the door. I began to think up ways to keep him close to me so when he lit the fire, he would burn as well. I remember thinking that even if he survived; I hoped there would be some effects of the fire on him as a reminder for the rest of his life.

It seemed to take forever before he spoke again. He asked if I was comfortable and if I wanted to live a little bit longer. I pleaded with him to stop. I knew the children were listening, and I didn't want them hurt in any way. He stood in front of me smiling. He was a sick man who loved to torture me. He gently shook his head and said he wasn't going to burn me, because he just couldn't do it. Instead, he handed me the matches and said he had done his part. My part would be the easiest—all I had to do was light the match. I could tell there were a lot of matchsticks in the box. My spirit was determined to live. Somehow I had to outsmart him. I had to destroy the matches. When Raj walked over to the door, I quickly got up, threw the matches into the sink and turned on the water. I hoped he didn't have another packet of matches or a lighter on him. This threw him into a rage.

***

Indeed I had narrowly escaped death; many are not so fortunate. Once while visiting my baby daughter in the hospital, I overheard the nurses talking about a female patient in the ICU. One described her as very scary to look at, while the other said she had nightmares last night. It was clear that there was something serious about this patient. Was there someone else other than me that was unfortunate? I knew I had to investigate this matter further. So I went closer to the nurses' station and asked who they were talking about. The nicer nurse leaned forward and whispered that I take a quick peek into the ICU.

Knowing I had only a few minutes to spare, I hurried past the cleaning lady, who showed no interest in her job. The floor was still very dirty except that now there was a fresh coat of bleach water. The smell was overpowering. I began walking even faster to make it through the flight of stairs without being caught by anyone. ICU was only restricted to immediate family members.

Someone flung open the door and there sitting were a couple of women and a very agitated man. I wasn't sure who I was looking for until my eyes landed on a woman who only had her face exposed. There was no way of missing her. She kept yelling "I want to die please end it quickly" and her eyes met mine. "Oh my god, what happened to this lady?" I felt like vomiting. I couldn't stand that sight. Who would do such a horrible thing to a young woman?

Covering my mouth, I headed out when a woman yelled out at me. Her eyes red and swollen, she looked so tired. "That woman lying in that bed is my daughter. This is the beast that tried to kill her." The man got up with one hand on his hip and the other pointing at the burned out woman. He began to call down every curse on her and her mother. A nurse demanded that he leave the floor immediately. He slammed the door wishing that they were all dead.

I could not get the image out of my mind. Her dull screams and short requests for death filled the room with so much pain. She wasn't the only one hoping to end it all – that man in the waiting room did too. What could have gone so wrong that it would bring someone to this stage?

The woman got up and walked towards me while wiping her tears with her wet handkerchief. "Please help my daughter – that nasty man burned her two days ago with kerosene. He accused her of having an affair and wanted her dead. This is my only daughter and I may lose her." By now she was wailing and trying to hang on to my shoulders. I wanted to run. What if I am caught by my in-laws? I will be in big trouble. Trying to get this grieving mom to sit down, I turned to the nurse and asked what her daughter's prognosis was. She said that it wasn't good.

After giving the mother a quick hug; I ran out the door to hold my daughter. "Is he going to get away with attempted murder? How dare he talk to her mother in that tone? What if she doesn't make it?" I picked up my daughter and held her tightly against me. No one would every hurt my babies like this. I will protect each one of them.

Just then I saw the nurse from the ICU. Holding on to my daughter, I asked if the police were notified. She said that she did not have all the details. She did say that there were burns to her entire body and she was in deep agony. She walked away shaking her head.

That woman's face haunted me for a long time. A few days later, I heard that the woman had succumbed to her death.

How do you get over the death of a child? How does a parent handle the death of her child? They are the flesh of your flesh and blood of your blood. To lose a child is the most devastating thing any parent has to face. No parent wants to outlive their children - especially when the death of that child is so barbaric. So many lives are changed forever. It is a grief like no other. All that the loved ones are left with is memories.

The families are given so much support during the funeral. But after that they feel isolated, fearful, ashamed, and overwhelmed with grief. Every spoken word haunts the family.

They are left with no answers; only questions. Could they have done something to prevent this from happening?

***

He checked the matches a few times. They were wet and unusable. Enraged he grabbed my hair and pushed me towards the door. He said I stunk and needed a shower. In spite of the pain and the shame, I still smiled to myself. "Maybe there was someone looking out for me? I had defeated death so many times. Was it just plain luck or was there a higher power helping me?" Whatever it was, I was triumphing.

It was the most painful shower I had ever had. The kerosene had burnt my skin. I wept under the cold water. "Is this what had become of my life? Am I really crazy? Was I the only one going through all these punishments? I could not stand his presence any longer. I had to fight back. I wanted to hurt him so bad that he would be paralyzed in his hands. I wanted to make sure he had to depend on someone else for the rest of his life. He could never hurt another soul, ever.

I had a rash all over my body. I wondered how I was going to put any clothes on. I wouldn't be able to sit or sleep. I knew the vulgar one wouldn't let me go to the doctor. I had nothing to soothe the irritation except for the baby lotion. I didn't want to come out of the shower. That was my asylum. Was there anything he hadn't tried yet?

Every time I turned, I had pain. The next morning I told Padma about his psychotic behaviour. I showed her my skin and asked for her help. She admitted that Raj had an anger problem but said I should stay away from him when he was in a bad mood. If I didn't bother him, he wouldn't do these things to me, she said. What a waste of time talking to her. Of course she will side with her son. I felt as if I had been thrown into a field of snakes. I constantly feared for my life. I thought about dying and my children having to grow up without their mother. I hoped they would all stay together and comfort one another in my absence.

CHAPTER EIGHTEEN

A Short Vacation

One day, my in-laws announced they were going on a two-month vacation. "You're on your own now," they told me. Raj's older brother, who hated me, had sent his wife and children to stay in Dubai. I realized that if I were killed, no one would know about it. Raj could dispose of my body any way he wanted. No one there really cared about me, so it wouldn't make any difference whether I was alive or not. The workers would no longer come upstairs. I was completely shut off from the outside world.

The prince still refused to work. I knew there would be no food for us. My in-laws had tried unsuccessfully to get him to work in one of their businesses. He had refused, always playing the "poor me" game. I wanted to tell him it was game over.

My father-in-law knew what I was going through, but he had to listen to what his wife said. There were a few times when he had caught Raj slapping me when I was trying to do my work. I remember once telling my father-in-law I was very tired of being beaten up and tortured. I suggested they send Raj away so that the children and I could live somewhat peacefully. I asked that he be sent back to the city (where he had been when my youngest had been born) to start a business there, so he would be away from us. When my mother-in-law found out about our conversation, she accused me of wanting to get closer to my father-in-law so he would give me money. She said people were already talking about me and now this would give them something more to talk about. It was a nasty thing for her to say. This old man was a father figure to me. Although he was not the best father, he was still my children's grandfather.

I knew people were talking about me and that many people in that community knew what I was going through. Many sympathized with me. However, a small number believed my in-laws were the perfect family. I had come to destroy their credibility and everything they had worked so hard to build. I really didn't care what people had to say because they were not living in my shoes. At one point, an older woman counselled me, at the request of my mother-in-law. She told me that I had to get my act together and start living like the respectable wife of a respected family. She asked that I stop telling lies about being mistreated. She said she had yet to meet a man like Raj. He was a kind and gentle man who spoke with respect. She said that whenever I had tried to commit suicide, he had stuck by me and had never let anyone influence him to divorce me. She even said that with my mental disorder, Raj continued to support me. He had given up working so he could help me take care of the children.

I was in total shock, not sure whether to laugh or get angry with this woman. I had to restrain myself from slapping her face. She wouldn't stop putting me down. Finally I interrupted her and asked if she wanted to switch places. I said that if she cared that much for Raj, she should give her own daughter to him. She got up and said I should be thankful this family kept me in their home.

I never thought a day would come where I would be sad to see my in-laws leave. They did play a small role in protecting me. My father-in-law's presence made me feel a bit safer. Raj was somewhat cautious when other people were around the house. What would happen once they were gone? Where would I get money for groceries? With Raj sleeping during the day and fighting most of the night, I figured we would starve to death.

My useless husband deserved that punishment but not my innocent children. I had to come up with a plan to keep my children alive. I didn't know what I could possibly do for them. I was falling into a state of depression, anxiety and desperation.

I had groceries to last only a few days. Raj would have another reason to fight with me now. One of the brothers had a whole warehouse business in the basement. In desperation, I snuck into the back of the warehouse and asked a worker for some food. One handed me a case of canned fish and another gave me some powdered milk. I hid these provisions under the bed. The workers were sympathetic. One day I wasn't so lucky. I got caught taking a bag of potatoes upstairs. Then Raj's younger brother called out all sorts of names and accused me of stealing. I gently told him that we had no groceries and the children were hungry. He went to confront the workers. I ran after him and told him that I had taken the potatoes myself. I didn't want the workers to lose their jobs because of me.

A little later, I heard someone call my name. I went outside only to be greeted by police officers. They asked to search my place because they suspected I was stealing groceries. They said I had no rights in that house and the brothers wanted me out. With tears rolling down my cheeks, I invited the officers inside. I showed them the inside of my suite and the two empty cupboards. My small children were all sitting quietly on their beds. Finally, I admitted that I had stolen from the warehouse, but that I had only taken food to feed my family, not for profit. I told them I had nothing and that some days I ate nothing so my children would have food. I told them I was willing to work in the warehouse in exchange for groceries but the family would never let me.

One of the officers took me downstairs and confronted the brother who had called them. He demanded the family give me proper food and clothes. I asked the officer to stay with me while I picked up the necessities for my children. I took much more than I needed, knowing there wouldn't be another opportunity like that. The officer told my brother-in-law to show some kindness towards the children.

I shared my pain with this officer, a kind man. He had just returned from a trip to London. He told me that many of his fellow officers knew what I was going through but they couldn't do much for me. He wished me well. The other two officers were talking to Raj. I heard them say that he should take better care of me and provide for his family. When they left my fear returned. Now all the brothers would make my life difficult. They were trying to embarrass me, but it backfired. Instead of being arrested and charged, I was awarded a lot of groceries for my children. I had never been inside their warehouse before. It was big. There was a lounge next to the office that was used for late night parties.

When the police didn't do anything to me, Raj's brothers weren't satisfied. The next day, they had a few workers break down the outside wood burning stove and empty the water tank. I hardly used that water tank. It was rusted and the water had been in there forever. The plumbing system was changed around so we couldn't get any water upstairs. I stood helplessly. They didn't stop there. Someone else cut the power to my suite. Now there was no water, no outdoor stove and no electricity. Dust and debris from the dismantled wreckage were everywhere. Water was gushing down into my suite. From that night on, we would be in the dark.

All the banging noises outside woke Raj from his beauty sleep. He peeked out the window and asked what was going on. I didn't bother responding. If he was a decent husband, we wouldn't be in this mess. He was too busy ruining my life. After the workers left I heard his brother laughing. I knew he would blame me. It wouldn't come as a surprise. I was used to it.

I walked around outside after the devastation to look for a kerosene lamp. I found a few old ones and some buckets. Padma kept all kinds of junk and it became my treasure. I gathered a few items together and brought them inside. When some of the workers came upstairs for lunch, they secretly told me which tap worked. I quickly filled a bucket with water and took it inside.

To my surprise, I saw Raj getting ready to go somewhere. He took Tony and the empty jug to the store next door to get some kerosene since the attempted murder had used up what we had. I cooked outside in the wood burning stove. Now that it was destroyed – I had no choice.

I was terrified of having the kerosene around since that frightening night. Now, not only would I be cooking with kerosene but I would also have to use it in the lamps. I went back into the storage area to see if I could find some more things to use and I found another empty gallon jug, a tub for washing and some old pots and pans. I felt like a street person collecting other people's junk. I brought the tub in and put it in the bathroom and, with the jug; I filled it with water to wash the dishes and clothes.

I had never imagined my life would come to this. I thought of my family often and wondered what they were doing and if they were thinking of me. I didn't think they knew the magnitude of my abuse. What would they do if they found out that we had no electricity or running water? I was completely isolated from the outside world. There were no newspapers around and no radio. I was a prisoner in this house.

During the two months my in-laws were gone, Raj fought with me in many little ways. There were a few slaps here and there, but the emotional abuse was constant. I learned new ways of coping every day. While the older brother was out with his mistress, I filled up as many containers as I could with water. I cooked early in the afternoon. Then I helped Hannah with her schoolwork and told stories to them. We had no other means of passing our time.

Inside, I fumed with anger towards Raj. He was the one who should have been providing for us and taking care of our needs. Instead, he chose to sleep through our ordeal. But I was learning to cope with the conditions and knew not to complain. He would simply turn everything around and blame me.

With fumes in our room from the kerosene stove and lamps, my nose bled all the time. I didn't want to take it outside to cook. Raj's brother wouldn't hesitate to destroy it. The fumes lingered in the house even with all the windows and door open. Never in my wildest dreams had I ever thought that a day would come when I would be missing my in-laws.

Even though Raj did not torture me during the time his parents were on vacation, I still lived in fear. I didn't trust anyone. Some glass levers were missing on the windows, and the door could be kicked down without much force. The men in this family were capable of anything. They had no regard for children and women. I didn't trust the man Raj's brother had hired as a security guard. One night, he and Raj got into a fist fight. Raj was trying to get into the warehouse to get some groceries for us. I was standing on the stairs, waiting for him to come back. As he made his way upstairs the guard confronted him. Raj told him to mind his own business, but then he became violent. I took the children and ran back into the house. Just then I heard Raj shouting at the guard telling him he had no rights there. They were fighting and threatening to kill each other. I was extremely nervous.

For a moment, I didn't hear any noises and wondered if one of them was either seriously hurt or dead. I feared for our lives. I held onto the children, hoping the guard wouldn't hurt us. I would plead with him for our lives and hope he would be merciful. Then Raj walked into the room covering his forehead. He had a small cut. I laughed to myself thinking "poor thing. He got hurt in a fight." The guard had walked away. I was so happy Raj got beat up. This was a moment I had long hoped for.

In a desperate attempt to regain some sanity, the woman began to plot her next move. She had to act fast. Time was of the essence. So she came up with a surprising thought. She needed powers far beyond any ordinary woman. She would need to wrestle her villain. She would have to have the super powers. Then she remembered her favourite TV show.

The woman always dreamed of possessing powers like that of a strong woman. She flashed back to, 'Wonder Woman', an Amazon champion. She was so strong she could lift up a plane and whales with her magic lasso. She had superhuman strength to resist blunt force trauma. Her tiara was a dagger and a throwing weapon. Along with her beauty, she was one of the famous super heroines. She was always on a mission to protect all mankind from the god of war, who was intent on destroying the human race. She had unique powers to boldly fight back against his destructive force. Wonder Woman was a perfect woman- beautiful, intelligent and strong.

The woman had been in a pathological relationship too long. She had lived her life hoping for a "happily ever after" future. She began her journey of fantasy believing her husband would be different and they would be happy. Whenever she looked at her black and blue bruises, she wanted to find a way out. She hoped vainly even as her marriage spiralled downward, that somehow it would get better one day. She wanted so much to live in peace.

She hoped and waited patiently for her perpetrator to die. She had sought help from his family to get him to stop, but no one cared. He had a grin permanently formed around his devil lips. She referred to him as the 'son of Sam'. All she wanted was a life free of violence.

She headed for the only bathroom near her suite, to avoid any further interrogation from her tormentor. As she sat on the covered toilet seat, she quickly checked one more time to see if the door was locked. This was her time alone with her fictitious lover. It would give her a few minutes and a chance to be in his loving arms.

She visualized her freedom with him and how that could change her whole world. There would be no more fear. This woman would become a superwoman who could now stand up and say whatever came to mind. She tried to cope by channelling her energy into other activities. Just to survive, she created work around the house so she could get her mind off him and onto something better. She laughed at her ignorance. She refused to give in, and kept on going.

She had thoughts of taking a stand and getting out of there quickly. It would be such a relief when she could just walk away.

She wanted to be liberated from him and his strongholds. She felt she had to adopt a coping mechanism around a fantasy of being in omnipotent control.

As soon as he raised his hand to slap her across her face, she would be transformed into this mighty woman. She had twice his strength. The moment he walked closer to her, she'd move closer to him, as if to provoke him. With one hand she would push him against the wall. Then with the other she'd begin to choke him while lifting him off the ground and then dropping him.

Shamelessly he'd fight back, unsure of what just happened. Her wrists were shooting bullets into him. Then he'd yell out, "Stop it". Her powers were on a timer. She had to use them all at one time. She'd throw him a few more punches to his face. He'd feel a drop of blood roll down from his forehead. He'd give her the look of death.

She'd pause and come back and hand-cuff him. He'd cry like a little girl when it began to tighten around his wrists. After asking him if he was comfortable, she'd kick him a few more times. Unable to stand the humiliation, He'd begin to curse her and shout profanities. She'd walk over to the sink and bring out the bar of soap to shove it into his mouth.

With a sense of accomplishment, she'd proudly walk over to the alcohol cabinet and slowly pour out all the alcohol from every bottle. She'd pick up the last packet of cigarettes from the table and break them into small pieces.

Satisfied by her achievements, she'd demand that he sit on the floor while she grabbed a chair for herself. Unwillingly he'd oblige. She would lay out the new rules. Their lives had just taken a new turn. It was called 'role reversal'. From this point on she'd be the master and he would be her slave.

There will come a day when I will smile again. I will look toward heaven with tears of joy and no more bruises.

That abuser was my husband. The dreamer was me.

CHAPTER NINETEEN

Return to the City

My in-laws returned from their Dubai trip. Although we had lost all of our privileges of electricity and water, I hadn't suffered harsh abuse while they had been gone. Many questions started to rise in my mind. "Why had there been some peace in their absence? Was Raj scared of his brothers? Had he realized he needed me? Had he been cruel to me before because he was always trying to please his mother? Now that his parents were back, would he revert to his former ways?" It didn't take long for things to change. In fact, it was just a matter of days.

Raj's brothers complained to their parents about both of us and demanded that we be kicked out. We left the next morning for Bombay. I encouraged him to apply for a job I had seen in the newspaper. He was successful in his interview and got the job as a sales manager. This job would require a lot of traveling. This was a huge relief for me. Someone was watching over the children and me. I even began to make some friends in our new neighbourhood.

I started to find things in Raj's bags that indicated he was having affairs while he was on his trips. I chose to remain quiet - I didn't want to ruin the peace. Eventually the women started calling my house. He brought one of them over one night, thinking I was asleep.

I also remember being asked at a resort in Goa if I was the children's nanny. The staff had been told the children's mom was dying of an illness. Raj was a frequent visitor there who threw large parties. Eight months into his new job, I received a phone call from Raj's managers informing me that he had been terminated. They asked that he return the company vehicle and the keys. I knew Raj's wild parties had finally caught up with him. When I confronted him he blamed me with the same old tale. That night, he overdosed me on Valium. Then, he brutally beat me up until I couldn't get up. I lay on the floor passing in and out of consciousness. I had no idea where he got these pills from. A doctor must have been prescribing them to him. Had he found a new way to kill me?

CHAPTER TWENTY

The People I Loved the Most

I woke up the next morning with a pounding headache. Every inch of me ached. The house was too quiet. I slowly got up from the floor and checked each room for Raj and the children. I thought they must be out shopping. I was still trying to remember what had happened the night before when Raj suddenly walked in. I asked him where the children were. Without answering, he threw me to the floor. I screamed in pain and begged him to stop, but he kept throwing me like a doll from one wall to the other. The walls in that house were made of concrete and every time I smashed against a wall, I felt the blood gushing. I feared I would have severe brain damage. When he decided to stop the beatings he began to speak. "You have made it your mission to destroy me—I have lost my job because of you. Now you F----- B---- you will pay for everything now." I could feel my body swelling up. The peaceful days had only been the calm before the storm. This episode was another way for him to shift his blunder on me.

He became aware that the neighbours were watching. So he went out to tell them to mind their own business. He returned to resume his rage and torture. By that time, I was too weak to say or do anything. I was disappointed with my neighbours. I hoped that some of the men would stand up to him and put an end to his macho behaviour. I just gave up, thinking it was my fate.

I lay on the floor until the next day. I was awakened by the sound of loud banging and kicking. I had been in so much pain I couldn't get up. I was too scared to open the door, so I just lay there until I heard a man call out. He identified himself as the local police. Very slowly, I crawled to the door and looked out. Some of my neighbours were at the door with the officers. I thought I was having a bad nightmare. It took a while before I realized where I was and what had happened. My body ached as if I had been run over by a truck. My head was spinning. I had no idea where everyone was. The police asked for the key to open the metal burglar bar. The big padlock was new and I didn't have the key. The small task of moving a couple of feet was an agonizing task. The neighbours told me that Raj had left early that morning with some bags. The police were trying to find out where he was headed.

With my permission, the policemen cut the lock and came inside. There was blood in the hallway. They began to point out the cuts and bruises on my face. I knew Raj had sent the children to stay with his parents. He had probably planned to kill me that night, that's why he fled. Maybe he had left me here to die. The sympathetic officers suggested that I pack up and leave. Since no one knew where he was, he would come back to check on me. I may not get another chance to live.

People finally believed me and knew what kind of monster I had been living with. I was taken to the hospital for a check-up and had some stitches on my head. I went to spend a few days with an acquaintance. She was a local prosecutor and an understanding woman. I also submitted a report to the police station so they could finally lay assault charges.

The police made contact with my in-laws and told them what had happened. They traced Raj to Dubai. My in-laws asked me to come back to the children. They promised to send us back to Vancouver. Happy with their decision, I went back to be with my children. I was excited to be finally returning home. The police spoke with my in-laws and told them what I had gone through. I felt pretty sure they were prepared to help us now.

My children were so excited to see me alive. We began to plan our trip back. I talked to them about their father's cruelty towards me. They said they knew that their papa was a mad man and they too were scared of him. They also asked me questions such as, "Mom, are you really crazy?" The most shocking one was, "Are you really our mom?" He and their *Bibi* had poisoned the kid's minds. All that these precious and innocent children wanted was a stable home.

How badly those questions and comments hurt me! I couldn't imagine how confused and hurt the children were. They had no sense of security in their lives. They had spent their lives being thrown back and forth from one bad situation to another. So many people were suffering because of one man's actions.

My in-laws kept telling me that they were working on getting our plane tickets. I lived with their lies, until one day the devil showed up again. He was angry that his parents were supposedly helping me. He got close to his mother again, and they began to plot against me. Inevitably, my father-in-law took their word over mine. The plan to send us back to Vancouver was over. I felt like such a fool for believing them. But I didn't regret the decision to return to their home; I was with the people I loved the most—my four precious little ones.

CHAPTER TWENTY-ONE

A Depressed and Deprived Woman

I had now endured so many months of hell in this dysfunctional house. I was depressed and deprived of any hope. I got rid of the mirror in my room. It only reflected the pain and scars. I had nothing to my name, not even a penny and went out very rarely. I returned to my fantasies. They had helped me before. They allowed me to temporarily get my mind off the brutality and picture myself in the arms of a loving husband. I had to fight more than ever, to survive and maintain some form of sanity.

A few times a week, I would be forced to sit outside our suite. I would only hope he would allow me back inside. I was scared. The creepy creatures that came out at night petrified me. One particular night Hannah stood up and told her father that Mom was not going outside because it was dark and scary. So he put both of us outside. She spent the night sleeping on my lap. Padma's dog had a better place to sleep than I did. He slept outside her door on a small mat with a blanket.

All the children had been abused in many ways. They were voiceless and defenceless. A small part of them still loved him. Children don't need both parents in a marriage like mine. I would rather be a single parent and provide a safe and loving home. Women who have lost husbands through death somehow make it. The only difference is that the society pities them over a divorced woman.

Hannah never spoke out in my defence again. It was probably better that she remained silent, rather than be punished along with me again. Seeing the faces of both of my daughters, I was determined never to let any man treat them the way I was being treated. I began to look for ways to secure a better life for my children and me.

One night, Raj drank and told some made-up stories that made the children laugh. He looked at me with his evil eyes and asked the children if they wanted a new mommy, one that would love them and give them everything they wanted. He said I was only there to take care of them temporarily. He kept telling them that I had destroyed their future and that I should be punished. Now he introduced the children to his lifestyle. He gave them permission to hit me for disciplining them. At first they hesitated, and then he brought them over to me and told them to slap me anywhere they felt like it. Reluctantly, they threw soft punches at me. I gave him the look and told him to stop it. He stormed over and punched me in my right eye. He told me to never give him that look. I fell to the ground, and he continued to punch me in the same eye, all along saying he was going to take it out.

If I could have I would have attempted to seriously hurt him that night. I had suffered so much and I just could not tolerate it any longer. He was getting away with everything. Whenever he got a little cut, he'd start looking for a band aid like a little boy. But to inflict so much pain to someone else meant nothing to him. In fact, he enjoyed every moment of it. There was blood everywhere, and the children started screaming. Once he saw that I was bleeding profusely and was struggling to see, he stopped. I was not allowed to go to the doctors for stitches or given a band aid. It slowly healed, leaving a permanent scar.

It became a way of life for him. Blaming me and the world for his pathetic life gave him satisfaction. Finally, one day, I snapped and told him to grow up. He slapped my face a few times but I didn't cease talking. I told him exactly how I felt about him. The more he hit me, the more I spoke. I continued to tell him that he was the most useless and obnoxious man God had ever created. That he had not only wasted his own life but all of ours as well. After venting and getting punched repeatedly, I decided to stop. He calmly walked around and said that he was just getting warmed up. He said he would decide when and how it ended. He grabbed me by my hair and threw me from one wall to another. Every time my head hit the wall, I felt blood gushing. At some point I fell and he came and started kicking me. I can't remember why he stopped. I slowly found some strength to get to the washroom. I fell on my knees wondering if there was a God. The only ones I knew were psychics and witch doctors – the so-called healers. They had brought more curses then blessings. And if there was a God, he must be blind. Why won't this man just die? If he is that miserable, he should commit suicide. I could offer him my sari, or the kerosene. I could drive to the ocean and push him over. Not to forget, he also had access to the Valium pills. There were many ways he could call it quits. I knew he was gutless. He was scared of dying but not scared to kill someone else. The only thing that I felt towards him was bitterness.

One evening Raj took the boys out for a walk. When he returned, he asked the girls to join them and they did. A little later, he came back and said he had taken the children for a ride to his aunt's house. He said they were playing there and he had come to pick me up. I refused to go because his aunt's house was on the road that led to the ocean. But he demanded that I get ready immediately. There was no escape.

We drove to his aunt's house. I found an opportunity to secretly tell her about the previous visits to the ocean. I made her promise that she would tell the police if I went missing, which frightened her badly. She was a kind woman.

They didn't have any large businesses or much property. All they had was a small farm and an old house. The older son worked with his father on the farm while the girls helped their mother around the house after school. The girls had dreamt of someday marrying a nice man from Canada. They longed to sit in a plane. Often they would ask me to tell them stories of snowfall, Christmas and shopping. Their faces would light up with each story. They confided that they prayed everyday for a marriage proposal from Canada.

I did not want to leave this aunt's place. I had been feeling such fear in me. "Should I run for my life while I still had an opportunity? But where would I run to? It wouldn't take long for the children to start missing me. Raj would have all the men with their flash lights scouring the neighbourhood looking for me, the runaway. That would only prove him right – that I was mentally insane. He would look so good in the eyes of all these people. He was the most conniving man I had ever met. I wanted to ask one of his male cousins to come along for the ride. But Raj would have made an excuse that there wasn't enough room in the car. He had a way with charming words.

***

Raj convinced me that I deserved all this abuse and had brought it on myself. I was lured into believing that no one else would accept me or want me. Soon you start to believe that this life that he offered was the only life.

I was raped, tortured and convinced that I was the most terrible person and not worth anything to anyone except him. Even though I had opportunities to leave, I couldn't.

The fascinating thing is how my mind and body reacted to living in constant fear and pain. I would freeze and shut out the pain. I would slip into a constant state of trauma. Somehow I became zombie-like. When it got worse, I would completely shut down. As years passed, he became certain I liked it, or that it was okay, since I didn't resist.

He had me traumatized to the point of complete submission. To run would mean potential pain and punishment.

Abuse is power and control. The abuser minimizes, confuses, ridicules and uses a variety of behaviours to break down their spouse so they have total control of the relationship.

One of the obstacles in recognizing chronic mistreatment in a relationship is that abusive men don't stand out. They have good qualities and show kindness towards others. People may think the world of them. He does not fit anyone's image as a cruel and intimidating person. People may not even believe your story that it was as bad as you made it out to be.

It is easy for bystanders, family and others to discount the abused woman's story because the abuser is friendly, charming and a sensitive person. He is judged by his appearance. They are so good at distorting the events.

The longer one stays in this kind of relationship, the more they deteriorate. The abused is no longer allowed a voice, it is silenced. Your right to being angry is taken away from you. No matter how badly you are treated you are not allowed to raise your voice. Rage is only reserved for him.

The chaos and abuse escalates. Even though you know you have to get away for sanity's sake, you cannot. There is just too much involved. The confusion, fear and craziness wear you down.

You are alone, you have no voice and you are blamed for everything. In the end there is only one question in your mind. "Have I allowed myself to be abused"?

***

With so much fear, anger and hatred towards this beast, I sat in the front seat feeling disabled. It was very dark with the exception of a few lights from the nearby houses. He made sure that all the doors were locked and the windows rolled up. He turned on the fan only to circulate hot air. Other than the smell of cow dung, the smell of fear was making me nauseous. As soon as the car rolled out of his aunt's driveway, I wanted to yell at the top of my lungs either for mercy or one last fight. He turned towards the ocean. His evil glares confirmed my earlier thoughts. With one hand he held the steering wheel, and with the other he held my hand tightly without saying a word. I wanted the children to start fighting with each other or scream – anything that would distract the deadly silence in the car.

As we drove through the rocky unpaved road, passing the jungle with the occasional coconut and mango trees, I wondered how happy the people living in the slums were. There wasn't a human in sight to give me some comfort. I had seen a couple of stray dogs and knew that there were many frogs in those bushes.

Tears began running down my cheeks. I knew these could be my last moments on earth. I was shaking with fear and regretted every word I had said to him earlier. Should I beg for his mercy or jump out of the running vehicle into the sugar cane fields? This time I blamed myself for his actions. But how could I get him to forgive me? We arrived at this unforgiving ocean. My heart pounding, now my entire body was shaking uncontrollably from the fear. The place was dark and quiet with only sound of the waves. The smell of the ocean haunted me. I had been here before. The cravings of freedom had been doomed.

He got out of the car and motioned me to get out. I kept tryimg to lock the door, but he would use his key to unlock it. He threatened to smash the window if I didn't come out. After a struggle, he managed to pull me out. I began to beg for my life, joining my hands together and pleading. He didn't listen. I looked in the back seat and saw my horrified children covering their faces. I whispered "bye" while weeping. I kept thinking about how the children would never see me again. I would never have the opportunity to see them grow up and get married. The cold water of the Indian Ocean swelled against my feet. I wondered if it was ready for me only to spit me out as quickly as it took me. Perhaps it was my own helpless fate causing my feet to keep moving.

Through my tears, I spoke to my children, even though they were nowhere near me. I told them that I loved them so much and wished our lives had never come to this. Naming each of them, I asked if they would always keep my memories alive in their minds. They had come here with their mother, and soon they would be going home without me and would never see me again. I didn't know how to swim or I would have jumped into the water and swam away. I could have pretended to drown and would have escaped.

Then I thought of my mom and dad, my brothers and sisters. Through my uncontrollable tears I mumbled how much I loved them. I hoped they too would always keep my memory alive.

It wasn't that cold but I shook from the fear of dying. Drowning is a slow agonizing death. I knew I would struggle desperately to stay alive. He would get away with murder. No one would be able to say that the drowning was a homicide. He was staging a murder to look like an accident. It was dark, and the smell of the ocean made me sick. I had heard that there were sharks in that water. But there was a bigger shark that had become a stench in my life. I resisted all the way to the end. He slapped me so hard that I saw stars. "I must continue fighting" I kept telling myself. Each inch was a measure of extreme torment. He tried to push me over the railing into the water. Instead I fell onto the deck and quickly found a secure rail to hang on to. I wasn't willing to give over to the sounds of death knocking at the door of my soul, yet I wondered if it would be over soon.

With his repeated kicks, punches, and slaps to my face, I was losing the battle. How was it that my face was enduring so many blows yet still remained intact? Finally, he pushed me down to the point where I was hanging onto the metal railings with both hands and half of my body was in the water. Pain was all I knew – I couldn't remember a time when I wasn't suffering with him. I was bearing down in extreme agony. He began to encourage me to scream for help from my friends and my mom. (My "friends" were the police who had arrested him.) I decided to scream. "But who was I going to scream to? A God who took pleasure in seeing my misery or scream to any God that may be around at this time of the night, when the rest of the country was sleeping?" I could hear echoes of my voice from across the ocean. The words echoed on a high-pitched yell that I could no longer contain. Even that was comforting. When I stopped screaming, he would kick me in my face and tell me to continue screaming. I screamed louder. "Help!" the echo came back. After a few more screams for help, the sound of the echo changed into a man's voice. He yelled back. I knew someone was very close by. I shouted back, saying that I was at the end of the deck. I screamed for help a few more times, so the stranger would hurry. In my excitement, I forgot Raj kicking me as if I were his football. Bright red blood leaked from multiple wounds all over my face and head and dripped into the water. I knew I could lose my grip and fall into the jaws of famished sea creatures lurking not far below. I was twirling from the rusted rails struggling to hang on and crying as I looked down at the high tides to see where I was going. It was just a matter of minutes before my life would end and Raj would be victorious in his fight to get rid of me. I had seen despair – every morning and every night. I felt so weak, morbidly suspending every limb, freezing me in my place. The water rushed past my thighs.

I kept thinking of the children, were the children safe in the car? Were they sleeping or crying? How would my parents react when they found out their daughter was dead? Their faces began to flash in front of me. I was crying out loudly, and then anger took over. "Why must I die? Why wouldn't he commit suicide if he hated life that much?" One of my hands could no longer hold onto the railings because of the pain and bruising caused by his continuous kicking. The rails were slippery and had rough edges, but I had no other choice but to hang on to it with all my might. With the other hand, I reached out and grabbed hold of his foot, digging my nails into his skin. I began to threaten him, saying that if I went down, I was going to take him with me. I shouted even louder, and when it became clear there was someone around, I shouted that I was at the very end of the dock. With loud shouts I urged whomever it was to please help me. I shouted again and asked the man, "Where are you?"

Then I looked up and saw a very bright light from the sky. It shone on us for a very brief moment and I thought that this man's flash light was extremely powerful. I was shocked that someone had actually responded to my cries. Raj left and headed back to the car. I quickly pulled myself out of the water. Drenched from the cold water and half of my body soaking wet, I felt such a sigh of relief.

Slowly, I began to walk back towards the car while still holding onto the railings in case he came back and tried to throw me over them. It was a dark night; the stars were hidden behind the clouds. Then I heard voices and struggled to make out what they were saying. I heard Raj identifying himself to the other man, saying he was the son of a well-known businessman. I guess people were supposed to bow down to his father's name or fear him in some way. I shouted to the man to please call the police because Raj was trying to kill me. Furious, Raj began to threaten the man, saying he would kill him if he called the police. I ran towards this man, hoping he would see my injuries and call for help, but he walked away. I began to frantically call out to him, "Sir! Sir, please don't leave!" But he had disappeared. I was frightened and angry at how easily this man had been intimidated by Raj. Why wasn't he using the flashlight he had used before?

Raj yelled to me to get into the car. I was so relieved. My children knew I was alive. I would live with them again. I was now determined to fight the good fight. No longer would I allow myself to be reduced to an animalistic mode of living. Up until now I was not permitted to move without his permission. He had recounted many sadistic fantasies of how he would like to kill me. I had lived under his threats of harming my family if I left. All these years I heroically refused to leave and gave him the power to rule over me.

I looked through the window before getting into the car and saw the children sleeping. I wondered when they had fallen asleep and what they had talked about while we were gone. It had been for over half an hour although it felt like hours. Were they crying? Were they comforting each other? Or were they blaming one of us? What had they talked about? They should not be going through such an ordeal. I worried about the long-term effects on them. Although I was exhausted and traumatized, I rejoiced inside. I would make sure that he wouldn't do this again. I had just survived the insurmountable, and all I wanted to do was sleep.

As soon as I sat down, severe pain took over. I had a foul taste in my mouth. "Could it be the blood?" I gently ran my hand over my face and felt the cuts and bumps everywhere. My lips had ballooned and my eyes were shutting. Raj demanded that I put on my seatbelt. He held onto the buckle so I wouldn't get out of the car, in case the police were on their way. No one spoke on the way home. I knew this would probably be my last narrow escape. Next time, he would kill me for sure. If I wanted to survive, I would need to come up with a plan to convince my father-in-law that his son had been attempting to kill me. What else could I do to get out of my terrible situation? I knew I had to devise a plan quickly because time was running out.

When we finally arrived at home, it was very late at night. All I wanted to do was sleep. I didn't want to wake up for a few days. My body was giving up and I had no strength left in me. How was I going to take care of my children and do all the housework? I walked up the long flight of stairs, carrying my youngest on my shoulders. Part of me wished I would collapse and end up in the hospital. No such luck.

A short time later, I heard noises and realized that Raj wasn't in the room. I figured he must have been talking to someone. The noises become louder; I knew the police were downstairs talking about me. I heard Raj say that everyone was sleeping and not to bother us. He was concerned about the children and didn't want to wake them up.

Although I wanted to run down and show the police my injuries, I knew the consequences of speaking out all too well. The police were very close friends with my in-laws. It seemed that they looked up to my in-laws, seeking their approval. When Raj returned, I pretended I had no idea where he had been. I had tiptoed to the top of the stairs to hear the conversation and moved away quickly so he wouldn't know. Inside, however, my anger and hatred towards him kept growing. Many thoughts raced through my mind, but the only thing I truly wanted was to return to Vancouver with my children.

I made up my mind to go to my father-in-law and threaten to expose the family. The next day, I told him about the drowning incident and said there had been witnesses. I had also seen a document in Raj's possession regarding some kind of income tax fraud. I told him that I knew about that. I added that one of us would end up dead if we continued to live together. He thought about it for a while and then agreed to send us back. He expressed his concerns over how lazy his son was and what a nuisance he had become since moving back. His other sons' were busy working in the family business and raising their families except this one. I couldn't agree with him more.

I was so excited and ran upstairs to share the good news with the children. We secretly began to pack our little bags. I made sure that the children kept the news to themselves. Their father must not find out about our plan. The children argued among themselves quietly who was going to get the window seat on the airplane. There was much joy in that dungeon. Some of the workers who had become close friends with me shared in our joy.

A couple of days later, my father-in-law brought me an envelope. I couldn't contain my joy...until the children insisted that I open it. Inside there was a single one-way ticket. With tears rolling down my cheeks, I ran back to him. I told him that the ticket agency made a mistake and there was only one ticket. I was missing four more. He stared at my face for a while and smiled. That smile was like a dagger going inside my chest. He said that I wasn't getting the children. If I wanted the children then I would have to find the money for their tickets myself. I cried and cried. I knelt in front of him pleading for my children and asking for one last favour, but he refused. Feeling like a total failure I wept and returned to my hell. I had so much anger towards this old fart. He was playing mind games at his age? No one in that house had any decency. I wished they were all dead. I hated them all and I was never going to talk to them again. From now on I would retaliate. Every time I'd see them I would swear and curse them. Hopefully one day my wishes would be granted and they would surrender to me. I hid that ticket from Raj.

I could not look at my children and tell them the truth. I had no answers. I debated whether I should leave and then send tickets for my children. How could I leave these small children behind with these monsters? But if I leave I can work and pay for their tickets and bring them back to be with me. What kind of treatment would they get from their grandmother? The boys would be well taken care of and maybe Manpreet because she was liked but I wasn't sure of Hannah. Padma did not like the birthmark on Hannah's arm, calling it evil. She had a tendency to blame all our problems on her birthmark.

That night, Raj sodomized me again and made me sit on the floor with few clothes on. I had fallen asleep, when suddenly he came over and kicked me in my stomach. I jumped up, not knowing what had happened to me. The devil was standing in front of me. He asked if I was comfortable on the floor. I nodded. He said that from that point on that was where I would be sleeping. I made up my mind that I was going to leave and come back as soon as I was able to, for my children.

It was the most difficult decision of my life, to leave the children behind and go back to Vancouver. To my surprise, Raj did not object to me leaving. It was probably the best day of his life. He most likely figured out that I was going to make his life a living hell. The family also knew that I could snap at any time now. After all, I was crazy and could poison them slowly. Their servants were getting closer to me. I also had some exposure to their textiles and metal businesses. Maybe one day I could overpower Padma and take her keys from her petticoat. Letting me go was a wise decision on their part. They still controlled a large part of me – my children.

To leave was probably one of the first decisions that I had ever made and I feared it—I had chosen to abandon my own children. Will they forgive me for this?

As I left my green cell, the children and I held on to each other, hoping that moment would never end. They pleaded with me to take them and that they were sorry for the times they were naughty. I held them even tighter and assured them that they were never naughty. I was the one that failed them. With limited time and my one chance to escape, I made them promise me that they would be good children. I was going to come back for them. They agreed with so many tears. The driver stood waiting anxiously.

How can I let go of my innocent little children? We held each other and wept. When I got up, a couple of them grabbed hold of my legs and wept. I thought of cancelling my ticket. I could not leave them. How could I leave them? No mother can do that. My girls' eyes were red from crying. Every inch I moved they grabbed me. This grief was boundless. With each tear we shed it pierced my heart. This was the most stressful act any human being could impose on another, the separation of children from their mother. It was an overwhelming sense of panic, rage and distress. There was absolutely no easier way of saying goodbye to the children. This was such an abrupt severing of a mother with her little ones. I kept telling myself that "I must be strong". My children need me and I will be back for them.

There is no relationship like that of a mother and her children. The bond between them is so powerful. No one can separate or take it away from them. I left lots of tears. I cried all the way to the airport. Raj chose to stay with the children at home. Through my tears I asked the driver to keep an eye on my children.

When the plane began to taxi from Bombay to the Delhi airport I wanted to scream. My heart ached and longed to hold my children one more time. I could still hear their cries and feel their tiny hands around me. Their screams taunted me. "Should I give up my own freedom to be with the children?" The plane was in midair and I couldn't return. "Were my babies still crying and looking for me? How long will it be before their innocent minds are poisoned and turned against me?"

While waiting for my flight to Vancouver, I stayed at a local hostel for a few days. I reasoned with myself that if I had stayed with Raj any longer, I wouldn't have been able to get out. I made a pact that I would get the children back one day and that they would live with me. At whatever cost, I would give them the life that they deserved. They witnessed way too much abuse. That's all they knew. We were a dysfunctional family.

I found out through a worker that Raj had also left for Vancouver. I knew that he would try and track me down. I had to stay behind for a few days. He decided to leave before I did. He was always was one step ahead of me.

My heart ached for my children. I wish I could smell them and hold them in my arms. The separation was so painful. I wanted to hug them. I would never stop missing them. I wondered what they were doing and if they were thinking of me. I wanted to phone them so badly but I knew that would be a waste. They would not give the children the phone or my messages. Instead they would rudely hang up. We had come here as a family, but now I was returning alone. I was determined to get my children back as soon as I could. I made a promise to get them out of that home as soon as I could. I would somehow get the money to buy tickets for my little ones. Finally, I left for the home I never thought I would ever see again. I vowed to come back one more time to pick up Hannah 8, Tony 6, Manpreet 4 and Satveer 3 years old.

She sat in a corner of a terminal, oblivious to all around her. She was a voiceless woman. All her power to act, or even speak had been taken away from her. She was still pale and ill-looking, still silenced by her perpetrator. All she could do was mourn and weep for her loved ones.

She could hear whispers among some of the people around her. But she did not turn around to look. The only voice that was loud and clear was the voice telling her, "What a terrible mother you have been. How could you do this? You should be punished for the rest of your life. You should have known better. You will always be a failure."

Her tormentor had seen her as a prize. He always got his way at whatever the cost – he was a sneaky manipulator. She was terribly bruised and beaten. Even her anger and outrage had been beaten out of her.

She was no longer beautiful to him. She knew that as a married woman, she would be considered worthless and even shunned by her own.

She missed her children terribly. She was so confused.

She would not allow anyone's sweetness to take the place where bitterness had been dominating for so long. Her eyes would never fail to see her horrific past.

Suddenly she was interrupted by someone with a message – especially for her. This stranger talked about the eternal and omnipresent conflict between good and evil and the tension between light and dark. The woman showed her the road to faith, hope and redemption. She talked about the Bible.

Perhaps there was some truth in what she was saying. Hoping for something better, the abused wife gave this God a chance to prove himself to her. She continued to get vital information from the stranger. She told how this Jesus had a special place in his heart for 'women', and how the Bible condemns violence and violent men.

Moving closer to the stranger, she looked in her eyes and thought, "Wow, someone is siding with me." She gave her full attention to the woman. She began hearing phrases like, "The Lord sympathises and offers comfort to those who are afflicted." This was music to her ears.

She longed to hear more soothing words. The stranger continued to talk about, "holding the abusers accountable and to help the victims. To shun those who consistently oppress and harm others."

Abandoned by all other so-called 'All knowing beings', she wanted to embrace this God who promised her a better life. Excited by this message, she asked to be introduced to him. She had never met a man like him.

For the first time, she gave her heart to Jesus – He would now become her Saviour. Though she was wretched, miserable and poor, she finally had hope. Hope for tomorrow. Hope for a better life. She was no longer alone. She would no longer carry the burden and the shame on her own shoulders. She was going to lift her head up high.

That stranger was a messenger. The new believer was me.

CHAPTER TWENTY-TWO

The Beginning of a Journey

My flight was to leave later that night and the airport wasn't busy, so I found a quiet place in the corner to sit and think. It had been a very difficult time for me. I did not know when I was going to see my children again. At that point, the only thing I could do was hope that their *Bibi* and *Papa* would treat them well. I worried about my eldest daughter the most. I was so lost in my thoughts and painful memories that I forgot where I was.

Suddenly, an Indian woman probably around my age in her late twenties interrupted my thoughts. Dressed in an expensive looking *salwar kameez*, she smiled and asked if I was traveling alone. With tears streaming down my cheeks, I nodded yes and looked away. Sensing that I needed company she sat down across from me. She politely asked her husband to take the children away. She asked me where I was going. I told her I was going home. Then she asked if I had come for a visit. I didn't want to tell her anything, knowing I would break down and end up with a pounding headache. I decided to ignore her questions, but she persisted. It was as if she could sense the deep pain within me. She gently reached out and touched my shoulder and smiled. Then she said she had lots of time before her flight left. All I did was stare at the floor and weep. She held my hands, saying nothing for a while and then she offered me a clean handkerchief from her handbag. It was nicely folded and looked new. I took it and wiped my tears away, but the more I wiped, the more my eyes flooded with tears.

Finally, in a very soft voice, this strange woman introduced herself and asked my name. I felt like saying my name was "Unfortunate." This lady seemed determined not to go anywhere until she was satisfied her questions had been answered. I gave her only one-word answers, but she seemed okay with that. I looked around to see if there were any newspapers or magazines I could read to avoid this woman, but there was nothing lying around.

I observed her gentle manner, her clothes and even her teeth. As she talked, I wondered whether she had ever been abused. Her husband seemed like a nice man, and their children were well behaved. He was taking care of them while she tried to chat with me. He didn't bring the children back to her or even try to get her attention. He must be a good man, I thought. She looked like a respectable young woman who loved her family. Now I wanted to ask her questions. So I finally decided to give in and talk with her a little bit more. I found out that her husband worked at a government agency and they were on their way to England to visit her family.

When this woman was done talking about her family, she asked me again if everything was okay with me. Again my eyes welled up and I told her who I was and what had happened to me. I talked less but my cries were continuous. I missed my children so much. Were they sleeping at this time of the night? I was sure that they shared one bedroom with twin beds and a foam mattress on the floor for the boys. Were they thinking of me as much as I was thinking of them? I could see their faces flash in front of me. How badly I wanted to run to them and hold them so tightly and never let them go. Was I ever going to have that opportunity again? Was I going back with false hope? What had I done to end up like this?

This was probably the first time in a very long time that I had not been afraid of talking. She seemed very patient, nodded her head when I talked and didn't interrupt me.

Suddenly, I began to wonder if my in-laws had sent her. Could this woman be trusted? Had they paid her to get information from me? Immediately, I looked away and began to regret telling her my pain. What if she was a spy? Were they trying to frame me for something and have me arrested? I got up and excused myself, hoping to get through Immigration as quickly as possible. She followed me. I turned around, thanked her for her time and wished her a safe trip. She kept talking and I kept walking. I asked a security officer if I could go through Immigration even though my flight wasn't leaving for a while. When he said I could, I turned around and waved goodbye to this woman. "Good riddance," I thought to myself.

After getting through Immigration, I made my way to the corner of the lounge, close to the bathroom. It was dark, but the lights on the runway lit up the airport. I found a newspaper and began reading it. Some men stood in a corner touching parts of the body that should be forbidden in public. They were trying every technique to get my attention. Even they could not be trusted.

Suddenly, I felt a hand on my shoulder. I jumped out of my seat, thinking it was a police officer and I would not be allowed to leave after all. But the gentle laughter and soft touch reassured me. It was the same woman and her family. She apologized several times for startling me. This time, she sat next to me and began telling me her story.

Life hadn't always been rosy for her, she said, but she had found faith in a God who had given her strength and hope. She gave me a brief story of her struggles as a young girl and what had happened after she had found this "living God" called Jesus.

I wasn't interested in her story, but I tried hard to keep focused on where she was going with it. Then she asked me a remarkable question: "Do you know Jesus? Do you know how much he loves you?"

I looked at her with an angry face and said, "No! And no one loves me!"

That strange woman refused to be put off by my anger. She just held my hand and said she knew I couldn't trust anyone and that was okay. "But," she said, "Jesus died for you and loves you very much."

I didn't believe a word she said but she kept talking. Leaning forward I began to demand answers from her. "Where was this loving God when I was going through hell? I had no one to talk to. No one to protect me from the evil man I had married. Now I had nothing; no possessions and no children. I didn't care about anything else but my babies and now I had lost them. I had failed them terribly as a mother". I told this strange woman how many times I had been close to death, how many times I had been terrorized. Where had this living God been during all of those times? Had he been sleeping because it was night-time? Had God been enjoying watching me suffer? Getting even angrier, I told her I had encountered many gods in my life, and the last one was my husband. Because of him, I had endured nightmare after nightmare. I told her that I just wanted to be left alone and not be bothered by anyone. I had planned to spend the rest of my life taking care of my children and keeping them safe from all kinds of evil. I had our new life planned out, and I did not want any "god" getting in the way of it.

But this woman, Shelly, reminded me that I should not give up. She agreed that it was very difficult for me to trust anyone. She said it was okay for me to express those feelings. She explained that she understood where I was coming from. She asked if I would be open to hearing about the true and living God. This God apparently had been with me even before I was born. She said he had been watching over me all my life. She said there was a devil that meant evil for me but God had protected me. Even though I had suffered so much, God had now taken me out of that situation because of his love for me. She asked for permission to pray for my children and me.

Reluctantly I agreed thinking that this would be the only way to get this "Jesus freak" away from me. Then she asked if I would like to know Jesus myself. I could talk to him and tell him exactly how I felt and ask him for things I needed. She said that God is not a God who is distant from us but that when we invite him into our lives, he will come and live in us. She explained that Jesus had died for me, to save me from evil. If I allowed him to take over my life, he would make my life into something beautiful. She continued to say that in Jesus there was no shame, that I am very precious in his eyes. She said that even if I were the only person on earth, Jesus would still have died for me. Through his sacrifice I would live forever in heaven.

I didn't understand everything the woman said, but I thought that if I agreed to give this Jesus a try, this woman might leave me alone. So, I repeated a short prayer after her. Nothing magical happened after that, but it left me thinking. I had learned of Jesus through my early years in the Catholic school. I thought if what she said was true, then it might be an answer to all of my problems. I wondered whether I should give Jesus a try. I had nothing to lose.

Finally, Shelly's flight was announced and she gave me a hug and left. I slowly began talking to Jesus in my mind. I asked him to prove himself to me. Shelly had said I could ask Jesus for anything. I had a bunch of things I wanted him to do for me. In fact, I asked him for a long list of things and everything was to be on my terms and conditions. I wanted my children back. I wanted a nice cozy home. I wanted my children and me to live in peace from here on. I wanted strength to raise my children on my own. I continued to talk to Jesus all the way back.

CHAPTER TWENTY-THREE

A New Home

I finally arrived home. I didn't know my parent's address or phone number. They had just moved to a new location and chose to keep their phone number unlisted. Raj had a habit of phoning and threatening them, especially at night. Once he made me call them and demand money to feed the children. He said that my mother and I had ruined his life and she should start providing for us as a form of retribution. Then he took the phone from me and told my mother that even I blamed her and did not want her in my life. I hoped that my mom didn't believe anything that he said. He was always good at starting fights. I wanted to somehow send my parents a message that I never blamed them for anything and that I loved and missed them.

I was not surprised to see Raj at the airport. He found out my flight number and showed up at the airport. With no other place to go, I took him on his promise –to get our children back. I wasn't sure if any of my family was willing to take me. The children's loud cries were still so fresh in my ears. I would do anything to have them back. He would be the only way to his parents. I agreed to live with one of his sisters, who was very nice to me. His good behaviour and promises were short lived. He reverted to his old nature. Whenever he fought with me, she and her daughter would come to my aid. One time he started hitting me in their carport and his niece came running to me. She managed to pull me out of the car while he had his fingers twined in my hair for a better grip. He kept hitting my head into the window. She demanded that he leave, but he wouldn't. He followed me into the house, threatening to kill me. His sister picked up the phone to call the police. Someone was able to calm him down. I thought finally someone from his family saw what I was going through and had stood up for me. Despite the beatings I felt that I had some support now.

There were some good days, and then there were some very bad days. Eventually, I threatened to leave if he continued his abuse. One night as I was falling asleep, I felt something on my neck. I quickly woke up to find him sitting and clenching his fists while twitching his jaw. I sat fearing that I would start receiving blows to my face again. He pulled me closer to him by my hair and hit my head against the headboard. I hoped that the noise would wake up his family and they would come running to my aid. He slapped me a few times demanding to know what I had told his family about him. I refused to answer any of his questions. Frustrated with my silence and disobedience, he threw me back on the bed and began to choke me. When I began to gasp for breath, I kicked him in his private place and ran out of the room. I told him that I would scream for help if he touched me one more time. After swearing and cursing for a while – he turned around and went to sleep. I decided to stay awake as long as I could, in case he choked me to death. Early the next morning when he left to go job-hunting, I finally did it. I left him. Freedom was long overdue. I found refuge at a women's shelter. Eventually I moved into a basement suite with another single mom. I could breathe without someone choking me. There was still a sense of fear of being found.

My freedom was short-lived. Raj tracked me down. He promised that the children would be coming back. He swore that this time he wasn't lying. I simply told him that I would come back once they were here. It had been over three months since I had seen the children. I was volunteering at a consulting office as a receptionist when I got a call from my roommate. Raj had gone there with the children. Not only did she see them but she had talked with them as well. I called Raj right away, and he and the children pleaded with me to come and stay with them. I gave my employer two minutes notice and left with so much joy. That same day, I left the basement suite I was living in, to be with my children. That was the deal he made with me.

Even though I was overjoyed seeing the children, I was grieved. It was a bitter-sweet reunion. Only two of my four children had been returned. My father-in-law felt that it was too much for his wife to care for four little children. They agreed to send the older two so they could start school. He accompanied the children to the Delhi airport and had the staff assist them on the plane. When I first saw the children, Hannah began with complaints that Tony had spilled orange juice all over her. Her cute little dress was stained and sticky. She swore she would never sit beside Tony again. It felt like they had grown up a little a more. I could not take my eyes off them. I became so possessive of them, wanting to know where they were going and for how long? I did not want them out of my sight. I would look for any opportunity to pick them up and cuddle with them. Hannah and Tony told me how Manpreet and Satveer had screamed and kicked because they couldn't come with them. They told me many stories of their younger siblings and how they had wanted to be put into their suitcases. They figured it was the only way for them to be with me. They promised they would behave and since they were small they could fit in their bags. My heart sank for my two little babies. What must they be going through now that they had lost Hannah and Tony? What hope do they have left? I wondered how long they must have cried for. Did they put themselves to sleep? Their room must be empty now. Why was this monster doing this to our family? Does he not care one bit for his own children? Or is it his way of punishing me? Whatever it was I was more determined to get my family back.

I left the room with tears rolling down my cheeks to have a talk with Jesus in the bathroom. Raj did not know that I was now talking to Jesus, and I wasn't ready to tell him. He was such a miserable man. I told Jesus that if he loved me enough to offer his life for me, then he had to bring the children back. I wanted to move on without their father. I no longer wanted to share my joy with him. He could never be trusted.

It wasn't long before Raj`s old nature returned. That night after drinking, he began to beat me up. Still unsatisfied with his actions, he raped me. It was a despicable act. The children were still awake. Even though they were in bed they knew he was hurting me. I felt so unclean and had extreme anger towards him. His empty promises and useless gifts were only to lure me into believing that he loved me. Satisfied with his act, he turned to go to sleep while I began to devise a plan of escape in my head.

That night, I decided it would be my last night with Raj; I was never going to spend another minute with him. I would take the children and leave in the morning. I was getting a little bit stronger, and I knew there was help for us.

Early the next morning, I got up from sleeping on the floor and got the children ready for school as usual. Raj was still sleeping with my purse under his pillow. I couldn't pack any of our belongings, but it didn't matter. I just needed to get away from him.

The children and I left the house, and once we were far enough away, we began to run. We ran to a shopping center and called a women's shelter. This time, I was determined that no amount of repentance from him would make me want to come back. I wanted to start a new life without him. We moved from one shelter to another fearing that he might find us. Although we were living with strangers—women and their children from many different walks of life—I felt safe. I was able to make decisions on my own. I wasn't sitting in a corner at night anymore; I was sleeping on a bed with my children nearby. I didn't have to try to please Raj anymore. No matter how much I pleased him – it wasn't ever good enough. No matter what I had done for him, it was always the wrong thing in his eyes. I had never been able to do anything right.

At the shelter, people called me by my name. They showed me respect. They did not use swear words or motion to me with their fingers. I started looking at myself in the mirror differently. I told myself that I was a beautiful person and my life mattered. The shelter had many donations of makeup and clothes and I was encouraged to take those things to use for myself. Some shelters had workers or volunteers who did the cooking and cleaning. Others even volunteered to take the children out so the moms could have some quiet time or counselling. I felt as if I had won a million dollars.

I remember a worker, whom I thought was a very beautiful woman, made a comment to me. She told me once that I was an attractive young woman. I almost fell out of my chair. I tried to deny it, saying this or that was wrong with me, but she began to point out all the things that set me apart from the others. She said I had beautiful eyes, a nice set of teeth and a pretty smile. She went on and on. Others in the room acknowledged the same things. I took it as a great compliment, especially coming from a woman who looked so much like a model herself.

I found a local church and continued to make my requests to the Lord daily. I longed to have all my children together, and I wanted a home. I looked forward to the day when all of my four children were together as a loving family. I looked at pictures in magazines and pictured my home. At the shelter I was able to collect lots of household things.

At last I received the news I had been waiting for. I was chosen for a home that was subsidized by the government. It was a three-bedroom townhouse and because it was still being built, we could move in a month. After that, I prayed even harder for my family to be reunited. This was my third big answer to the many requests that I had made to God. The first was getting my children back, second finding the courage and strength to leave my abuser and now getting my own brand new place. This place will give each of us our own rooms. Wow, God was coming through for me! He indeed loved and cared for me and my children. Well, I loved him back.

CHAPTER TWENTY-FOUR

Friends Who Did Not Give Up

I made some friends in my new church. They prayed for my children and me regularly. They knew I was very bitter against my husband. They also knew a little bit of what he had put us through. Very gently, they would show me verses from the Bible and although I didn't understand or read the Bible much, I began to believe that the Lord Jesus was with me. I was getting stronger in my faith and was getting involved with small groups of Christian believers. I was still shy and spoke very little. I guess I was more of an observer. Many times my mind would drift away and I would wonder what these people's lives were like. Did these women have loving husbands? I felt like asking them about their personal lives.

Whenever I was asked to share my story or introduce myself, I would just say my name and sweat nervously. I didn't want to tell anyone about my miserable life. I didn't want my new friends to know anything about my past. What if they judged me or didn't want anything more to do with me? I was carrying a lot of baggage, and I didn't want to get hurt any further. It would be too devastating to my self-esteem. I was just beginning to see some good in me. I didn't want to lose this growing sense of worth, since it had taken me so long to feel that well. I chose to keep everything inside and only talk about issues I was comfortable talking about.

Some of the mature women, however, were a bit more discerning. Little by little, they started inviting me to their homes for Bible study and prayer. I went often and would take notes and make prayer requests. These requests were very discreet—I'd say only vague things such as, "Please pray for my family." A few women began to share their hearts with me. One thing I would hear from them often was that I needed to forgive my abusers. Politely I would smile and nod my head, not wanting to lose my new friends over this forgiveness talk.

I wasn't much of a Bible reader. The occasional times I did read, I would see verses such as, "If you forgive men when they sin against you, your heavenly Father will also forgive you." I knew I wasn't perfect, but neither was anybody else. And there was no way I could forgive my abusers. So I let go of that idea. Good for those who can forgive, I thought. I began to avoid these women. Every time they saw me, they asked if I had forgiven those who needed to be forgiven. Tired of their nagging, one day I gave in to them in order to please them and get them off my back. I prayed a little prayer with no real effort. It was a meaningless prayer, but the ladies were very pleased with me. I scored some points with them until they realized, from something I said in another prayer meeting, that the forgiveness hadn't come from my heart. Finally, I told them I wasn't ready to forgive and they should stop asking me about it.

I decided I wasn't going back to that group. I felt overwhelmed. They had no idea what I had gone through. How could they tell me to do something my abusers didn't deserve!

But then these ladies started coming to my home. I tried to be as polite as I could, until one time when I couldn't take it anymore. In a rather rude tone, I asked them how much they knew about my past. They said it didn't matter, God knew everything, and he wanted me to live a life without anger and bitterness. I told them that if God knew what I had gone through, he wouldn't ask me to forgive. With anger overwhelming me, I told these women and God very frankly that I would make them a deal: I would have to first take revenge. My plan was to bring Raj home under false pretences, tie him up, beat him, burn him with his own cigarettes and shave part of his head. He had to feel the pain I felt all those years. Then I would forgive and let go of all my anger. I wanted vengeance.

Gradually, the women stopped coming over, but I was sure they were still praying for me. After Sunday morning service, often one of them would tell me they were praying for my family. I would kindly thank them and leave before they began on the forgiveness thing again.

She rose early that morning after a sleepless night. She had been living her life like a second-class citizen. It was in the same building where the two were joined in Holy matrimony in front of family members, where she would end her marriage. Only this time, she would be going there alone. As she took a deep breath, she silently whispered that this would be her last time here.

She had hoped at last to come to a place where her voice could be heard loud and clear. Her fight for peace and safety had led her to the steps of the lawmakers. She would enter the arena of family law where her future would be in the hands of the same judicial system that had failed many mothers before.

Was she a courageous mother who fought the system to protect her children from further abuse? For the past eleven years, she and her children had been sentenced to a life of pain. Now she was before the courts asking that the sentence be overturned.

She had clung desperately to an unhappy marriage, because of the many hidden fears, not only for herself, but all her loved ones as well.

She wondered if there would be any true winners from this painful process. Closing her eyes momentarily, she thought of the many more battles she'd have to fight because of the stigma attached to being a single parent. But she would take this bittersweet consequence.

She had always been told that she was neither a good wife nor a good mother. As she sat listening to two strangers dissect her life in an empty court room, she prayed, "Lord, what if money wins the war?" The awful thought lurked with her. She lowered her head; too tired to hear what she had hoped for.

All she wanted to tell the judge was that "rest and sleep were luxuries that she never had."

She had put herself at risk, and hoped with all her might to dissolve this marriage. Now she would not remain silent anymore. She would cut all her ties with him. Why should she go on with this dangerous life?

The air filled with confidence. Maybe a solution was possible.

She took a deep breath and exhaled slowly as she walked out of the court room free at last. The woman was finally free – she was no longer legally attached to her mate. From that point on, she had no obligations to him.

Some have criticised her for abandoning her ties, suggesting all she wanted

was her independence. Others have wished her well.
  She hopes now that her life would have some normalcy.

  That man was now my ex. The independent woman was me.

CHAPTER TWENTY-FIVE

Please Complete My Family

Some of my closer friends, who were very caring, continued to pray for my younger children. Although I wasn't willing to forgive, I still prayed asking God to complete my family. As a young Christian I didn't see the contradiction there, believing that God could not expect anyone to forgive such gross violations. My heart ached every day. All that was missing from my life was to have Manpreet and Satveer with me again. I didn't get to talk to them because they were never given the phone. Whenever I called, my in-laws always made excuses, saying the children weren't available. Eventually, I stopped calling. It was very hard to be rejected and not be allowed to talk to my own children. I prayed even harder. Every night, Hannah, Tony and I would pour our hearts out to God. We asked him for our family to be complete. I longed to see Manpreet and Satveer. I wanted them to have the same lifestyle and love Hannah and Tony had.

Many times when Hannah and Tony were given new clothes, toys or treats, my eyes welled up because Manpreet and Satveer were missing out on all these things. It wasn't fair that we had to be separated. I felt like a failure to have let my younger children down like this. I had never intended to go such a long time without having all of them with me. It had been nearly two years. That was not what I had promised them when I had left. I prayed that they wouldn't forget me or blame me for leaving them behind for so long. Every day I would think about what they were doing and what they were eating, trying to imagine the details of their lives. I wanted to see them so badly. Even to hear their voices would have given me some comfort.

Birthdays and holidays were the hardest. On those days, I would cry myself to sleep. I wondered if anyone even acknowledged their birthdays. Did they get any gifts? I knew no one would throw a party for them and there would be no birthday cake. Did the children even know it was their birthday, I wondered.

I was determined when we reunited, I would give Manpreet and Satveer so much love that they would forget their pain. I would make their favourite foods and take them to the park. We would go for picnics and camping. I had so many things planned for our reunion.

Raj couldn't bear to see me happy. He continued to harass us. The thought of me being independent didn't suit him at all. He found our address through one of his friends. He began to come around at nights and leave notes with his phone number, saying it was urgent. He tried very hard to scare me, saying that if I didn't reconcile with him, I would lose Hannah and Tony. He said he was the more stable parent and was working, so he wasn't a burden to society. He would threaten to tell the courts that I had been in a mental institute and I couldn't provide proper care for the children. I knew he would have no problems getting documents to indicate that I was a bad parent. To make us suffer he could forge any documents he wanted. His family would be more than happy to help him with it. I hoped and prayed that his lies and threats would come to an end.

I wasn't afraid of him or his threats anymore. I believed in Jesus more firmly now, and reading the Bible gave me more of an understanding of who Jesus was. I understood that not only would He provide for us but He would also protect us from our enemies. I let the police know of Raj's threats. A couple of times I called 911 when he showed up at my door with gifts for the kids. One evening, he brought some small tools with him to help him get inside the house. After hearing noises in the backyard, I turned on the light and saw him sitting with the tools. Terrified for our lives, I locked the children and myself in the bathroom and called the police. He was arrested, and further charges were laid against him, but that did not stop his behaviour. Another night we were awakened by a phone call from a social worker. He said he was calling because Raj had them very concerned about the safety and welfare of the children. As a regular procedure, social services had to check up on all such calls, whether they were legitimate or not. Thankfully, after an investigation, I was cleared of all of Raj's allegations.

The children were doing well in school and made friends with some neighbours. Hannah, a beautiful little girl, began to take modeling lessons and although she was never chosen to model for anything, her self-esteem was boosted. She was beginning to feel good about herself. She had also seen some doctors about removing the birthmark from her arm. We knew it would be a major surgery so we took our time to pray about it. Hannah would need a lot of support and care, and that meant that we all needed to be strong, both physically and mentally.

Yet the months of prayers that had been offered for my Manpreet and Satveer almost seemed worthless. Even though many other prayers had been answered, I couldn't figure out why God wasn't answering my prayer to be reunited with my two babies. The more desperate I became, the more I prayed and studied the Bible. I would quote Bible verse after Bible verse reminding God of all his promises to us. I knew that Jesus was my only hope to bring my children back. I decided to ask Raj for his help, but he said no because he wanted to continue punishing me, even though in reality, he was only punishing the children. So I gave up on him.

One day while driving I heard a little whisper: "Go get your children." I immediately slammed on my brakes, thinking it was Raj speaking to me from the back. I turned to look in the backseat to see if he was there. But there was no one around and the cars next to me were driving by very fast. Who had spoken those words? I decided to turn around and go home. I had wanted to hear those words so badly for so long, but who could have said them to me? Confused and somewhat scared, I phoned a friend and shared the mystery with him. After a while, he called back and said he believed God was speaking to me and I should be obedient to what God had told me. I prayed for direction again and asked God to help me. I was excited and scared. What if I was hallucinating? Did I really hear those words spoken that clearly? For the sake of my children I was willing to take that risk.

There were so many things I needed to plan. I needed money for tickets and clothes and other traveling expenses. I went back to God and told him that if it was his voice I had heard then he would have to provide. I gave him a list of things I needed and added that I would like to have them pretty quickly. It didn't take me long to figure out that maybe God, who is really in charge of the universe, doesn't always work on my timetable. Although I was very impatient, I was learning that I had to wait for God to work out a perfect plan. I had no idea how or when I would get my children, but because God had spoken to me, I had new hope that things would work out.

Within a couple of weeks, I had enough money to buy three tickets, for the children and me and some clothes for the children. I even had some money left over. I knew all of this must have come from God because there was no other way I could have received all this money. Only a handful of people knew my plans. I decided that it was better not to tell Hannah and Tony where I was going. Children are so innocent and they could casually mention it to someone and the news could very quickly get to Raj. They were happy to spend some time with their cousins at my parent's house. They would be safe there. I told them that I had to leave town for some business and would be back soon.

When the day came to leave to go to pick up my babies, I was so excited. I forgot how nervous I had been and I didn't worry very much about how I would get them. I had all the important information written down and had been given some contacts for some important people by a trusted friend. When I arrived in India, however, I became very frustrated. Nothing was working out the way I had planned. I spent a couple of days trying to find a way to get to my in-laws town. I kept going back and forth with the plans. I was very anxious. I was on a very tight schedule and I desperately wanted to see my children after such a long time. At a certain point, I realized I had stopped praying and asking God for his guidance. I guess I had felt that I didn't really need him anymore since I was so close to getting my children.

At that point, it would have been easy for me to blame God for the delays, but instead, I asked God for forgiveness for taking over and pretending I could handle everything. I had to have faith that if he really was in charge of this trip, he wasn't going to stop halfway. If God really is all-powerful, then whatever God starts, he also finishes. From that moment on, I let God take over. I still worried a little but didn't stop praying in my heart. Still, hours seemed like days, and sometimes I wondered if God was at work.

During that time, I met a few very influential people through a friend of a friend. He promised to help me. Then I took the train to the town where my babies were. Some of these people asked for bribes openly but they came through for me. I prayed that they would both be in school so I could avoid a direct confrontation from my in-laws. They were on the board of directors for the education department. They held high positions in the government. Most of the staff members were loyal to them. So I had to be extra careful. I began talking to God as if he were a person walking beside me. This was going to be a very fast kidnapping scheme. Time was ticking. This would be my only opportunity. There was no way I could blow this one. I had to remain calm and maintain my composure. Feeling like a criminal I hired a taxi. With my heart pounding and fear gripping me – I knew it was a point of no return. I had to get my children out.

When I stepped out of the taxi, I saw hundreds of children playing outside. It was their lunchtime. The girls were all dressed in dark blue dresses and the boys in blue shirts and khaki shorts. How was I going to recognize my two children? There were little skinny children everywhere and I felt I was looking for a needle in a haystack. Just as I was reaching the middle of the playground the bell rang and all the screaming kids ran past me into their classrooms. Now what? I couldn't go classroom to classroom looking for my babies. Someone would call the police or my in-laws and I would be locked up before even seeing my children. I felt nauseated but continued praying as a last resort. I kept walking towards the classrooms and peeked into the principal's office. No one was there. So I walked to the classroom closest to the office. I called the male teacher and introduced myself to him. He took me to the Principal's office and told me that my son, Satveer was in his class and my daughter was in the class next to his. I couldn't wait to see them and my excitement showed. He walked over to his class and called Satveer to come out. Then he walked over to the next class and asked the teacher to send Manpreet to the office. Very slowly, a very young and very timid little boy walked into the office. The moment he saw me, he began to hide his face. I ran to pick him up, but he turned away from me. When I asked him if he knew me, he said I was Aunty.

Then Manpreet came in and walked towards her brother. She was a tiny, yet very cute little girl. I quickly went over to hold her in my arms, she too resisted my hugs. It was horrible for me to see them like that. I kept smiling at them, hoping to get a smile back. Why were they acting like this? I kept telling them very softly that I was their mom, but they remained distant. The teacher would soon get very suspicious and would ask me to leave. The children were not showing any affection towards me. The harder I tried to hold them the further they moved from me.

Knowing that I was losing precious time, I asked the teacher if it would be all right to take them home. He said that was fine. I lied and told him that their *Bibi* and *Papa* didn't mind them coming home early.

The teachers brought out their school bags. My children reluctantly took them. As soon as the teachers turned around, I grabbed the children by their hands so they couldn't run away from me. Tears filled their eyes, and I could see the fear in them. I reached for some chocolates and candies I had brought for them. This worked for a little while. I ran quickly to the waiting taxi and told the driver to drive as fast as he could. I began to change the children as we drove to the airport. I had bought some clothes for them. I knew I was going to be there only for the day and there was no use for excess baggage. They were excited to see their new clothes, but they didn't want to go with me. They asked if I was taking them to their *Bibi* and *Papa*. I tried to get them excited by telling them that we were first headed to the airport in a big plane. Then we would come back to visit them. They didn't like my idea. Once they realized that we were heading to the airport, they began crying loudly and throwing tantrums. They demanded that I have the taxi stopped. They were determined to get out and walk back to their grandparents. Although I had taken a train coming here, I chose to fly out of here. I had no time to waste. We had a flight to catch. If anything went wrong, I could end up losing my children forever. Quite firmly I told them I was their mom and we were going home. Hannah and Tony were waiting for them.

When we reached the airport, the plane was just taking off. We had missed our flight. I knew I was in big trouble. I ran towards the ground crew, pleading with them to stop the plane. They shook their heads and said "sorry madam, next time be here early". The next flight was four hours away. I feared that Manpreet and Satveer would make a scene and let people know that I kidnapped them. With the state of mind that they were in anything was possible. I also had to calm the taxi driver, who knew that if he was caught, he too would end up in a lot of trouble. Feeling totally frustrated and helpless I booked us on the next flight out. Where would I go, and where could I hide the children? I knew they would be found. I was scared; I phoned a friend and asked for his help. The driver demanded that I pay him so he could leave. As he left with hands joined together he requested that I never mention his name to anyone. He had a family to feed. One of the airline workers found a taxi nearby and sent us back to the town. They gave me their word that they would not disclose any information to anyone else. In fact they even changed our names to protect us from my in-laws.

This kind driver parked in the alleyway and made sure that no one was around. Then he whisked us into the back of the lawyer's office. I sat in the back of his office with my two very terrified children, who kept asking for their Bibi and Papa. It was obvious that they were attached to them and didn't know me. I tried my best to keep them entertained with some small toys in my backpack, I also had pictures of Hannah, Tony, me and our new home. The children were easily distracted, but they knew it was after school and one of the workers would have a snack ready for them when they got home.

As we began to talk about Hannah and Tony, the children asked who I was. I had told them numerous times that I was their mother, but this time they asked with seriousness and concern. I didn't blame them—after all, it had been over two years since they had last seen me. Again I told them I was their mother. They had a confused look on their faces. Then Manpreet blurted out that their mom was dead. Tears filled my eyes when I asked them who had told them I was dead. They said their Bibi and Papa had told them about my death. They truly believed I must be one of their aunts.

How was I going to convince these children that I was alive? As we went back to looking at the pictures, I said again that I was their mother and they looked at me with fear and asked if I was a ghost. I just held them and wept silently. What had my in-laws done to these innocent children? They were brainwashed. That's why they were so scared of being with me. I needed to get them as far away from them as possible.

While waiting for the next flight, I decided to call my in-laws and let them know that I had taken the children out of school. I knew someone would be going to pick them up from school. They would call the police right away. The first place they would look would be the airport then the train stations. My mother-in-law did not come on the phone, so I left a message with the maid. I told her not to bother picking up the children because they were with me. I needed to protect my children. Still not satisfied and fearing the worse I called again just before school ended. This time, Padma came on the phone and spoke with kindness and invited me to come to her house. Then her husband took the phone. He said that he felt sorry for me and he knew what I had been going through with Raj. He, too, insisted that I come back and visit them. I lied. I told them that I was on my way to Delhi. I promised to call them later in the week.

We started to walk towards the car for the airport when I was confronted with a few police officers. I knew I was caught. Fear gripped me. My first reaction was to grab my children and head back inside for help. How did they find out that I was hiding there? Did someone from the lawyer's office leak this information to them or did they trace my line? The police told me they were there to take the children back and they would be arresting me for kidnapping. No matter what I said or how much I pleaded, they didn't listen. Finally, we went to the police station, and I asked to use a phone. I had to get out of here with my children.

Little did I know, but God had orchestrated a plan. It was so awesome. I had made some connections with a couple of high profile people. The interrogating officers would not allow me to use the phone. When I mentioned the names of my contacts they reluctantly handed me the phone. At first he laughed and said that I was a criminal. They said that criminals are not given any special privileges other than to be locked in a cell. A dear friend from church had given me the name of a person as a contact. He turned out to be the breakthrough I needed. He knew people in high places. More importantly, he was a caring person.

After negotiations with the officer, I convinced him to let me use the phone. I made a phone call to a prominent politician, who had offered to help me if I got into trouble. I told him briefly what had happened. He asked to speak with the police officer in charge. The conversation was brief. All I heard was "Yes Sir, Right away Sir". When he hung up, I was told I was free to leave with the children. They would escort me to the airport to avoid further harassment. My in-laws and a couple of male employees were standing outside the police station, waiting for the children. They were all laughing and mocking me. Little did they know that I was a free woman. For the first time in my life, I had victory over them. I felt powerful. The children didn't ask for them. We walked to an unmarked police car and drove off. All I could do was thank God for being so powerful and doing the impossible. The police officers wished us well and stood around until the plane disembarked. Throughout the flight, I just held my children, vowing never to lose them again.

Once we landed in Delhi, my next tasks were to get birth certificates and passports for my children. When my in-laws refused to give them to me, I had to use the limited amount of time that I had there. I asked my new friend to talk to the right people and speed things up. It didn't take long for the birth certificates to be ready. Of course, all this required a lot more bribing. The passports were ready within a few days. Then I had to apply for visas to allow the children to travel with me. I decided to go to the American Embassy to apply for a temporary US visa to Seattle. Once there, I could apply for a Canadian visa. Finally, I entered the guarded Embassy and was given a Visitor tag for clearance. I was so excited that we would be going home the next day. When my name was finally called, an employee handed me the documents and I left quickly. Running down the stairs, I decided to look at the children's passports for their visa and to my shock and horror, all I saw was "Denied" stamped on both passports. Now what? By this point I was in the lobby and heard the security ask for my Visitor tag back. I reached for the tag but it wasn't there. The security officer demanded that I go back and find it; otherwise I would not be allowed to leave the building. Totally stuck, I had to trace back my steps floor after floor. At last I saw the tag on the floor where I had received my documents. I was feeling like a total failure—with no other way to take my children back. As I bent to pick up the tag, a voice in me said that I should talk to the consular. I quickly got myself together and asked the same gentleman who had given me my documents earlier if I could speak to the consular for a minute. He pointed to the clock and said that they were closing in 10 minutes and I should come back on Monday. I tried to reason with him and showed him the tickets for the next day. He refused to listen. I pulled out some Canadian bills and folded and handed them to him. Pleased with my gift, he asked me to have a seat. Five minutes later, a younger woman walked towards me and asked if I was waiting to speak to her. With tears welling up, I showed her my children's passport and that my request for a temporary visa was denied. She listened to my plea. I don't remember what I said to her but whatever it was proved to be good. She smiled and told me to come back on Monday. I quickly interrupted her and showed her the tickets. She motioned to the waiting area and said that she would be back in a while. As she was leaving, I managed to see the application. In red ink, she checked off "Approved, 3 months." The joy in my heart was so overwhelming that I couldn't sit. I had just conquered the world and I wasn't about to sit quietly. As soon as I got those two passports I ran with such excitement, smiling at everyone who passed by me. I thanked the security and wished him a blessed life. I treated the family that put us up with a cake and pastries, and gave gifts of money to their children. By the grace of God, everything was ready one day before we returned.

Meanwhile the children were getting acquainted with me. They had so many questions about me. At times they insisted that I take them back to their *Bibi* and *Papa*. Finally, the day came when I could say that my biggest prayer request had been granted. We were going to be a complete family! For the first time, I would be in control of my life. At last I would be able to give the children the life they deserved. I decided to check in five hours early to avoid being seen by any familiar faces. I knew that we weren't out of the woods until we were in the plane and departed.

The three of us were allowed to board the plane early. As we made our way to our seats in the middle of the plane something happened. The head stewardess looked at her sheet and asked us to get up and follow her. "Oh my God, is it over for us? Why Lord, after all this, and now—why Lord?" As I began to gather my things, my face turning red, I felt other sets of hands reaching for my hand luggage. We were moved to the front of the plane, to the first class compartment. The stewardess said that their manager, who was a friend, put in a request to get us more comfortable seating. The manager had always been a nice guy. He knew the family well. He came over and gave a hug and wished us a better life. Wow this was getting even better. I was so happy.

Then came the best moment of my life: the plane started to move. Both of the kids were so excited that they wanted to get out of their seats and look out. Then the announcement came, that we are "cleared for takeoff." Wow! We were finally going home to be a normal family.

We arrived in Seattle around noon. My family informed me over the phone that Raj had been leaving threatening phone messages. He demanded that I return the kids to his parents; that he had deliberately left them behind to help their grandparents. He also informed the Immigration Department and my neighbours that I was a criminal.

I was determined to make it through with my children at any cost. They were not illegal immigrants to the US—they had valid visas. We got into the car and drove to the Canadian border, a two and a half hour drive. I answered all the questions from the Customs officer and he said, "Have a good day." I stared blankly, shocked that he didn't treat me like a criminal, and thanked him. All the way to my parent's house I screamed with joy. I laughed and thanked God for the victory and for what we had accomplished. Up until that moment I had not realized the intense pressure I was under. Now that huge load had been lifted.

Unable to contain my excitement, I started to honk the horn as if I was in a wedding procession. My parent's house was a block away. It was time to celebrate. The neighbours looked out their windows and my family came running to the car. It was the biggest group hugs that I have ever seen. Then my dad walked over to me with so much pride and gave me a new title. He said "what you have done today, no one could do, so from this day, I call you my son. You have proved everyone wrong and have done the impossible. I am so proud of you." I treasured those words so much.

We spent the weekend enjoying each other. We all acted like silly kids, making a mess, eating on our beds, and chasing each other around the house. We had so much fun.

Tony and Hannah were waiting anxiously to see their younger siblings. Before I left we had already set up their beds. The girls would be in one room with two single beds and the boys in another room with a bunk bed. I was so excited, but I also knew it was a very sad moment for my children. They had to leave behind the only people they knew. Hannah, Tony and I and were all strangers to them.

Then the next working day we went to Immigration and started the sponsorship process. It was challenging going through the Immigration but in the end it all worked out. When Raj found out what I had done, he raised a big fuss with them. I had to wait months before everything was settled. It would take a while for the children to go to school. It was the best time I had with them. We visited the school where they would eventually be enrolled and they were given new nicknames: Megan and Shawn.

CHAPTER TWENTY-SIX

Difficult Adjustments

It had been a long time since we had had so much fun as a family. My four children and I ate well, slept well and watched TV, all without anyone's permission. They were doing well in school and were also involved in the Sunday school programs. My neighbours kept a vigilant eye out for Raj. With my parents' assistance, I bought a small car so we could be mobile. I also enrolled in a two-year social services program at a local College. We began to make more friends. One of my closest friends was a young Christian woman named Caroline. She often encouraged me when I was feeling down. Some of the other students called her "the religious one."

I found college very challenging because helping the children with their homework, cooking, cleaning and running errands left little time for my own homework. I was getting behind in my assignments and felt like a little girl constantly in danger of being sent to the principal's office. My instructor had a chat with me and reminded me that I was losing marks when my assignments were handed in late. I did not have the best grammar or a good understanding of the work required of me. I didn't speak out in class much. I was still dealing with fear and insecurities. I was afraid of offending others and didn't want to reveal much of my past to anyone. I was fearful of being judged. When I had to speak in front of the class, I would lose sleep over it. I hated public speaking. I shook so badly that I started wearing clothes with pockets, so no one could see my sweaty, shaky hands.

The first semester was the hardest. It didn't get much easier afterwards, but I started attending a learning assistance class to help me with my lessons. I enjoyed doing research; this gave me an opportunity to work closely with my friends. Yet I dreaded the days when our group had to make a presentation to the whole class.

Eventually, my schoolwork began to be affected by the lingering problems in my personal life. Although I had been doing well, getting A's and B's, I knew I couldn't keep it up. I hardly got any sleep at night, and there was no way I could attend classes full-time, five days a week. Although I was enjoying my program, I didn't want to drop out. My instructors were very understanding of my situation, but they couldn't break the rules. I decided I would just do my best and leave the rest to God. I finally finished two semesters of the program.

I had also been attending another group from church, a women's Bible study with craft and cooking classes. I couldn't attend regularly because of my school assignments. I missed the morning coffees and the pastries the women baked. Compared to my schoolwork, the assignments in the church group (lessons from the Bible with a study guide) were pretty easy. We were given one lesson per week, and most of the lessons asked us to talk about our past experiences. I hardly ever shared with the group any of my messed up life. I was in a community of people where everyone seemed to get along with each other. The women presented themselves as organized and quite disciplined. They dressed well and walked hand-in-hand with their husbands into the church. They all went out for lunches after the Sunday service. They often met each other for dinner and coffee. I felt that I was coming into this community with a lot of baggage and was afraid of being judged. I didn't think they would understand what I had been through. I feared they would blame me and distance themselves from me. I didn't want to be rejected anymore. I really wanted to fit in. And the best way to do that was to pretend that everything was just fine with me.

My children were also getting involved in different activities at this church. At times, the members of the congregation would sponsor my children for certain events. Every summer they attended a week-long camp and they would take turns spending a week at my parents. They did well, especially after much counselling.

It was finally time for Hannah to begin her long journey to have her birthmark removed. She needed several surgeries, and it would take a number of months to grow skin for the graft. We were then living in the suburbs and had to drive 50 kilometres in to Vancouver two to three times per week. The doctor injected a solution into the area where the skin was growing. This meant I had to juggle my schedule. All the children helped out and took on a few more chores. A very dear, elderly friend volunteered to take the children after school for a few hours. She cooked and took them out for some activity. I was so thankful for the help I received from family and friends. Some of my neighbours were very good as well, keeping an eye on my home while we were out. God always seemed to provide someone in my life who came just when I needed help.

Hannah was a very brave girl and took the needles and surgeries very well. By the time she had begun to heal from her surgeries, I was scheduled for surgery. This was for a hysterectomy. I was very generously given a homemaker from social services for the few days I was hospitalized. My surgery also went smoothly and I was home in a few days and healing well. I was surprised to see how many people came with food and gifts. The children were enjoying the attention and the company. I was very proud of them. They had been so good during my surgery and they attended to Hannah's needs as well.

I also had other nagging problems. My violent headaches continued and I was becoming addicted to painkillers. Some nights it was so bad that I ended up in the emergency room. The doctors concluded that I was having migraines. They would give me more painkillers. Sometimes depending on the pain level, they would give me medication intravenously. All of these were just band-aid treatments. I suffered these migraine attacks at least two to three times a week. This meant the children would have to be very quiet, and I would stay in a dark room. Often I would throw up because of the pain. I felt I was in bondage from something. Even though I was free from abuse, I was still in so much pain.

People from the church began to pray for me. It helped for a short while, and then I would be sick again. Some friends thought perhaps my home was making me sick, but the doctors told me the headaches were stress related and I should learn to relax a little. I decided not to work for a while until things got better with us.

CHAPTER TWENTY-SEVEN

Custody Battles

During this time, I got myself a lawyer to get full custody of my children. I had already obtained an interim order, but I needed to protect my children and myself from any surprise moves by Raj. I was very glad when a legal aid lawyer agreed to take on my case.

When Raj was served with the papers he immediately got himself a lawyer. Within days, we were going back and forth with the lawyers and the courts. I had to keep proving that his statements in the affidavits were lies. It was time-consuming and very frustrating. Raj was not going to give up without a fight. He couldn't stand the fact that I was finally free and living a good life with my children.

Somehow Raj would get my unlisted phone number and start calling me at odd times of the night. The children and I had to secure our home with metal bars. We unplugged our phones at night so we could sleep. But if Raj's phone calls didn't keep me up all night, the nightmares did. They were so terrifying that it felt as if there were demons in my bedroom choking me. It was getting very difficult to stay awake in school. I was too embarrassed to tell anyone about my nightmares. I figured people either wouldn't understand what I was going through or they would think I was losing my mind. I often woke up screaming. At other times, one of the children would wake me up as I struggled to snap out of my sleep. It got so bad that we decided to leave most of the lights on at night, but that was only a temporary solution.

Since the start of the legal battles both lawyers argued over the custody of the children and the allegations we made against each other. The court appointed a counsellor to meet with each of us separately. My home was checked out, and the children were interviewed one-on-one. Then the investigators went to the school and spoke with the children's teachers and the principal. Finally, the investigators met with Raj and then a report was prepared. I was waiting nervously for this report, but my lawyer told me it looked good for us. I was very particular about how my children dressed and their manners in public. Whenever we went out even for a short while, they had to be neatly dressed, and behaved. I didn't want anyone taking pictures of the children scrubby looking. I was proud of them and wanted to show them off.

A date was set for our custody trial but Raj's lawyer would ask for adjournments. After a couple of adjournments, the lawyers finally presented their cases to the judge. After hearing the arguments from both sides and reading the court-appointed counsellor's report, the judge awarded me full custody of the children. Raj was not even given visitation rights and ordered to stay away from us. He was also ordered to pay $2,000 a month in child support, effective immediately. Finally! People believed me. Everything he did to me was overturned. He was the one with the problems. I was over the moon.

I was relieved that this ordeal was finally over and a new chapter had begun for us. My children and I had been through so much misery and uncertainty that we were ready to welcome some stability into our lives. We needed closure. Also, with the support payments we would finally be able to get back on our feet, and wouldn't need any assistance from the government. The child support would be enough to pay all of our bills every month. We began a budget sheet to plan our monthly expenses. It was very exciting. We would even have savings for ourselves.

That excitement was very short-lived, however. Within days, I found out Raj and his lawyer had appealed the judge's decision regarding the support. So quickly, Raj became sick with back problems and could no longer work so the judge lowered his support payments to $600 a month. This meant I would still have to depend on the government until I got a full-time job. I began by taking on volunteer work for which social services would pay an additional $100.00. A few hours a week worked well for me. I chose not to work full-time until the children were much older. I also still had the migraines to deal with.

Unable to contain his anger and loss of power and control, Raj went into a rage.

After being charged with breaching the court order, Raj left the country. He had an order from the Supreme Court prohibiting him to make any direct or indirect contact with either my children or me. Neighbours often found him looking into my house through the blinds. Sometimes he would show up and leave presents for the children at the door. He was caught a number of times by the police and arrested. His lawyer informed us at the next court session that he was out of the country and wouldn't be returning soon. It was his way of punishing me by refusing to pay the child support. It really didn't matter because I had all my children, and I knew that somehow we would make it. With Jesus my Lord at my side, nothing was too difficult. Through all of this, my faith was greatly tested. God never let us down.

Here and there my parents helped with groceries. During Christmas and Easter our family received a hamper from the church. Even though it was embarrassing to receive assistance from strangers, I knew it would help us greatly. I only hoped that one day I could return that same generosity to others. I had to let go of my pride and accept things from others. Looking back now, I believe there are times in our lives when we need to be on the receiving end. God allows different seasons in our lives so that we will put our trust in him completely. But for me then, it was very hard to keep my faith in God strong when things were not looking good at all.

There were times when the refrigerator was completely empty and I had no money. At such times, I was angry with Raj for leaving us in that situation. Would we ever get to a place where we wouldn't have to worry about our next meal? Bills were piling up and I was sinking deeper into a depression. Sometimes I would be reminded by someone that I needed to praise God in all situations. Easy for them to say that—they weren't the ones who had nothing, I would answer them. It was hard to praise God in that kind of situation. I would read the Bible and see God's promises. His word says that he will always provide for us and feed his children. Somehow I did not have the faith to apply that for myself.

I continued to hold a grudge against Raj. He had betrayed us and had left me in much pain, emotionally and physically. Although I was free from all the abuse and torture, I still had many other things to deal with. There was the continual fear of him harming us, making it difficult for me to live with total freedom. There was little chance of him accepting that we were separated and I had enough of his abuse and had moved on. He still felt that I was his possession; that he owned me.

I really couldn't understand this man. He couldn't live with me, and he couldn't live without me. Why couldn't he accept the fact that I was stronger now? I do give him some credit for making me a stronger person. I was learning new things to protect my children and myself. These were mostly just basic common sense things, such as letting the neighbours know that he was a violent man. Calling the police whenever he came by, even when he had gifts with him. I secured all the windows and doors. My answering machine had someone else's voice. I slept with flashlights beside my pillow, and I had important phone numbers programmed into the telephone. Many nights, I would leave the downstairs TV on all night. I was always looking for ways to secure the house and keep us safe.

I did not allow the children to have sleepovers at their friends' houses. I was so afraid something might happen to them that I became over-protective. The painful months and years I had spent without them had given me every reason to stay close to them. My children had friends and were allowed to play with them, but I was always around to monitor what was going on.

I knew that they wanted to be a little freer, like the other children in our neighbourhood, but they knew there could be consequences. Just like me, they had to deal with abandonment issues. They had been little when I had had to leave them. They must have lived with the fear of being forsaken. Not having any idea if I would come back for them. I can't imagine how many lonely nights they had spent just holding on to each other. I wondered if they cried themselves to sleep, waking up to face the same loneliness again. They would have eaten whatever they got and worn the clothes picked out for them. They must have learned not to be fussy. No one cared about them like their mother did. Having to deal with those sad memories, these children didn't complain much.

We also didn't invite anyone to spend the night at our home. It was just too dangerous to have someone else over. Nights were the worst. Given Raj's past actions, anything was possible. If he wanted, he could find a way into our home. As soon as it got dark outside, my past fears returned. Every night after the children were washed up and changed into their pyjamas, we would all sit on my bed and take turns reading the Bible. That was our comfort. After that, I would ask them for their prayer requests and we would begin to pray. Night after night, we prayed for God's protection over each one of us and over our home. When morning came, the first thing I would do was check on each one of the children. I would praise God for his protection over my family that night.

I could never tell when Raj was in the country, when he left or when he returned. He somehow managed to call me from wherever he was. His calls would start out smooth and sweet but quickly turn into accusations. He wanted to reconcile and start fresh. I would laugh and ask him if he was joking. Now that I had tasted freedom there was no way I would ever give that up. I knew him all too well to believe anything. There was nothing he could bribe me with or threaten me with this time. The children deserved a life with some stability. It would be very unfair to put them back in that dysfunctional lifestyle.

Then late one afternoon, Raj showed up at our house while the children were outside playing with their friends. He got out of his car and started handing the children toys he had bought for them. They were still in their store bags with the price tags on them. He had a bag for each of them. Then he handed another small bag to the children and told them to run and give it to me. As the children were running inside with the bags in their hands, I ran to the door to see what the excitement was all about. They shouted that there was a bag for me too. As they handed me the bag, one of them said that Papa had brought all these gifts for us. They insisted that I open my gift too. When I reached to close the door, a stronger hand blocked it. Raj was standing at the door, hoping I would accept his gift and let him into the house.

In a very firm voice, I told him to leave. He said he was leaving the country and wanted to leave the gifts he had bought the kids. I handed him my gift back without even looking at it. I wasn't interested in his gifts. I didn't want anything from him except to be left alone. He became very angry when I rejected his gift and said he had spent hundreds of dollars on it and he regretted buying it. I told him that I could care less for his gifts. I nodded my head in agreement and told him to return it. To my surprise, he left without forcing his way into the house. I locked all the windows and doors and shut the blinds, fearing his return. He hated rejection, and knowing his history the chances of him coming back with a vengeance was high.

The children were showing each other their gifts. They loved their new toys. They had never received such expensive toys before.

That had not been my priority. I made sure they had good meals and clean clothes to wear. I gave them tons of love and spent quality time with them. That was something I treasured and invested in them.

There was another knock on the door. It was Raj. I opened the door a bit with the chain still on. He said he wanted all the toys back. I shook my head in disbelief that he would do this to the children. I told him the children were playing with their toys. When he insisted, I closed the door, grabbed all the toys from the children and gave them back to him. Slamming the door, I went to comfort the children. They were crying and didn't want to talk and blamed me. I couldn't make them any promises to replace what they had lost. I would be lying to them.

Yet, slowly, our lives were becoming somewhat normal. The children never forgot those lost toys, but they got over it. I found out from some people that Raj had left the country again. He had told them he would be back soon. I felt a little bit safer knowing he was gone, but I was still on my guard. I had stopped changing my telephone number. Somehow he had always been able to find out my number and call anyway. I had also stopped recording his phone calls for the police because many of the calls were from pay phones.

I began to receive calls from him again. He told me he had gone back to his parents and things were much better there. He encouraged me to come for a visit. I didn't have to think about an answer. I declined his offer immediately. But I wished him well. In later calls, he promised to treat me well. He said he was building a house for himself and he wanted my help in designing and decorating it. I firmly told him there was absolutely no way I would come there and he should give up on that thought.

The calls became less and less frequent. When Raj did call, it was only to talk to the children. He began to make false promises to them. He would promise hockey equipment, money, and so on. The children would get their hopes up waiting for the presents to arrive in the mail.

One day, a reporter from a local TV station approached me, looking to interview me on deadbeat dads. I agreed to do an interview for their six o'clock news. The interview was aired about a week later. Shocked and betrayed at the report, I heard Raj's voice in the piece as well. The reporter had tracked him down and asked for his side of the story. Raj stated plainly that he wasn't paying child support. His excuse was that since he didn't get any rights to see the children, he didn't see why he should pay for them. He also said that if he did pay child support, he didn't know how the money would be used.

This led to the family maintenance enforcement unit filing a claim in India. When he received the letter from this department demanding that he pay all arrears and continue his monthly support, he called me. Though he was very angry about the interview and the fact that I had gone public with my story and embarrassed him, he said he had decided he would pay us all the money. I was glad that for once in his life he had agreed to do something good for his children. Maybe it was because he had no way out of the court order. They were strictly enforced. Supreme Court orders had to be taken very seriously.

While all this was happening, my church friends continued to pray for us and visit us often. Every opportunity they had, they gently reminded me of the importance of forgiveness. To please them, I would agree and say a prayer offering forgiveness to all who had hurt me. But I never really forgave them from my heart. I still held on to the hurts and nursed my deep wounds. I hoped that if I could inflict on them the same kind of pain I had suffered, then I would forgive. I did not understand the power of forgiveness. I knew the Bible was clear on forgiveness, but I felt it was for others and not for someone like me who had suffered so much.

When we spoke one evening on the phone in late April, Raj sounded willing to help support his children. He said he was missing them and hoped to come back soon. After we talked for a little while, he promised to call me again in a few days.

For some strange reason I kept waiting for his call, although I wasn't expecting much. I was used to his broken promises. Why should this time be any different? He always had a way with words. No matter how many times he had hurt us we still held on to a little bit of hope. Maybe he will come through for us this time. I expected him to comply with the court order. I waited with anticipation for the phone to ring.

That call never came.

Every morning some of the local fishermen and women went out to the sea hoping to make a catch. Some were just out scavenging. That particular morning she had not caught anything. She said to herself, "surely I must find something for my family." Most often she caught enough fish in her net. She'd take them to the market place and sell them.

The middle-aged woman walked slowly, with her head bowed, along the shore as one who was in sorrow. She climbed up on a small hill and stood under the branches of a young hornbeam looking towards the unforgiving ocean. She sat under the shade of the tree to shelter herself from the sun. She was weary and had wandered away from the rest of them to find dry shore.

Just then a black dog ran toward her and snarled. It made her shiver. Looking around to see if there were other animals to watch out for – she noticed something odd. The area was littered with cigarette butts, bottles, cans and other trash people had thrown.

The woman saw what she believed was a mannequin of a man in the thorn bushes laying upside down. It was just a few feet away. She quickly flung herself down to see if he had passed out. Something didn't look right. And then her gaze drifted toward his face. She looked around for any evidence. She yelled frantically to the others, while also speaking to this naked man. There was no response from him.

She quickly checked for a pulse while her imagination was running wild. "Who could this man be? Is he a local or a wanderer? What a tragedy." She asked others if they heard of anyone missing from their village. She couldn't help but wonder who this man was, "Does he have a family?"

She thought of her own family. Her grownup sons, whom she loved, had a future unlike this man. He was robbed of the experiences that the future promised. She felt for the individual and his family. "Were they looking for him?" she wondered.

Her breath didn't return – she thought she would die. She knew the person was gone when she forced her gaze to rest upon his face. She closed her eyes for a long minute hoping it would disappear.

The women consoled each other for the man who nobody knew yet. A small group of men gathered around the body making small talk. Hardly anyone spoke – only a strained silence. There in front of the group was stretched out before them the dead body of a young man.

This would be a horrible tragedy if it was a murder. Her initial reaction was shock, shortness of breath, terror and dizziness. Who would do such a horrendous thing to this man? Despite the heat, this middle-aged woman stood off a ways while glancing at the investigators. With her head bowed down and tears rolling down her face, she couldn't believe that a mother had lost her young son. She couldn't get rid of the lump in her throat.

She had lived in this small fishing village for the last twenty years and she had never witnessed a death here. A cold sick feeling rushed over this woman. She felt like throwing up and running away. But she was now a witness to a possible murder, or a suicide investigation.

As she stood waiting impatiently at the crime scene for the detectives to take her statement, she tried hard to regroup her scattered thoughts. Her heart froze and skipped a beat when the police rolled the body onto its back. She moved closer to look at his face. She thought to herself, "If this man was suffering, this death still wouldn't give him any peace."

Her eyes dropped from his dead gaze to the bloody cuts and bruises all over his thin body. He lay awkwardly half-propped on a rock. She knew he was beyond comfort. This death was unusual.

She had looked death in the face. She told the police and some of her friends standing beside her that she would be haunted by the sight of the dead man forever. "How can one stop thinking and get the image out of their head?" she questioned.

That dead man was my husband. The woman was a local.

CHAPTER TWENTY-EIGHT

Closure

Now here I was in late April 1998, returning with Hannah and Tony to the place I swore I would never visit again. This place held so many painful memories. I had received news that Raj had drowned. One of his relatives called me to give me that 'tragic news'. They told me to get ready to go for the funeral. I couldn't believe that the man who was trying to kill me throughout our married life was actually dead himself. Was this some kind of a trick to get me to come back? And how did he drown? According to the family, he had gone boating and hadn't come back. A woman walking the beach found his body a few days later. Is that why he didn't call me back as he had promised? But could this family be trusted?

Hannah and Tony were clearly distraught while Megan and Shawn weren't sure how to react. My anger subsided and I began to mourn for him. "Was I crazy to be sad over this man?" I made a couple of calls to my trusted friends in India to find out if he had in fact died or was it all a big joke. They confirmed that he had drowned.

After talking it over with my family and close friends, I decided that I would take Hannah and Tony to the funeral for a few days. We needed closure and this would help us heal our wounds. There was a lot of concern for our safety. My plan was to be in town for the day.

We would return to Delhi the same afternoon.

Two days after receiving the news, we headed to the airport. Raj's younger brother told me that the funeral would start as soon as we landed in Bombay. As the plane took off, I held my children and whispered to them that it would be okay, even though I myself was numb. Tony was terrified to be going there. One of his uncles told him on the phone that he was expected to light the fire to cremate his dad's body. On the plane he made me a promise that he would do no such thing. I told him that he must stay with me at all times and only listen to me. I had never expected to get this news. I didn't know how to act in the traditional manner that was required of me. I felt too young to be in this situation. I had undergone a great variety of experiences at the hands of Raj—he had always been full of surprises, and this time was no different.

After he had gone back to be with his parents, I had heard rumours that he was living with someone. He planned to marry this woman. I didn't know who she was, but I felt sorry for her. Who would want to marry this man? Was it for the love of money? People were aware of his behaviour and the way he had treated my children and me.

In some ways I was glad to be free of Raj. By no means would life be a breeze. It only meant that I would no longer be looking over my shoulders. I envied couples that did things together. I knew every family had some problems, but not many husbands tortured their wives. There had been minor problems in our home growing up, but my parents had dealt with them in an adult manner. There had been two failed marriages in my extended family. They parted ways like mature adults.

Most of my siblings were well educated and held good positions. They were respected in the community. In comparison to them, I felt like a total failure. Ironically, when I had first gotten married, I thought that out of the nine children, I had been the luckiest to marry into an extremely wealthy family to a smart and handsome man. I had been so wrong.

Sitting in that plane, I went through many emotions. "Why was I even going? No one really wanted me to come. Raj's family just wanted the children to come and fulfill their cultural duties and show everyone how much they loved the children." There was no way I would let them go alone. In fact, Tony had not wanted to go there at all. I had to bribe him. He did love his dad and wanted to say his good-byes. I felt bad for forcing him into going. Life had been so unfair to them. I didn't fully understand what effect this trip would have on him in the long run. I didn't have the strength to think that far ahead. Hannah was a bit stronger and was handling the situation pretty well.

I had left the younger children behind with my parents. It would have been very difficult to deal with the funeral while taking care of four children. I was also afraid of losing them again. We had decided it would be safer to leave them behind. I didn't want to expose them to anything that would leave a lasting effect on them. It was bad enough taking Hannah and Tony.

I was praying that God would take care of us on this trip. I no longer made any hasty decisions on my own. I got into the habit of praying first. I trusted God was in this situation and he would protect us from any danger.

I shed many tears on the plane—most of them for my children. They had suffered way too much. I prayed that God would give them the strength to handle this difficult situation and for total healing in their lives after this. From their birth until now, all they had seen was misery and loss. "Would God finally put an end to all of our suffering and restore some form of peace and healing to our lives?"

Reflecting back, it had been easier for me to begin the healing process because I had been able to talk to people. My children hadn't. As a result, they had been acting out in different ways. Hannah had chosen to talk a lot. In contrast, Tony became very quiet and withdrawn. He had a hard time making and keeping friends. He would get himself into trouble at school for fighting. He had little interest in activities other than school. His principal suggested that we put him into karate. That lasted for only two classes. Counselling hadn't worked for him either. He had enjoyed being with his cousins, so we tried to visit them weekly. Now how would this trip affect him?

None of us ate anything during our long flight. No one had any appetite. I should have been much stronger by now but I wasn't—I was falling apart. I wasn't prepared for what was ahead of us. It would be a long day with all the funeral rituals. I prayed that we would be able to handle whatever would come our way. I prayed that this would be the last chapter of our troubled life. We had endured over fourteen years of misery.

We arrived in Delhi early in the morning. I purposely missed our next flight to their home town. I wasn't ready to deal with the family and all the drama. I had never been their favourite person, and that day would be the worst day to face them. I was so afraid of what was waiting for us. I decided to leave all of our travel documents and our bags with my family in Delhi before boarding the next plane.

I had a quick shower and changed into a traditional white *Salweer-kameez*, while the children napped. Over breakfast my niece turned on the radio just in time for the funeral announcements.

When I checked in at the airline counter for the smaller plane that would take us to Bombay, a very rude and hostile employee greeted me. He didn't know who I was. But he began to insult me. He said I was very disrespectful to this family and I was delaying the funeral ceremonies. He told me that I should be very thankful that he was allowing me to get on this flight. If it hadn't been for this family, he would not have let me on. I was too tired to argue with him or explain why I delayed leaving. Apparently this man had received several calls from my in-laws demanding that he find us. There were people looking for us.

As we made our way to the chartered plane, I introduced myself to this man. I also told him never to talk to me like that, especially when he did not know the reasons for my delay. He apologized.

It took us two hours to get to my in-laws' house—the place I dreaded the most in the whole world. I had promised myself I would never return to this house ever again, but here I was, and hopefully for the last time. I knew there would be a lot of people there, most of them spectators. People would have been going to the house for the past few days to mourn with the family. As we got closer to the house, my heart began to pound. I did not know what to expect. The two employees that picked us up were very respectful towards me. They referred to me as *bhabiji*, sister-in-law. They quickly got out of the truck and opened our doors. They asked if our luggage would be coming in the next flight. I told them that I wasn't sure.

I held my children's hands as we walked up the long flight of stairs. I heard loud cries like women wailing. I didn't know what I was supposed to feel: anger, sadness or relief. As we entered the home, all eyes were on me, waiting to see my reaction. I was led by some of the elders to the front of the room where Raj's immediate family sat. My heart lurched. In the centre was an old wooden coffin. The only nice thing about it was the beautiful wreaths. What I had been told was true. It was over. But were my troubles over as well? I tried to get closer to get a better look at the body, but I couldn't see much. There were garlands made from fresh flowers placed around his neck. For some strange reason his head was covered with a red cloth.

The brown coffin brought back so many past memories. Raj's mother and her family sat on one side, and his sisters on the other. As I got closer to the coffin, I didn't recognize the person inside. Was it because there was a cloth tied around his face, or was it because he looked different. Whatever the reason was, I started to get nervous. "Had this been a trick to get me there so the family could punish me for the things I had done?" I turned around and asked one of his sisters whose body it was. She said it was Raj's. Then I asked why he looked so different. She said it was because he had drowned. Wanting all my questions answered right away, I asked why his face was tied up. Reluctantly, she answered that he had a broken jaw and it had had to be tied up for the funeral. But his face still looked very different. I had been with this man for many years, and I knew what he looked like. This deceased man did not look like him.

Since so many eyes and ears were trained on me, I chose to re-main quiet while trying to come up with a plan to escape from there. It had been very wise of me to leave our documents behind. We had traveled light. The children had just one change of clothes with them in their backpacks. Our return tickets for the flight back were tucked away in a safe place.

Then the priest started the ceremony with speeches. First, he read the sympathy cards and the telex messages. Most of them were from dignitaries and important officials. Then he began the religious prayer.

I still wanted to know who the man was in that coffin. Every so often, I looked at Raj's mother and tried to gauge her reaction. She looked very tired and sad. Her sisters were consoling her. If this re-ally was her son, I felt very sorry for her. No parent ever wants to lose a child at this age. In fact no parents should outlive their chil-dren. Even though I knew she was going through a very difficult time, I didn't talk to her. I wasn't sure if she was going to talk to me. In the phone conversations before we had left for the funeral I found out that most of them did not want me to attend. They had asked one of Raj's sister's to bring the children, but I had refused to send them with anyone else. Although I was very sorry for his parents, I was not willing to sacrifice my children's safety.

Midway through the hour-long funeral ceremony, while I was debating with God why he had allowed me to attend this funeral, Raj's mother reached for a glass of water. Then some men came over and removed the cover from the coffin. I moved closer to the body. I wanted to know what was so different about him. I didn't know why they were exposing his body and what the rituals were. I saw many bruises and cuts on the body, but I couldn't pinpoint exactly what was wrong with the features.

While the ceremony was still going on, I prayed that God would show me who this person in the casket was. Until then, I had just sat wondering how I had been fooled into coming to this funeral.

Every part of that house held so many terrible and painful memories. I did not want to look around. I focused my eyes on the body and prayed for a sign that it was truly Raj.

Then I noticed Raj's mother filling the teaspoon with water. She began to lower it as if to feed the body in the coffin. I wondered why she was doing that. If he were dead, he wouldn't drink the water or even open his mouth. I didn't think he was thirsty. I guessed it must be some kind of religious act. With one hand she held onto the spoon, and with the other hand she moved the lower lip in order to pour the water inside his mouth. As she did, I almost screamed because of what I saw.

One compliment Raj had given me was that I had a nice, even set of teeth. I, on the other hand, had always teased him that he had crooked teeth because of his foul mouth. Now I recognized his teeth. "Yes, it was Raj, but what had happened to his face?" Immediately, I turned to his sister and asked what really happened to him. She said he had drowned, the fish ate his eyes. Because his body had been pushed back and forth into the rocks, he received those bruises. I thought he had too many injuries on his body for them all to have come from the rocks. I was getting more and more nervous sitting there.

Then the Priest announced that the body would be taken to the *gurdwara* for a final prayer and then to the cemetery for cremation. I quickly followed the crowd right behind the casket. I didn't want to get left behind to be grilled by the family. They were already giving me mean looks and I could tell they weren't happy to see me there. From the day they had found out about Raj's death, they had made it clear that I was not to be at his funeral. I wasn't there for anyone except my children. They needed me.

There was a police escort for the body. A few uniformed police officers rode their motorcycles, followed by the hearse and the immediate family. Most of the people chose to walk to the *gurdwara*. It was about a ten-minute walk. The men slowly took the casket out and placed it on the porch of the *gurdwara*. I could not believe that this man was dead. I sat close to the casket this time and observed the cuts and bruises on his face. I couldn't help but compare them to the ones that I received many times before. As I sat there totally oblivious to the others, I had flashbacks of the times he talked about my death and planned my funeral. Numerous times I was so close to death. "Why was I spared?" While the priest was praying over the body Raj's brothers came over to get Tony. He said they were taking the body to the cemetery after the prayers. This young boy was so traumatized that he began to shake when he heard he was expected to go without me. I had talked to him about the possibility of cremating his father. When he refused to go they insisted. He did not want to go without me. When I saw them coming towards him, I decided to raise my voice to the priest.

I asked him very politely if I could go with Tony because he was scared and very emotional. The family tried to answer before the priest could. They said women were not allowed at the cemetery. The priest knew of the many incidents when I had had to flee from Raj's violent outbursts. He looked at me with sympathy and gently said, to everyone's surprise, that I could go with my son. They allowed me to go to the cemetery with Raj's sister and my children. We followed the procession to the funeral grounds. In the centre of the cemetery was a shed where the cremation ceremony was to take place.

By the time we reached the cremation site, the body had been taken out of the casket and put on the pyre. I walked quickly with the kids towards the body to get a better look at the body and bid him a final goodbye. It was a warm day, and flies were all over him. I stood by, thinking about how this man had driven by this area and asked the children to pick out the spot where I should be buried. Now the tables had turned. I was here with the same children in the same cemetery. We were well-prepared and ready with the matches in our hand to burn his body. He would have melted butter poured over him – instead of Kerosene. The tortures I had endured at the hands of this man flashed like a movie in front of me.

At that moment, a small voice inside of me said, "Will you forgive now?" Then I heard the same voice saying, "Vengeance is mine." I can't really say how I felt at that time.

I began to understand how much Jesus loved me and how he had protected me all those years. God did not allow Raj to kill me – no matter how he tried to. I remembered so many times through his words in the Bible and through people, God spoke to me about forgiveness. How important it was to forgive and release my wounds to the Lord. I now saw God as a loving and compassionate father. I knew he remembered everything that had happened to us; he had not been slow in coming to our aid.

This time, I didn't have to negotiate with the Lord. All the years of my suffering had come to an end. I reached out my hand, touched Raj's arm and forgave him and his entire family. No one knew what I was doing, but I had a moment when no one interrupted me and I quickly whispered words of forgiveness to him and his family. Even though he was dead his soul was living.

Just then, Raj's father announced that the time had come to cover the body with a white sheet. The men brought over logs and laid them on top of the body. Liquid butter called "*ghee*" was poured over the entire body to start the fire. Then one of the brother's came over and helped Tony and I light the match. This time I had no hesitations. We were in charge of the final rite. We walked around lighting everywhere we could until we couldn't stay there any longer. That was the end of Raj. Within moments he was burned to ashes.

Within seconds the flames grew. We kept moving further away. From a distance, we waved goodbye. The children wept. The older men came by and gently touched the children on their heads as a way of comforting and consoling them. I felt someone touching me from the back, but I didn't turn around to see who it was. I heard a voice very unfamiliar to me. She spoke very softly. She said that she was the one who came across his body. I quickly turned to talk more with this woman, but she disappeared into the crowd. I looked around desperately but there were too many people. I regretted not making any eye contact when I had the opportunity.

I whispered to the children that we would leave as soon as possible. I could not stay there any longer. I was scared for our lives. After seeing the injuries on Raj's face, it was obvious that there was trauma. I could not accept the fact that he had drowned and had a broken jaw. Something didn't seem right, and I wasn't sure how he had died. All I was told was that he had drowned.

In the car I announced to Raj's sister that we would be leaving later that afternoon. Shocked at my decision, she insisted that I tell her parents myself. I dreaded going back up that long flight of stairs. I had hoped to avoid going back into that house. Knowing my sister-in-law wouldn't leave, I reluctantly went. I was trying so hard to be brave. My mother-in-law and some of the immediate family members met me at the top of the stairs. If I wanted to leave I had to be very firm with my decision and not give into their sweet talk. As soon as we approached them, the sister announced loudly that I was leaving and wouldn't be staying for the three-day prayer service. Raj's mother agreed that I should leave since it was no longer my house. Raj was no longer alive and I was not considered part of the family. Besides, we already had a bad history between us. She probably meant it as an insult, but I was so relieved to hear her say that.

Some men and Raj's father were inside listening to what was being said outside. In a loud voice, he called us inside. The sister followed us. He asked why we were leaving and not staying for the prayers. I said that we had to go back. I thought that I should be very sincere with him – after all he did understand and witnessed most of the violence. I began by saying that it was very hard for me to come back. I had been trying to get back to some normalcy. To hear that he had died was very hard on the children. He said he understood my feelings. He asked that we sit for a while. I quickly told him what time our flight was that afternoon. Raj's sister and the oldest brother, who had made our lives a living hell, also pulled a chair to listen in. I figured they were there to see what my father-in-law was offering us. Raj did have shares in some of the companies.

The dad pulled his shirtsleeves to show me his arm. He pointed out spots where he was hurt. With all the dark hair on his arm, I couldn't see anything. I cautiously asked what he was pointing to while trying hard to ignore the other two. He answered with some emotion that a week earlier they had an argument which erupted into a physical fight. He had been thrown onto the floor and hit a number of times by Raj. He shocked me by saying that I had made a wise decision leaving his son. He was not going to hold onto the money that Raj had left behind. He would give it to us.

But there were conditions attached to this decision. I would have to leave the children with him. He promised he would take care of them and give them everything I couldn't. That possibility, too, I had cautioned the children about. They were not to give in to any promises *Bibi* and *Papa* would try to bribe them with. I quickly got up and said that I didn't accept their offer and that I had to leave. "Were they out of their minds to think that I would leave my children with them—especially after everything they had been through?" I told them that we would use the money from the estate wisely. We need our own home and the children would need funds for college. Then the three of them forcefully took the children into the bedroom and asked them if they would like to stay for a better and prosperous future. I walked in and heard Hannah and Tony say "no" to their proposition.

When they realized we were not giving in and were determined to leave my father-in-law demanded we leave his sight immediately. I waved a quick goodbye to everyone and headed downstairs to get a taxi. Instead Raj's younger brother offered to drive us to the airport. I trusted this brother and his wife.

Before we left for the airport, they drove us to the place where Raj had been living just prior to his death. There was a small boat on the side of the house. They told me it was the same boat in which he had drowned. I went out to look at it and noticed small blood stains inside. The children also noticed them. They asked if I wanted to go inside his house. I declined and instead took the next plane to Delhi.

CHAPTER TWENTY-NINE

Aftermath

I was now left with two grieving children. We arrived at my brother's house later that evening. My sister-in-law was tired and decided to go to bed early. I too was suffering, dealing with my own grief and trying my best to console the children. Tony was in such a bad state that it was impossible to comfort him. That night was the worst night, full of nightmares and flashbacks. We lay on the bed just staring at the ceiling. Earlier, Tony asked me if we killed his father by setting his body on fire. The funeral had left him with a great deal of emotional trauma. Then he asked me, "Would he have died if we had been living together?" Shocked at his question, I simply said, "I don't know".

There were questions and accusations from many other people. One thing I heard was that I had been the reason Raj had died. Some said he had slipped into such a deep depression because I had taken the children away from him. That's why he had committed suicide. They said I was the one who had killed him by taking everything away from him. He couldn't bear to live without his wife and children. His life was meaningless. I decided I wasn't going to play the blaming game. They forgot all those nights of torture and attempted murders, hanging, choking, and soaking in kerosene, forced into the ocean and so many other abuses. Do they all have a short term memory? Was this behaviour okay with them? I realized that regardless of my innocence, the family needed someone to blame. I was an easy target. I was thousands of miles away when he died.

I had to stay away from this entire family and all their gossip. We had started our journey to recovery. I needed to be there for my children. They would need a lot of help, counselling and support. I couldn't afford to waste my energy on people's opinions.

A few days later, we returned home. It was such a relief to see the younger ones; I was so glad they hadn't gone on this journey. I was so thankful for the wisdom the Lord God had given me. Their *Bibi* and *Papa* would have bribed them into staying. They still had a bond with Megan and Shawn. God was with me. He was true to his promise "He would never leave me or forsake me."

The more I began to reflect on my past life, the clearer it became how much God had saved me from death. I had questioned where God was when I had been suffering through all those unthinkable things; if God is a strong and mighty God, he could have protected me. And he did. If he hadn't protected me, I would have been dead the first time Raj had beaten me or the second time or any other time, but he had not allowed death to take me.

My prayers had all been answered. I was safe. I had all my children with me. And I now had Jesus to walk the rest of my journey with. He is more than enough.

Although I had forgiven Raj's family earlier, I did not want to be around their venomous ways.

CHAPTER THIRTY

Abuse Must End

Abuse is never justified. Abuse not only wounds physically, but destroys people emotionally and mentally. It is a systematic breaking down of the person you were meant to be.

Abuse is not limited to women and children. There are some men who are also victims of domestic violence. Often times, out of shame and embarrassment, these men do not tell others they are in an abusive relationship. Compared to the resources now available for abused women, there are very limited resources for abused men. But the reality remains that there are far more abused women than men, and that abuse in any form should never happen. No person should ever live in fear in their own home. All people should have the freedom to be who they are.

As a little girl growing up, I never thought I would be a single mother or a battered wife. I had a dream of being a loving wife and of having a loving husband and a big family. Even after I married, I did my best to try to save our marriage until I was too exhausted.

So, what happens when such dreams never come to pass? What happens when a woman's dreams slowly die inside her and she feels herself becoming numb? Friends and family are a thing of the past. The phone begins to ring less and less often. The house seems to get darker during the day. The blinds hardly open.

That is how the cycle of abuse begins. First it is emotional and verbal abuse. Then comes a slap, followed by many more slaps and punches. Night is the best time for a husband to beat his wife the TV is loud, and other people aren't around.

At times, the built-up anger makes a woman in this situation want to leave, either to start a new life or to teach her husband a lesson. Then he apologizes profusely and makes promises that he will get help. He swears that he loves her and that he can't imagine his life without her or the children. She agrees to stay. The honeymoon is short-lived.

There were many times when I thought of leaving Raj. But I knew that it would most likely cost me my life and the lives of my family as well. Raj made many threats that he would kill my parents and me and escape the country with the children. It was safer to stay in the horrible marriage than to flee. I was more fearful and concerned for my family than for myself.

I did not have a lot of skills to live on my own. My husband controlled all the financial matters. The only thing I wanted was revenge. I wanted the situation to be reversed, so that I could do to him what he had done to me. I wanted to tie him up, kick him and punch him until he bled and asked for mercy. Whenever he would begin to torture me, I would wish in my heart that he would be paralysed. I did not want him to die. That would be too easy. I wanted him to suffer.

The sad reality is that it takes many attempts before a woman decides that she has had enough; that the cycle of violence has to end. Even sadder is that some women are murdered while contemplating a new life.

Every woman who has died as a result of domestic violence was someone's daughter, sister, mother, aunt and a friend. Their life mattered just like mine. Though she is no longer suffering, she has left many others who are suffering for her. I cannot imagine the pain of losing a loved one through a tragedy like this. It could have been prevented.

When I was first married, the laws weren't very strict concerning abusers. With increased awareness and a growing number of resources, the laws are also changing. Police have more power to arrest abusers and lay charges against them. But it is not enough.

I would like to see our community leaders, religious leaders and elders, take a different approach. Instead of telling the government what it should do and wait for government funding, we all need to do our part in educating future generations. Our sons and daughters need to be treated equally. Parents need to be taught basic life skills, such as respecting women and letting their sons be adults. Parents need to teach their sons to participate in the daily household chores along with their daughters. If our *gurdwaras* and churches began weekly classes on parenting, legal rights of individuals and on-going support groups, then we could see a decline in the abuse and death rates. Let's not wait for a tragedy to happen. We need to take action before abuse begins.

If you are being abused or have been abused, there is absolutely no shame in telling someone. There are many forms of abuse. The most obvious form is physical abuse, but there are others, such as isolation from family and friends, constant phoning to check up on you, verbal abuse, shouting, rage, sexual abuse and even withholding money from you. If you feel violated by the actions of your husband, it most likely means that you are in an abusive relationship.

If you are being abused, I urge you to tell someone. Tell your doctor to document any injuries or past abuse. Have a journal hidden away. If your children are of an understanding age, speak to them. Teach them how to call the police by dialing 911. Make some friends in your neighborhood.

Your life is precious. Protect yourself and your loved ones. Even if you call 911 and hang up, the police will still show up at your door.

Despite what you have been told about yourself, you are not

worthless or useless, and you are not the cause of the abuse. You are unique and precious in God's eyes. No one deserves to be treated abusively. You are entitled as God's child, to be treated with dignity and respect.

A small group of my friends from our town house complex decided to attend the breakfast meeting at our local church. We were told that she was an author and a public speaker on abuse related issues. We had never heard of her. She would speak on Tuesday morning. Everyone was encouraged to attend. Our church was privileged to hear her story.

We found our table and quickly settled in. The Pastor's wife made a brief announcement to take our little ones to the nursery. After a short prayer the breakfast was ready. Our guest of honour was the first to get her plate. Then the others followed.

Immediately following breakfast, she was introduced. She looked like an average North American woman. Then she began to speak with such humility. Her opening words were "It wasn't by chance that I was invited to speak at your church – God has a message for each one of you. God is present in this room to set captives free." She admitted that she always got nervous before any speaking engagements and asked us to pray for her.

Then she began to share her unthinkable hurts. Everyone wept with her and for her. Others wept for themselves. She touched everyone with her pain, her joy and her unusual sense of humour. Her life story was a very heart-breaking one. As we wept tears of sorrow and of joy we thought about her being healed of this magnitude of tragedy. It was mind boggling.

She had a special way of presenting her story to her audience. She was very informative and yet sensitive at the same time. Her story kept us reaching over to our tables for more tissues.

Her humble and gentle presentation of her horrific story gave me goose bumps. The atrocity inflicted on her by her abuser was beyond human. She had been betrayed and battered in so many ways that I wondered if he were the devil. But she remembered a policewoman telling her that she would be praying for her many years ago. That faithful young cop was the reason she was able to stand before us and speak.

She suffered great evil yet she learned so much from it. She had become a stronger person and moved forward with courage and a dream. Although she had no power to change her past, somehow she found power to design her future. "Survivors must break free from their past hurts and pain", she told us. "Don't think *that time will heal your wounds."*

Through her unimaginable abuse, she triumphed. Then she spoke about overcoming our pains, through God's grace. We were personally challenged to take the step through "forgiveness to freedom", from a lifelong burden of our lives, no matter where we've come from.

Her message was so powerful, I knew I had to let go of my unforgiveness towards my offender. She did not sugar-coat the truth. Her message was a healing salve for each one of us. She extended and showed us God's love, grace and forgiveness through her own life.

Some people think that we dare not touch the truth. As she put it, "The pain is not abstract – it is tied to anger and rooted in pain, injustice and abandonment. It is very debilitating."

Remarkably, the anger and resentment that I held onto towards my abusers, lost its power that morning. I experienced a shift in my heart. It meant that I wasn't going to tolerate their behaviour in the future – this would enable me to maintain my dignity. I too, like the speaker, now choose to live each day in abundant freedom and hope.

That speaker was me. The narrator was from the audience.

CHAPTER THIRTY-ONE

Princess

One good came from his death: we wouldn't be looking over our shoulders anymore. Raj was dead and was completely removed from our lives forever. He had died the way he had intended to kill me, not far from the place where he had intended to drown me. During the final cremation, I had been able to forgive him completely and release it all to God.

As I journey back in my mind to the day I was married and through our time together, I realized that I experienced life in ways that are hard to fathom. What began with a fantasy of being a princess in my new home, turned into a life of complete terror and uncertainty, always asking myself "what's next?" There were countless sleepless nights. I remember begging to die. I had given up all hope that there would ever be any future for me. I was lonely, depressed, deprived and scared.

After Raj's death came a time of total dependence on God. I asked my church to pray for us. My church became my family. Some days were much more difficult than others. I knew I had a long way to go before I would be totally free from bondage. I was very fearful and had low self-esteem. I was nervous around people. When I made friends, I tried very hard to please them for fear they would either mistreat me or desert me. I was always trying to do things on my own, unwilling to accept the help that was available. I failed God many times, but He never failed me.

I often wondered if my children would ever find complete healing. Would they ever get their inheritance? Would we ever really know how their father had died?

I finally realized that it really didn't matter if those questions were ever answered. The only truth I came to know was that God was in control and that we were his children. He would take care of us. I learned to depend on his promises even when it looked as if there was no hope.

Since Raj's death, my children and I have had many challenges. There were health issues, financial issues and unemployment issues. We moved many times from one basement suite to another. Life on a very limited income was very difficult. As the children grew, so did the demands, but we just worked with what we had. I knew that if I was faithful with the little that I had, then I could be trusted with more.

Today, after many years of journeying, my oldest daughter is married and has a bundle of joy named Caleb. The Lord has provided us with many gifts and blessed us with a home where I am able to meet with many people and share God's love.

Many people are looking for signs, wonders and miracles in order to believe in God. I myself have experienced few miracles in my life, but I have experienced the presence of God. I can look back and see that when people abandoned me, God took over. He took my suffering away and gave me blessing instead.

God has never promised us a life without problems, but he has promised a way out. Every day I face challenges and some are very painful. We have a God who loves us unconditionally, but we also have an enemy, the devil, who tries to deceive us and destroy us. What the devil meant for harm, God has turned into joy. The devil wanted to kill me, but God had a greater plan for my life. I have walked with Jesus for the past seventeen years, and I feel I am just beginning to learn of his love for me. Though there are days when I stumble and fall, he is faithful and always picks me up again.

I would like to share with you what a strange woman shared with me in a tiny airport. My prayer is that you, too, would come to believe in a living God who gives strength and hope. I ask you what she asked me: "Do you know Jesus? Do you know how much he loves you?"

I accepted those words then, but it has taken me a long time to fully understand them, to come to a place of total freedom. I have finally understood God's promise that everything has been done for me on the cross at Calvary. Jesus died and paid the price for my sins and my pain. I am no longer a slave to men but a child of a loving Father in heaven. He is the King, and that makes me his daughter.

I am finally a Princess.

"So I now sit again, trembling at the foot of my master. This is a different Master. He loves me and gives me power instead of taking it. The power to love and the power to forgive."

Forgiveness

Many of you will ask "Why? How could God allow such suffering to happen? Why did it take so long for Him to intervene?"

I don't pretend to understand.

There were a number of reasons for writing this book. The first is so that we all will understand—no one has the right to hurt you.

Do not be ashamed to admit that you have been abused and ask for help. Seek help as soon as possible. Keep a diary, or choose a couple of trusted people as confidants and know that there is hope for you and your children. There is a better life after abuse.

Another purpose in writing this book was to share the freedom I found through forgiveness. My prayer is that it will be used to help others who are, like I was, locked in a prison of unforgiveness. I have found that forgiveness is the secret to living free in this world in spite of the unfair hand that life may have dealt us.

I am not saying forgiveness is easy. It will be the hardest road you have ever travelled. The greater the sense of injustice, the harder it is to forgive because the more justified we feel in holding on to our anger.

This book would be nothing more than an epistle of suffering, were it not for the final freedom I discovered through forgiveness. If, through my life story, I can bring this freedom to others, then it has been worthwhile. It was very difficult. As things were getting better for my children and me, I desperately wanted to take revenge on Raj. When I was living on my own with my children, I began to get stronger and started to see the emotional and physical prison cell I had been locked in and I wanted him to pay for all the injustice that he had done to my children and I. So I came up with a plan.

To forgive my offender seemed impossible at that time; I felt that the man who had abused and tortured me for years, and even tried to kill me, did not deserve to be forgiven – ever. My thoughts of him centred on wanting vengeance against him. I wanted the extent of trauma that I had suffered, to be returned to him many times over. I wanted to tie him up, beat him, shave his head, burn him with his own cigarettes as he had done to me, and much more. He had caused so many deep wounds in me. I was weak and vulnerable and he took advantage of it and me; he was a monster who wasn't worthy of any mercy. I wanted to hang on to my pain and my anger, which I felt was fully justified, so that it would not abate. I felt that if I let my anger subside, he would get away with something.

But the truth was that he was not even around to feel the impact of my anger and it was only hurting me. Because he occupied much of my thought life through my anger and thoughts of retribution, he still had power over me.

As long as I gave place to that anger and unforgiveness, Raj, even though dead, continued to have control over my life, and I was giving in to him. Thoughts of revenge, which of course centred on him, meant that he continued to occupy first place in my mind and heart. Just as he had held that primary place all those years out of fear and intimidation, after I left him he continued to hold pre-eminence in my thoughts through my unforgiveness. The abuser continues to hold control over us as long as we allow the anger and resentment directed towards them to control our thoughts and emotions.

"Forgiveness doesn't make the other person right; it just sets you free!" By forgiving them, it does not mean that reconciliation will happen or that you agree with what they did. You can acknowledge that it was very wrong; it was a sin. However, by forgiving you are nullifying the negative effect that such evil has over your heart and severing the hold it has over your mind and soul.

How does it have that hold? What do I mean by bondage to un-forgiveness? Un-forgiveness can be compared to drinking poison while hoping that the other person will die from it. The target of my anger remained blissfully unaware while I slowly decayed inside. If I had continued to harbour unforgiveness, I would have become more and more bitter.

The walk of forgiveness has been compared to an onion with many layers: as you deal with the biggest hurts, you think you are over it, but then other levels of hurt will be revealed. Although it won't seem like it at the time, this is a good thing. God wants to free you from all deep hurts and those things rooted deep down inside. He desires you to be completely free.

There is another aspect of abuse that must not be overlooked. After being treated that way for so long, I was completely submerged in the "victim mentality". I had lost ownership of my own actions and felt helpless and intimidated and like I had no power over my own life. There was a desire for me to justify myself through exposing the abuse of Raj, even through subtle emotional manipulation. I used to have day-dreams of me dying and imagined the world's reaction as they realized how bad he really was. The victim mentality had become such a big part of my life that I wasn't even aware of it. I had a deep desire to have someone take care of the children and me, and I craved the love, affirmation and acceptance that I'd longed for, but never received. At times there were tendencies to seek another man to fulfill those de-sires. I thought this would help with the hurt. Thankfully I never sought the temporary relief provided by alcohol, drugs or sex. I did however start working three jobs – hoping to give the children things that they wanted. My workaholic behaviour was also another way of masking my pain, but this was only a temporary fix.

I was once asked if it was easier for me to forgive Raj since he was dead and I thought about this many times. "Is it easier since he is no longer around?" Yes and No. In some ways, I wish that he were alive because I'd like him to see me the way I am today; how much my life has been transformed since I left him. It has gone from ashes to beauty. I am no longer begging him to spare my life. I am no longer afraid to stand in front of him. I am no longer trembling with fear in his presence. So many times he was planning my funeral and asking the older children to pick a burial plot, and who would light the fire for my cremation. Yet it was I, with the same children, cremating him some years later.

Now I own a beautifully furnished home and a vehicle and my children and I live normal and healthy lives. I would have liked to invite him to my home and have him see how beautiful the children have grown up to be. I'd like him to think about all the good things that he missed out on, like our oldest daughter's wedding, the birth of her son and his birthdays, other family gatherings, graduations, engagements and even funerals. After showing and telling him all the good things, I would love to give him a hug, tell him that I forgive him and then ask that he never come back into our lives again.

I was deprived of the basic fundamentals of life – sleeping and eating, loving and being loved, being a mother and wife. I felt that my life was so programmed that it only revolved around him. As the days drifted into evening and the workers were going home, I'd imagined that this may be my last day on earth. Now there would be no witnesses. To live under that much fear and oppression is death in itself. I would often wish that something bad would happen to him. Maybe he would get into a car accident or collapse and end up in the hospital. This would give me a few days of peace to enjoy with the children. Then the sound of his footsteps – oh how painful they were to my ears; I hated hearing him come home.

I knew that if I wanted to live a life that was free of abuse, I needed to make some major changes in my life. Weeks, months and years went by after our separation, and I was still bitter towards him. After much counselling, I had to make a choice, either to live in my world of self-pity or to forgive him and start a new life – a new beginning. I chose the latter. Bitterness was killing me inside. I had four beautiful children and I wanted to be a positive role model for them. I wanted healthy and happy children who would grow up to be good citizens.

That is my prayer for you. If you are in that kind of bondage, choose to forgive, not for him but for yourself. I guarantee that this is one decision you will never regret. Live the life of fullness and freedom that you were meant to. Suffering will make you into a strong person and help you to become a positive role model like I am starting to become. God has a big plan for you. He will take all the ugliness and make something so beautiful out of it.

I never in my wildest dreams pictured myself speaking about my abuse, yet God wanted to expose this hidden secret and my hope is that through my difficult journey and the lessons I've learned, maybe you will find your freedom and live the life you deserve.

Even though I live in a lot of physical pain, I will still continue to speak out for all those who are suffering at the hands of their abusers. What limitations have you put on yourself? Step out in faith and make a difference. If we all do our part – this world would be a more peaceful place to live in.

Through all of this, I have to say that I have finally become the Princess that I had dreamed of as a teenager. This life has given me so many challenges – but it was all worth it. Had I not gone through these entire traumas in my life – I wouldn't be a voice for the voiceless and I couldn't offer any hope to people.

Raj was a tornado that ripped through my life, destroying everything in his path.

My prayer is that you all find strength to make wise decisions and live the life that God intended for you.

May you be safe and enjoy life.

When you don't forgive, they keep the power.

Take back the power and walk in freedom.

I now stand trembling in fear. This fear is in the presence of my Master, my Jesus.

AFTERWORD

I want to break the stigma attached to single parents that they won't make it or they will just get by. As a single mom of four children, I want to be a living testimony that we can not only make it, but also raise healthy children. I understand that there will be challenges, but we must set goals and stay focused. We are not to be ashamed to ask for help. Find a counsellor who can lead you into the right direction. There is hope for each one of us and there are many resources to take advantage of. As I began my new journey with my children, I felt like a teenager experiencing new things. I needed to learn the basic things that we all take for granted, like opening an account, writing checks and learning how to shop on a budget. It was difficult, but it has helped me to be a more complete person.

Another reason for this book was to expose the violence that happens behind closed doors. We must not be ashamed to talk to our neighbours, report to our doctor or talk to a friend or even leave a note somewhere. There is nothing that we have done or can do that means that we deserve to be abused by someone.

Lastly, please remember above all that no matter what you have done and what your situation is – there is a loving God who is waiting with open arms. He longs to have a relationship with us and He is our only Hope for the future.

Some of the things to recognize as warning signs in an abusive relationship:
- Your isolation from friends and family
- You are being questioned every time you've been out

- Your bank account is being monitored
- Turning your children against you
- You are being made to think that you are losing your mind
- Name calling
- Verbal threats
- Physical assaults
- Withholding money or privileges

There are many other things to watch out for and becoming educated about this matter will help you to avoid abuse in your life.

There is life after abuse. In fact, there is a better life. As long as you are spiritually grounded, have a good support system and stay focused. When I first became a Christian, I had a long list of things I wanted God to accomplish. Some of them included:

- Getting my children back with me
- Owning a home, nice car, good furniture
- And being a voice to the voiceless – to expose the violence against women and children

I have had all my expectations not only met, but God went beyond that and has given me so much more. I have learned to depend on Him for everything.

There are times when I do feel anger towards my abuser when I hear of another murder or spousal assault. I always wonder how people can be so cruel. Then I think of my blessings and how God spared my life to be a witness for Him and my peace returns to me.

Although it has been many years since Raj died, to this day I have trust issues, which is probably why I chose to remain a single mom. I didn't want to put my children through another round of misery with another man. I believe there are many wonderful men out there, but I never did find one for myself—maybe I wasn't really looking. There was a lot of fear instilled in me and I have needed space in order to heal. I have daily reminders of the abuse that I suffered through the hands of Raj: I live with an artificial jaw and the constant pain and limitations that go along with the implant have become a daily struggle. The nagging headaches, the physical and emotional scars are all evidence of what I have come through. Although my pain limits what I can do, I have made a commitment to God, and to all vulnerable people whom I meet, that I will continue to speak out on their behalf.

FROM THE CHILDREN

Fourteen years later, many unanswered questions, one common understanding needing closure. My constant child like questions were: "Why is my dad like this? Why can't I have a normal life? Why does my mom go through this?" I felt no love for my father as he abused my mother, and destroyed our family, but all the while wanting nothing more than for him to hug me and make it all better. At the time I thought that he made it all bad and was the only one who could make it better. Having survived my father I know now that he couldn't make it better, ever. Although many details of my childhood I have deliberately stored away in an effort to forget, I still will never stop knowing the reason for who I am today:

My mom, a true warrior in God's blessed army. A woman who taught me mostly through her silent battles how to have a loud voice and win. My mom, my hero, my mentor, my go to woman of the world, has taught me one lesson and that is "Lean not on your own understanding, but that of the Lord's."

Those who know me well today would say Hannah is a no-nonsense individual and I would agree. I acknowledge that my witnessing this horrific life growing up has made me more aware of various feelings especially that of hurt, fear and distrust; I always have my guard up. I am not that scared little girl anymore, rather a wife and mother of a beautiful Boy (Caleb), who fills my life with joy and laughter.

–*Hannah*

***

It's been 15 years since my father died. Growing up as a child I always wanted a normal family life. I now have realized family doesn't mean

2 parents. It means people who care about you. My father was a good person for what I remember, but also an evil man who drank too much. I remember as a child watching my parents fight and it usually turned into my father abusing my mother. I grew up watching my mother struggle but never give up to finally earn the life she deserves. My dad left my mother with only promises yet my mother delivered.

Growing up fatherless was very difficult due to the fact that many friends always talked about their dads, but my mother always made us feel loved.

If I could go back in time I would change things. I'm not sure what I would change because I have never been through what my mother has.

Enjoy reading this book and thank you Mom for everything and every time.

–*Tony*

***

For many years I have heard my mom tell her story to countless people. She has overcome death and is fighting to educate men, women and children about the effects of abuse.

I can to this day recall when my mom walked down the hallway looking for the principal to help find her youngest two children. I remember seeing her and when she spoke the words "I'm their mother," I had never experienced so much joy. She is our ray of hope and I hope this book will inspire you to help us to end abuse for all.

–*Megan*

***

I must say that I am so proud of my mom. She has overcome many obstacles in her life. I see her determination to make each one of our lives fruitful. I hope that through her sufferings, you may be able to find some comfort in your life.

–*Shawn*

For speaking and workshop
inquires, please visit us
at www.blackandbluesari.com